ALL ALONG THE RIVER

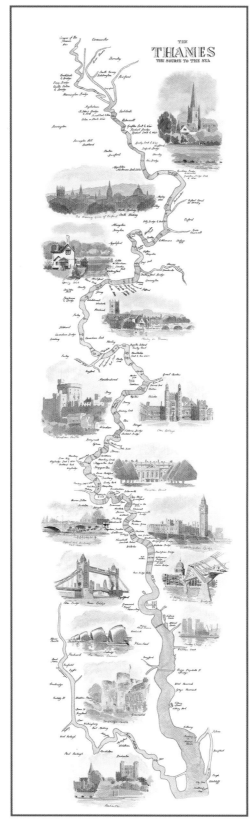

ALL ALONG THE RIVER

TALES FROM THE THAMES

Pauline Conolly

ROBERT HALE • LONDON

© Pauline Conolly 2013
First published in Great Britain 2013

ISBN 978-0-7198-0798-5

Robert Hale Limited
Clerkenwell House
Clerkenwell Green
London EC1R 0HT

www.halebooks.com

A catalogue record for this book is available from the British Library

2 4 6 8 10 9 7 5 3 1

Designed by Eurodesign
Printed in Singapore by Craft Print International Ltd

Serene yet strong, majestic yet sedate,
Swift without violence, without terror great.

Matthew Prior, 1700

For Rob, my companion on so many journeys

CONTENTS

ACKNOWLEDGEMENTS

Many thanks to my editor at Robert Hale, Nikki Edwards.

I would also like to express my appreciation to Bill Wilson and to all those who provided stories and recipes relating to the River Thames, or who simply shared a friendly word on our wonderful journey from the source to the sea.

Two other people deserve special thanks; artist William Thomas, for allowing me to use his illustrated map of the Thames Path – www.riverthamespath.com and miniaturist Kiva Atkinson, for her quirky representation of eel pie and oysters – www.kivasminiatures.com.

Finally, my love and thanks to Rob, whose help has been beyond words. His photographs have added so much to the book that his name deserves to be on the cover.

PROLOGUE

S tanding in a remote Gloucestershire field, I ceremoniously primed the Thames by pouring two pints of water into a dry well of pebbles. As water now rarely appears at the river's source, my partner Rob and I had brought our own supply, drawn 112 miles (180 km) downstream below our holiday home at Marlow. We had filled an old beer bottle, purchased at exorbitant cost from a Henley antique shop and supposedly tossed into the Thames by an eighteenth-century bargeman. I would love to believe the story, though perhaps the dealer recognized a pair of gullible Australians.

Priming the Thames with middle-Thames water!

The head spring of the Thames was wont to disappear even in medieval times. During an extensive tour of the country between 1535 and 1543, Henry VIII's historian John Leland noted that it rose in a field called Trewsbury Mead near the Gloucestershire village of Kemble:

> *In a great somer drought there appereth very little or no water, yet is the stream servid with many of springes resorting to one bottom.*

As our water resorted to the bottom, I wished I had thought to add a few drops of crimson dye: we may have been able to spot a faint pink stain as it flowed past Marlow again, on its way to the sea.

Rob and I were intending to make the journey from source to sea ourselves, via the 180-mile (288-km) Thames Path. We had discussed the alternative of walking upstream from London, but decided it would be an anticlimax to run out of river in the middle of a field.

Following decades of negotiation with landowners, the Thames Path officially opened in the summer of 1996, coinciding with our purchase of a lodge on the historic Harleyford estate, bordering the Thames in Buckinghamshire. We felt we were *meant* to complete the walk after discovering that a footbridge on the edge of the property was built to span the last gap in the path. Nevertheless, it was several years before we drove to the source armed with our bottle of middle-Thames water.

Regardless of whether it is walked in a downstream or upstream direction, the Thames Path does not present a severe physical challenge. It winds through a gentle landscape with plenty of riverside pubs and teashops. From Oxford to London, it is so well served by public transport that if you get stung by nettles or your boots start to leak you can simply throw in the towel and catch the next bus home.

Over a period of six months we slowly made our way down to the Flood Barrier at Greenwich. Since then we have retraced our steps on many sections and on many occasions, both on foot and by car. In the summer of 2003 we were fortunate enough to view a long stretch of the river from a completely different perspective when our next-door neighbour took us on a magical helicopter flight upriver to Wallingford. The trip ended back at Harleyford, with a final sweep around the golf course followed by a gentle touch down a few hundred metres from our front door in the old sheep paddock.

This book is an attempt to share our fascination with the Thames, particularly its folklore and rich social history. There is a good deal of 'sight-seeing' involved, despite Charles Dickens' son (another recorder of the river) warning against such frivolity. I did decide to follow one piece of advice from Mr Dickens, albeit delivered tongue in cheek. It was borrowed, he said, from American tourists whose principle was 'never to enquire how far you may go, but to go straight on until you are told to stop'. He suggested that this, combined with an understanding of the value of 'palm oil', would guarantee the tourist seeing everything he cared to. As a rule my arms are too short and my pockets too deep to contemplate bribery, but if truly pressed …

I am no *cordon bleu* cook, and can only explain the emphasis on food by confessing that fresh air and exercise greatly increased our interest in the subject. Of course, food has always played a large part in the lore of the river. Take the contents of Ratty's picnic basket in Wind in the Willows, for example: 'coldtonguecoldhamcoldbeefpickledgherkinsfrenchrollscress-sandwichesmeatpastegingeralelemonadesodawater –'. To which, egged on by Mrs Beeton and her ilk, I have taken the liberty of adding: 'cakestartssconessweetbunssyllabubssuet-puddingsChristmaspuddingsmincepieseelpiesandsavourymeatpies –'.

Much of the first draft of *All Along the River* was written at Harleyford, where inspiration was frequently outweighed by distraction. I was captivated by the wide variety of birdlife, from swans, coots, herons and kingfishers to soaring red kites and the area's many woodland species. In spring, the opposite Berkshire banks are overhung with flowering horse chestnut and the softest veils of weeping willow. In autumn, beech trees emerge from the mist to provide a molten-gold backdrop to eighteenth-century Harleyford Manor. By Christmas, water shines through the leafless branches of sycamore and beech all the way down to Bisham Abbey. My computer often went into automatic-save mode as I gazed out the window.

Throughout the writing of the book the irrepressible spirit of my late mother Myra often appeared. Her favourite expression upon hearing anything extraordinary or shocking had always been: 'Oh my hat!' Given the number of sexual scandals, sinister deaths and tragic accidents I recorded along the Thames, Myra would have had occasion to invoke her hat on a great many occasions!

Head Spring to Ashton Keynes

We had left the head spring and were negotiating the first squeeze-gate on the journey downstream when I looked back to see a group of serious 'leggings and stick' walkers approaching the source from another direction. I thought of turning back to explain the damp patch in the well of stones but when I heard their excited shouts I could not bear to disappoint them. If an article appears in a ramblers' journal celebrating the miraculous reappearance of water at Thames Head, please disregard it.

The path crosses the old Roman road, the Foss Way, via stone steps and the first of more than 100 stiles en route to London. Stiles may be old-fashioned and quaint, but they are also an extremely civilized means of negotiating fences. I swear it would be possible to climb one with dignity whilst half shot, wearing stiletto heels and a tight skirt.

Further down, even in the driest of seasons, one of Leland's 'many springes' bubbles to the surface (see page 10). Eventually, several puddles join to form a slow trickle, hidden from view in a reed-filled channel. At Brooklands Farm in the nearby hamlet of Ewen, the tiny stream suddenly spills into a meadow. Despite my ceremony at the official source, I looked at cows standing ankle-deep in water and understood why the Saxons named this place *aewylme*: start of a river.

As a dairy farmer's daughter, it is embarrassing to admit that the sight of those cows produced a frisson of fear. Newspapers had been reporting nasty incidents involving cattle on the country's public footpaths. One woman had every rib broken after being trampled by an angry herd and another was killed when her dog barked, causing a stampede. Seven deaths in less than a year had prompted a spokesman from the government's Health and Safety Executive to comment: 'We are hoping this is not the beginning of a trend.'

The notion that an English cow could be dangerous was so shocking I began to fear everything except voles and rabbits. Only the degree of perceived danger varied; a charging sheep could possibly be side-stepped but I decided to give a wide birth to dogs of any description, domestic geese, breeding swans and adders.

There is a famous old pub at Ewen called The Wild Duck, which dates from the sixteenth

© Rob Conolly

On a hot day these cows could drink the infant Thames dry!

century. Inside, a portrait of Princess Diana looked slightly incongruous among a collection of stuffed fish and animal heads. As we waited for our drinks I read the verse on a framed piece of embroidery celebrating Cornelius Uzzle, who once visited the pub and demolished 12 lb (5.5 kg) of bacon at a single sitting, half of it raw. The lines are illustrated by a needle-work map of the area, complete with a single-strand Thames. Presumably Cornelius's huge appetite resulted from walking to The Wild Duck from London rather than nearby Kemble.

In olden days Cornelius Uzzle
Performed a gastronomical puzzle
Twelve pounds of pig he put away
And lived to eat another day.

According to the *Oxford English Dictionary*, the origin of the word guzzle is unknown, but it is tempting to imagine it derived from Uzzle.

Not far from Ewen is the town of South Cerney, located on the River Churn, a major trib-utary of the Thames. In fact some argue that the true birthplace of the Thames is not Trewsbury Mead but Seven Springs, where the Churn rises in the Cotswolds. Rob and I later visited South Cerney, partly in acknowledgement of the alternative-source theory, but also because we wanted to visit All Hallows Church.

During the early years of the twentieth century, the churchwarden was a Mr E. T. Cripps, who lived next door to All Hallows in Atkyns Manor. In 1913, Mr Cripps and his young daughter were present when workmen found the head and foot of a rare twelfth-century wooden crucifix in a wall of the church. It had been hidden during the Reformation and is considered to be the earliest example of wood carving in the country. A replica is on display at All Hallows but the original fragments are held at the British Museum.

Before our visit we had made contact with Raymond Fenton, Mr Cripps' grandson, who met us at the church and kindly showed us around. Later, over lunch at a village pub, Raymond confirmed his grandfather's connection with another All Hallows story. The church's tenor bell was cast in 1721 and was supposedly stolen from a neighbouring village because its metal contained an unusually high proportion of silver. Not everyone believed this tale but when the bell cracked and had to be recast in 1911, the vicar and churchwarden Cripps took the precaution of standing guard at the foundry.

When we met Raymond he had been organist at All Hallows for thirty years. He was christened in the Norman font, as were his children and grandchildren. In an increasingly rare example of continuity, three generations of the family were still living at Atkyns Manor, parts of which date back to the fifteenth century.

Across the Churn in Silver Street is the old vicarage, now a private home. For some years in the nineteenth century it was occupied by the Revd W. W. Liddell, uncle of the real-life Alice in Wonderland. Lewis Carroll (Charles Dodgson) knew Revd Liddell well and was a regular visitor. A tiny door under the stairs is said to have inspired the opening Alice discovered when she disappeared down a rabbit burrow on the banks of the Thames near Oxford.

It was bitterly cold when we visited South Cerney and no doubt the steamed pudding we enjoyed during lunch with Raymond was named for its popularity among English country vicars. I could imagine the aroma of orange and ginger wafting across to All Hallows on wintry Sundays, prompting the Revd Liddell to cut short his sermons and hurry back to Silver Street.

I hope the White Rabbit was not intending to time our journey down the river!

VICARAGE PUDDING

175 g (6 oz) self-raising flour
60 g (2 oz) shredded suet
120 g (4 oz) currants
60 g (2 oz) soft light-brown sugar
1 teaspoon ground ginger
grated rind and juice of 1 orange
50 ml (2 fl oz) milk

Sift the flour then beat all ingredients together in a bowl adding enough milk to produce a firm dropping consistency. Turn into a greased 1 litre (1.75 pint) pudding basin. Cover with greaseproof paper and foil and secure with string. Stand the basin on a saucer in a large saucepan which has been half filled with boiling water. Cover the saucepan tightly and steam the pudding for 1½ hours. Turn out and serve with custard and cream.

Back on the Thames Path, the river threads its way through flooded gravel pits via a strip of land so narrow we were tempted to scratch a channel with a stick and stop the tiny stream in its tracks. Butterflies and clouds of iridescent blue damselflies rose as we passed, but our presence scarcely disturbed the rabbits nibbling the grass verges. Far from hurrying by like the White Rabbit, they waited until we were within inches of them before looking up and making a languid hop or two into thickets of hawthorn. Walking in the unworldly glow of late-afternoon sunshine, we felt we might easily slip down a burrow ourselves, emerging back in Australia, or as Alice suggested: 'Where people walk with their heads downward! The Antipathies!' In rawer areas of the gravel workings, putting a foot wrong could prove fatal. Signs warn of deep, numbingly cold water in the pits and of bottomless ponds of quicksand.

The flooded quarries form part of the vast Cotswold Water Park, where wetlands provide an ideal habitat for insects, including thirteen species of dragonfly. The nineteenth-century English poet Jean Ingelow captured the elegance and beauty of dragonflies in the following lines:

And forth on floating gauze, no jewelled queen
So rich, the green-eyed dragon-flies would brake
And hover on the flowers – aerial things;
With little rainbows flickering on their wings.

In turn, insects attract birds; hobbies and sand martins nest in the quarry faces and there are songbirds such as reed and willow warblers, whitethroats and the elusive nightingale. From hides along the banks of the lakes, bird lovers watch the autumn arrival of around forty different species of waterfowl. A 10-hectare (24-acre) reed bed has been created, encouraging the birds to stay and breed, and perhaps even increasing the population of otters. In November 2011 a herd of Dexter rare-breed cattle was introduced to the reeds beds. These diminutive but hardy animals perform a valuable service by grazing on invasive willow. Aquatic sports such as jet skiing and sailing are also popular in the water park and anglers can test their wits against carp, bream, rudd, perch, pike and tench.

The first true Thames-side settlement is the Cotswold-stone village of Ashton Keynes, where the river flows straight past the front doors of cottages under miniature bridges. William de Keynes held the manor here in 1256, but it was first mentioned in Saxon times, when King Alfred bequeathed it to one of his daughters. Its name was Aesctun in the eighth century and Essitone in the eleventh, with numerous other variations before it evolved into Ashton Keynes. Sections of the double moat which encircled the original manor house and church can still be seen. The village has four medieval preaching crosses, all rather knocked about by Cromwell's Roundheads during the Civil War. Their presence in such a small community is a mystery but no doubt explains why the parish church is called Holy Cross.

It was in this church that twenty-three-year-old Andrew Lloyd Webber married his first wife, eighteen-year-old Sarah Hugill, after the pair had met two years earlier at a party in Oxford. The ceremony took place on 24 July 1972, just months before the musical *Jesus Christ Superstar* opened on Broadway and became an international success.

At the time of the 1851 census, Ashton Keynes' main thoroughfare of Gosditch consisted of about thirty buildings, including a dairy and a pub. Households in the street included a number of cottage-based glove makers, who were paid a pittance for assembling and stitching leather gloves. It was considered such lowly work that pride often forced the women to hide their materials if anyone called, although the smell of leather and dye must have been a giveaway.

The Gosditch pub mentioned in the census was the Horse and Jockey, which has stood for over 400 years. In mid Victorian times it was a simple scrumpy house, selling cider pressed from local apples and offering a limited bar menu of cheese and onions (probably all its patrons could afford). There was a major culinary advance in the 1950s when locally made pies went on sale and we were pleased to find that steak and ale pies remain on the menu. The pub's old stables have been converted into a skittle alley.

While cottagers were happy to drink the Horse and Jockey's rough cider, country squires preferred to pour hot spiced wine or ale over baked apples to make a drink called Lambswool. According to one theory, the name referred to the fluffy apple pulp, but I have also read that Lambswool is a corruption of *La Masabul*, the angel of fruits and seeds.

LAMBSWOOL

2 litres (8 cups) ale
3 cooking apples
1 cinnamon stick
3 cloves
½ level teaspoon ground ginger
½ level teaspoon ground nutmeg
½ cup soft brown sugar
white sugar to taste

Core the apples and fill the cavities with brown sugar. Bake in a moderate oven until very soft. Remove the skin and mash the pulp. Heat the ale with the spices and pour over the apple pulp. Add white sugar to taste. Remove the cloves and cinnamon stick before serving.

CRICKLADE TO LECHLADE

Five miles (8 km) below Ashton Keynes is the Saxon town of Cricklade. Thames Path walkers approach via North Meadow, protected as a nature reserve since 1974. For generations this 100-acre (40-hectare) meadow has been farmed according to the medieval practice of allowing common grazing from Lammas on 12 August until Lady Day on 12 February, then letting the grass grow for hay throughout the summer. Carved stones in the field still mark out each farmer's portion of the crop.

Wild flowers seed and multiply in the uncultivated soil and in early spring there is a magnificent display of the increasingly rare snake's head fritillary, which cannot tolerate the high nitrate and phosphate levels of improved pastures. In a good season there may be one million of the chequered purple bells, which naturalized in water meadows after escaping from gardens in the sixteenth and seventeenth century. Picking the right time to see the flowers is now a bit of a lottery: due to global warming, the peak flowering period can occur as early as the end of March.

Cricklade is where the River Churn joins the strengthening Kemble spring. It is now widely accepted that the Churn is a Thames tributary rather than its mother stream, but this question has been argued for a long time and in very high places. During a House of Commons debate over the issue in 1937, the MP for Stroud argued strongly for the Churn and Seven Springs, which was in his constituency. Maps erred in showing the source at Kemble, he insisted, because the spring there was known to dry up. His words prompted an opposing MP to quip, 'Why don't you?'

Not to be outdone, the Welsh have been known to claim that the Thames actually rises in the Black Mountains, eventually trickling across the border into England.

Cricklade was first occupied by the Romans, but the most lasting impression was left by Alfred the Great in the ninth century. To counter the invading Danes, King Alfred built a series of forts called burhs, which were also commercial and community centres. The idea was that locals could seek refuge in the burh in times of danger. Plots were laid out on a rectangular grid measured in poles (one pole equalling about 15 ft, 5 m). Some say this measurement originated from the length of a pole put across a room to dry armour. Another theory suggests it was the length of a stick required by ploughboys to reach the front pair of eight yoked oxen. Apparently there are houses in the High Street which have retained their original Saxon frontages of two poles. I wanted Rob to check this for me but he was worried he might be taken for a property developer.

Cricklade later provided shelter for Henry II's mother Queen Matilda, during her protracted struggle against her cousin, King Stephen, in the twelfth century. The local museum displays a copy of the charter granted by a grateful Henry, exempting townspeople from paying tolls or customs fees throughout the kingdom. Unfortunately for present-day residents, the charter was only renewed until the reign of James I.

There is also an interesting display at the museum on leather making, an industry that survived in the area until 1994. The Ockwell tannery was Cricklade's largest employer until the 1930s. In the early days, dog excrement was an ingredient in the process of softening sheep skin and the pungent odour must have been difficult to cope with.

Our first day's walk ended here and we retraced our steps to the source, where we had left our car. Some weeks later Cricklade became the starting point for our walk along the most isolated section of the Thames Path: the 42-mile (67-km) stretch down to Oxford. Bill Wilson, a friend from Harleyford, kindly dropped us off on the High Street by St Mary's Church as birds were chirping the last bars of the dawn chorus. Almost immediately we found ourselves in the middle of a farmyard, our steamy breath mingling with that of cows waiting to be milked. As we cautiously squeezed past, I was reminded of lines from Oscar Wilde's poem about the Thames, 'The Burden Of Itys', in which a milkmaid leaves her lonely bed at dawn to follow the same daily ritual as the herd:

... the heavy-lowing cattle wait,
Stretching their huge and dripping mouths across the farmyard gate.

The seventeenth-century English antiquarian John Aubrey noted that dairy produce was a mainstay of the North Wiltshire diet, although in his view the locals failed to flourish on it:

They feed mainly on milke meates, which cools their braines too much, and hurts their inventions. These circumstances make them melancholy, contemplative and malicious.

Despite Mr Aubrey's report, the cottagers were inventive enough to get their hands on the odd rabbit, legally or otherwise:

RABBIT IN THE DAIRY

8 rabbit joints
60 g (2 oz) chopped ham
1 small onion, finely chopped
1 celery stick, finely chopped
2 bay leaves
300 ml (½ pint) milk

Place the celery, onion and ham into a casserole dish. Arrange the rabbit joints on top with the bay leaves. Bring the milk to the boil then pour over the rabbit. Cover tightly and bake in a moderate oven until the joints are tender (approx. 2 hours).

Rural poverty not only encouraged petty crime such as poaching, but made villagers susceptible to political corruption. Prior to 1780, Cricklade voters willing to be bribed would chalk a grid on their front door, made of five vertical and five horizontal lines. It signalled their willingness to sell a vote. The going rate was ten guineas if the candidate was elected, five guineas if he failed. Of course, by polling day the chalk grids had been rubbed out.

A report in 1821 described the harsh conditions still being endured by local farm workers. Livestock grazed the meadows while labourers and their families existed in hovels squeezed onto muddy roadsides. They were said to be eating food barely fit for pigs and using wheat stubble for fuel. In those days the Thames was navigable as far as Cricklade and the bulk of farm produce was piled onto barges and sent downstream to fill the mouths of city dwellers.

Smallholders who could keep a few chickens were able to add eggs to their 'milk meates', and to bake simple supper dishes. The following recipe dates from 1818:

CHEESE PUDDING

90 g (3 oz) tasty cheddar cheese
155 g (5 oz) white breadcrumbs
120 g (4 oz) butter
150 ml (¼ pint) milk
2 eggs
Pinch of Salt
Parsley to Garnish

Grate the cheese and mix with the breadcrumbs. Melt the butter in the milk and stir into the cheese and breadcrumbs. Add the well beaten eggs and a good pinch of salt. Bake at a moderate heat for about half an hour until golden brown. Garnish with parsley.

With so little to spare, strangers were hustled out of town, regardless of their circumstances. In 1800 the overseer at Cricklade's St Sampson's Church made the following entries in the parish records:

Black man in distress for Liverpool – 6d.
Gave a woman with 3 small children all with the small pox upon them to get them along – 2s.6d.

Life was a little easier by the early twentieth century but there were few luxuries. Francis Norris Cuss was born in 1911 and grew up in Cricklade, where his mother eked out a living making leather gloves. Francis earned the odd penny himself by picking blackberries and gathering watercress from the Thames.

During the First World War there were additional shortages and when the local shop ran out of sweets Francis was offered a ha'penny of locust beans, normally used as sheep fodder. It is hardly surprising that his early memories should centre on food, especially puddings. Top of his list was boiled jam roll, which I later discovered had been a favourite among inmates at Oxford gaol, further down the Thames. It was a comforting reminder of home and, more importantly, rhymed with parole!

Francis fondly recalled his mother's Christmas puddings and would have appreciated a Wiltshire dialect verse written by Edward Slow:

THA GIRT BIG FIGGETTY POODEN

A used ta come in steamin hot,
Nearly as big's a waishen pot.
Wie vigs an currands zich a lot,
In thick ar Crismas pooden.

Between Cricklade and Castle Eaton, smaller tributaries flow into a Thames now strong enough to support banks of water-loving willows and alders. It is perhaps this section of the river that best fits William Morris's line from *The Earthly Paradise*:

By this sweet stream that knows not of the sea,
That guesses not the city's misery.

This little stream whose hamlets scarce have names,
This far-off, lonely mother of the Thames.

Approaching Castle Eaton, a row of farm cottages has a plaque expressing gratitude that the area was spared a fatal cattle plague in 1866. It is impossible to read the words without remembering the devastation caused throughout Britain in recent years by foot and mouth and mad cow disease. In 1866 the problem was *rinderpest*, a highly contagious viral infection capable of wiping out entire herds overnight. The relief at being spared must have been overwhelming for a community so reliant on dairy produce. In 1922, a married couple from nearby Castle Eaton claimed their longevity (they had both reached 100) was due to a diet of butter, milk and 'skim dick', a cheese made from skimmed milk. The old people said meat made them ill, possibly a result of consuming huge quantities during the rinderpest plague when the local maxim was: 'Let cattle be slaughtered and eaten today, for tomorrow they may die.'

As we walked into Castle Eaton village, a middle-aged lady rode past on her bicycle and called out: 'Good morning! If you would like a cup of tea, follow me.' She led us to the community hall, where we joined a weekly get-together of locals. It is hard to say what we appreciated more – the tea and home-made cakes, the use of the loo, or the friendly conversation.

No trace remains of the castle from which Castle Eaton took its name, but down by the river the village church has Norman doorways. There is also a slate-covered bell turret containing the original thirteenth-century sanctus bell. On our most recent visit to the church we noticed a bird had built a nest in the turret. According to William Cowper, it is likely to have been a jackdaw:

THE JACKDAW

There is a bird who,
By his coat
And by the hoarseness of his note,
Might be supposed a crow,
A great frequenter of the church,
Where, bishop like,
He finds a perch
And dormitory too.

The Thames Path skirts around neighbouring Kempsford, but the village's massive 1390 church tower is a focal point for miles. In AD 800 the Anglo-Saxon Chronicles recorded a battle at Kempsford between Ethelmund of Wessex and Wechsen of Wiltshire. When Ethel-mund and his men crossed the Thames, 'A terrible conflict ensued, in which both commanders were slain but the men of Wiltshire obtained the victory.' The clash of battle axes that shattered the peace of this area in Saxon times has been replaced by the roar of high-tech military aircraft. Behind the village is Fairford RAF base, also used by the US air force. The base was built to accommodate British and American planes used during the D-Day invasion of Normandy. In 1969 it became the UK base for testing Concorde.

During the 2003 war in Iraq, long-range American B52 bombers were loaded here before making return missions over Baghdad. At the height of the conflict I was touched to find pamphlets at the church asking visitors to pray for peace in the Middle East, with suitable prayers provided for those of Muslim, Jewish or Christian faith.

In the mid fourteenth century, the manor of Kempsford was held by the 1st Duke of Lancaster, whose only son drowned in the Thames while crossing the ford. The heartbroken Duke rode away, never to return. According to tradition his horse cast a shoe as he left and it was nailed to the door of the church by sentimental locals. There is a rusting horseshoe on the door to this day, reminding me of a rhyme from a mummer's play performed at Kempsford many years ago and recorded by a local family:

I comes from the country where they knits horseshoes and spins steel iron bars and thatches pigsties with pancakes.

The unhappy Duke of Lancaster was succeeded by his daughter Blanche, who married the nobleman John of Gaunt, fourth son of Edward III. Blanche was a patron of Geoffrey Chaucer and is remembered by him in *The Book of the Duchess*, commonly believed to be an elegy to her. Blanche's sister Maud also has a memorial. By the river at Kempsford is a terrace known as Maud's Walk, where she once paced the banks grieving for her drowned brother. Another story has Lady Maud ending up in the river herself, murdered by her husband after becoming embroiled in a medieval saga of slander, jealousy and political intrigue.

Thankfully the story surrounding Kempsford's George Hotel is more positive. It was built by John Arkell, who was born in Kempsford in 1802. Arkell emigrated to Canada in 1830 and made his fortune there. When he returned home he established a brewery and several pubs, including The George.

A little way downriver is all that remains of medieval Inglesham, one of many riverside settlements lost to plague, economic depression, or both. In one field it is possible to distinguish the pattern of ancient ridge and furrow farmland. A laneway leads to Inglesham's thirteenth-century St John the Baptist Church. Thanks to the enlightened Victorian William Morris, the church has retained its Jacobean pulpit and box pews. There are wall paintings from the thirteenth to the early nineteenth century. But one of the most intriguing features in St John's is a Saxon section of stone frieze, which until 1910 was located outside forming a sundial. Now in the south wall of the nave, the fragment shows the Virgin Mary and child being blessed by the hand of God.

At the rear of a farmhouse back at the riverside is a brick round-house; one of five built along the Thames and Severn Canal, which left the river at Inglesham on its way to Stroud and beyond. The creeper-covered building resembles a romantic folly but was actually very functional. Horses were stabled on the ground floor, the lock-keeper lived on the first floor and a lead roof served as a water tank. The three levels were connected by a spiral staircase built into the building's thick outer walls.

The Thames and Severn Canal was completed in 1792, principally to transport coal from the Forest of Dean to London. It stretched for 29 miles (46 km) and required forty-three locks. Unfortunately there were regular water shortages through seepage and later canals provided more direct links to the Midlands. The arrival of the Great Western Railway dealt the waterway's final blow but for Thames Path walkers there is a wonderful legacy in the towpath that allowed teams of horses to haul barges up the Thames and along the canal. From Inglesham the towpath continues all the way down to Putney, just 20 miles (31 km) short of the Flood Barrier.

One of the greatest engineering feats along the canal was the 2½ mile (4 km) Sapperton Tunnel, said to be so straight it was possible to stand at the entrance and see a pin-point of light at the other end. For bargemen, the only practical way through was to lie down and push along the walls with their feet; a painstaking four- or five-hour process known as 'legging'. The men often suffered from a condition dubbed lighterman's bottom, a painful variation of housemaid's knee. There is a colourful account of Horatio Hornblower legging through the tunnel in the opening chapter of C. S. Forester's *Hornblower and the Atropos*.

It is possible to walk to the pillared tunnel entrance by continuing on past the source of the Thames back at Kemble. An interesting old pub located just above the entrance, the Tunnel House Inn, was built to serve the needs of the miners who spent five long years burrowing underground by candlelight. The inn held a special place in the heart of the late Sir John Betjeman: 'My father took me here as a child and the romance of the place has never diminished.' Today's visitors will find plenty of local beers on offer, a great accompaniment to one of the pub's most popular dishes: a plate of Gloucester Old Spot pork sausages.

The poet Percy Bysshe Shelley thought of exploring the canal system when he rowed to Inglesham from Old Windsor in 1815 but was put off by its steep £20 toll. He continued upstream via an increasingly reedy Thames then, like countless boaters before and since, gave up and floated gently back to the market town of Lechlade. The town's Halfpenny Bridge has an unusual hump-back design that allowed the passage of tall-masted Thames barges. It was named for its halfpenny toll, levied on all pedestrians except those on their way to church or to a funeral.

By 1327 there were fifty-eight taxable inhabitants at Lechlade, including Thomas la Taillur, William le Tanner and John le Botlyer. There were probably several le Bakyers as well, although the town lost a master of the craft a few years ago when the Flour Bag Bakery was sold. Slabs of their rich, lardy cake sustained many a Thames Path walker. Regrettably, all things change but an echo of the old Gloucestershire scrumpy houses remains in Lechlade Cider Cake.

LECHLADE CIDER CAKE

2 eggs
120 g (4 oz) butter
120 g (4 oz) sugar
250 g (8 oz) plain flour
½ teaspoon ground nutmeg
1 teaspoon bicarbonate of soda
1 teacup of cider

Beat the eggs thoroughly. Cream the butter and sugar and beat in the eggs. Sift together the nutmeg, bicarbonate of soda and half the flour, then stir into the egg mixture. Pour in the cider and combine thoroughly, then carefully stir in the remaining flour. Put into a well-buttered shallow baking tin and bake until firm at 190°C (375°F) for about 45 minutes.

At the town's St John's Lock is a sculpture of a reclining Old Father Thames, commissioned for the Crystal Palace Exhibition in 1851. The reason for its inclusion in the exhibition was that it was made of concrete, then an experimental material. Having survived the fire that destroyed the palace, the sculpture was purchased by the Thames Conservancy and eventually erected at Thames Head in 1958. Repeated vandalism prompted its move to the lock in 1974, where it has remained ever since.

Father Thames is surrounded by barrels and wool bales, symbols of a once-thriving river trade. The 'lade' in Lechlade means 'to load' and goods sent downriver included dairy produce (especially cheese), salt, raw hides, stone and wool. Here in 'Cotswold Thames', the sheep industry was well established by medieval times. Riverside meadows provided good grazing and under the soil was a rich supply of Fuller's Earth, an aluminium silicate that absorbed grease and was used in wool scouring.

By the fifteenth century, farmers were reaping the benefits of an improved breed of sheep

© Rob Conolly

Old Father Thames reclines at Lechlade Lock

known as Cotswold Lions. Tradition has it that when the Flemish Princess Philippa of Hain-ault married Edward III, her dowry included twelve huge Flemish rams. Cistercian monks acquired several of the animals and managed to cross them with their flock of smaller, native sheep. The resulting 'Cotswold Lions' could weigh up to 16 stone (100 kg) and produce fleeces of about 25 lb (11 kg).

The great manor houses and churches of the Cotswolds were funded by the wool industry and Lechlade Church has a chapel dedicated to St Blaise, patron of woolcombers. By 1600, raw wool and woollen cloth made up an astonishing eighty per cent of the English export trade. Its importance to the country's economy was reflected in the fact that at Westminster the Lord Chancellor sat on a large bale of wool. The Chancellor's seat is still referred to as the Woolsack.

During his visit to the town, Shelley composed verses in Lechlade churchyard and he is remembered by Shelley Walk. He spent a couple of nights at the New Inn, which still stands by the church in Market Square. Another lovely place to stay is the riverside Trout Inn, appro-priately decorated with stuffed trout and pike. It was built beside St John's Bridge in 1472, by monks who had established a nearby priory two centuries earlier. The inn was used as a religious guesthouse and was originally known as the St John the Baptist's Head (no wonder they changed the name!). When the priory was dissolved in 1475 by Edward IV, one monk remained behind, in charge of the bridge.

BUSCOT TO WYTHAM GREAT WOOD

Beyond Lechlade the river winds through open meadows, occasionally looping back on itself so completely that walking the Thames Path can be like negotiating a lawn maze. A number of small concrete pillboxes in the surrounding fields were erected during the Second World War as part of a last line of defence against an enemy force trying to reach the industrial Midlands. Originally the pillboxes were covered with feathers, an attempt at camouflage which failed miserably when grazing cattle rubbed against them. Their presence is a reminder of the country's quiet desperation at the height of the war, when German invasion was a serious threat.

Downstream is the village of Buscot and the National Trust property of Buscot Park, built in the 1770s by Edward Loveden Townsend. Townsend did much to promote the area's cheese trade and in 1808 3,000 tons of Gloucester cheese were loaded at the estate's tiny wharf. Gloucester cheese is particularly good accompanied by beer or ale, which may explain why it remains so popular in Thameside pubs. It is most often served with bread and pickles in the traditional Ploughman's Lunch, but I prefer the following hot snack:

GLOUCESTER CHEESE AND ALE

250 g (8 oz) thinly sliced double Gloucester cheese
1 teaspoon English mustard
4 thick slices wholemeal bread
3 tablespoons brown ale

Place the cheese slices in the bottom of a shallow ovenproof dish and spread the mustard over the top. Pour in enough brown ale to just cover the cheese. Cover with foil and cook at 190°C for about ten minutes. Meanwhile, toast the bread and when the cheese mixture is cooked, pour it over the toast and serve immediately.

In 1859, Buscot Park was sold to Robert Tertius Campbell, who had made his fortune in the Australian gold rush, not as a prospector but as a gold trader. In a bold move, Campbell turned the estate over to the production of alcohol made from sugar beet and beetroot. Instead of double Gloucester cheeses, barrels of spirit alcohol were sent down the Thames and across to France to be used in the production of brandy.

The entrepreneurial Campbell introduced steam-driven ploughs at Buscot, fitting them with lime-light flares so that work could continue after dark. Water was pumped from the Thames for irrigation and a narrow-gauge railway installed to collect the beets. He also began building Buscot village, erecting the world's first concrete barn, which still stands. Sadly, the venture failed, partly because Campbell was unable to recoup his huge capital outlay, but also because he provided his farm labourers with unusually generous working conditions.

At the height of his financial troubles, Robert Campbell's eldest daughter Florence was involved in a notorious unsolved murder. In 1875 she had married a young barrister, Charles Bravo. On 18 April 1876, Bravo retired for the night in the couple's south London home but became violently ill after drinking from his bedside water jug. He died in agony several days later, having ingested 1 oz (30 g) of the corrosive poison antimony. The circumstances of his death suggested foul play and Florence became the prime suspect after lurid details of her private life were revealed. A coronial inquest returned a verdict of wilful murder and although there was insufficient evidence to take the matter to trial, Florence's reputation was ruined. She died from alcohol abuse just two years later. Her body was brought back to Buscot by her heartbroken parents but the gossip and innuendo remained so intense that she was buried in St Mary's churchyard at midnight, in an unmarked grave.

Campbell's distillery closed in 1879 and when he died in 1887 the estate was heavily in debt. It was purchased two years later by Lord Faringdon, who finished building the village and established Buscot Park's famous art collection, which includes works by Murillo, Reynolds and Rembrandt. Of particular interest to visitors is a series of Pre-Raphaelite pictures by Edward Burne-Jones known collectively as 'The Legend Of Briar Rose'. They hang in their original, highly ornate frames designed by the artist himself. For aspiring art investors the paintings provide a classic example of how fashion can affect value. Lord Faringdon bought the pictures for £15,000 but by 1940 they had fallen from favour and were valued at a mere £2,000. Today they are worth around twenty million!

The sole memento of the Campbell family's time at Buscot Park is a bible which belonged to Florence's sister Alice. An inscription notes that she was born at Woolloomooloo, Sydney and that she was married at Buscot's twelfth-century parish church in 1874, the year before her older sister married Charles Bravo.

The church benefitted from Lord Faringdon's patronage of Burne-Jones. In 1891 the artist created St Mary's beautiful 'Good Shepherd' stained glass window, in the chancel.

A rare photograph of the Bravo household, taken shortly before the suspicious death of Charles Bravo (centre) in 1876. Florence Bravo (née Campbell) is seated on the right

Appropriately for an area so long associated with the wool industry, it shows Christ carrying a lost lamb on his shoulders.

Between Buscot and Kelmscott the Thames Path passes lonely Eaton Footbridge. In 1937, Eaton Weir and its flash lock, one of the last on the Thames, was removed. Flash locks were a primitive means of taking boats over weirs in a sudden surge or 'flash' of water. During the Campbell era at Buscot Park it was rumoured that the innkeeper at Eaton Weir would buy spirits illegally from passing bargemen and hide it in kegs chained to the riverbed. It was true moonshine liquor, as he would quietly retrieve the kegs at night. Tragically, the old inn was destroyed by fire in the winter of 1979 and the landlord, his fiancée and business partner all lost their lives. The pub has never been rebuilt and an air of sadness lingers.

A little further downstream there is warmth and life at Kelmscott Manor, country home of the prolific writer, artist and craftsman William Morris from June 1871 until his death twenty-five years later. In his utopian novel *News From Nowhere,* Morris's travellers row to Kelmscott from London, where the character Ellen expresses her joy in the old manor to the story's narrator:

> *She led me up close to the house, and laid her shapely sun browned hand and arm on the lichened wall as if to embrace it, and cried out, 'O me! O me! How I love the earth, and the seasons, and weather, and all things that deal with it, and all that grows out of it, – as this has done!*

The stone-gabled house with its mullioned windows was built in 1571, and was described by Morris as 'heaven on earth'. In 1895 he published an article titled 'Gossip About An Old House On The Upper Thames', which includes a lovingly detailed account of the view from the manor's 'best room'; a panelled parlour:

> *Another charm this room has, that through its south window you will not only catch a glimpse of the Thames clover meadows and the pretty little elm-crowned hill over in Berkshire, but if you sit in the proper place, you can see not only the barn aforesaid with its beautiful sharp gable, the grey stone sheds, and the dovecot, but also the flank of the earlier house and its gables and grey sealed roofs and this is a beautiful outlook indeed.*

The elms have succumbed to Dutch elm disease but otherwise the view to the barn, dovecote and gables is unchanged. In spring, haze-blue ceanothus brushes the window and there are roses blooming against the grey stonework.

Kelmscott Manor was, as Morris put it, 'within a stone's throw of the baby Thames', and its flora strongly influenced his work. His designs for wallpapers and fabrics featured the boughs and leaves of willow, as well as wild flowers: creeping bellflowers, bluebells, snakeshead fritillaries and forget-me-nots. The river also played its part in Morris's revival of the art of natural dyes:

> *I was at Kelmscott the other day in that beautiful cold weather and betwixt the fishing, I cut a handful of poplar twigs and boiled them, and dyed a lock of wool ...*

For three years Morris and his wife Jane lived in a difficult *ménage a trois* with the widowed artist Dante Gabriel Rossetti. Rossetti had fallen in love with Jane and, to complicate matters, he was often under the influence of drugs. He finally stormed out after a row with local fishermen, even leaving his precious paintbox behind. There is another poignant reminder of Rossetti at Kelmscott: Jane Morris's jewel box. It was decorated by Rossetti's dead wife, Lizzie Siddal.

Morris's search for a country property was prompted by his desire for a refuge from his busy life in London. He was also thinking of his family, particularly his daughter Jenny who suffered from epilepsy. On 17 May 1871 he wrote to a friend:

> *I have been looking about for a house for the wife and kids and wither do you guess my eye is turned now? Kelmscott, a little village about two miles above Radcott Bridge ...*
>
> *Young Jenny and her sister May thoroughly enjoyed the novelty of floods at Kelmscott, especially when the baker had to aim loaves of bread through the upper window of the house with a pitchfork.*

May Morris (left) with the formidable Miss Mary Lobb

Morris died in 1896 and was buried in Kelmscott churchyard, the coffin conveyed on a haywain decorated with willow and alder. In 1896 Jane Morris paid for the building of what are known as the Memorial Cottages, easily distinguished by the carving on the front showing Morris sitting in Kelmscott's Home Mead.

When her mother died in 1914, May Morris became guardian of the Kelmscott estate. In 1917 she met Mary Lobb, who was working as a landgirl in the village. May engaged Mary as a companion and the pair spent the next twenty years together. Miss Lobb was a solidly built, formidable character who wore her hair severely cropped and habitually dressed in knickerbockers and a tweed jacket. She could produce a startling stream of invective when annoyed. There is a wonderful cartoon of her on display at the manor. After May died in 1938, Miss Lobb lost all heart and reportedly took to her bed with a bottle of brandy and a loaded pistol!

Just below Kelmscott is a view across the river to the village of Eaton Hastings, named after Ralph de Hastings, lord of the manor in the twelfth century. The Norman church of St Michael and All Angels was built to serve the needs of the manor house and both tenant and freehold farmers, but in 1348 the Black Death ravaged the population. Those who survived faced increasingly harsh winters, regular flooding of the Thames, and above all the devastation of land clearance.

Although Lechlade benefited from the expansion of the wool industry in the fifteenth century, for tiny settlements such as Eaton Hastings the opposite was true. In the church notes at St Michael and All Angels the following rhyme appears: 'Horn and thorn have England all forlorn.' 'Horn' stood for sheep and 'thorn' was a reference to hawthorn hedging, which was used to enclose large tracts of land for sheep runs. As a result of the enclosures, tenant farmers were ousted and villages depopulated.

The English statesman and humanitarian Sir Thomas More realized what was happening in the countryside: 'The shepe that were wont to be so meke and tame and so smal eaten, be become so great devourers and so wylde that they eat up and swallow the very men themselves.' Of the displaced tenants he wrote sadly: 'By one means or by another, by hooke or crooke, they must needs departe away, poore wretched souls.' With no alternative means of earning a living, many took to the roads as tramps.

At Eaton Hastings, the nobleman who enclosed the village fields was a member of the Fettiplace family, whose extreme wealth prompted a mention in another old rhyme:

The Traceys, the Laceys, and Fettiplaces,
Own all the best manors, the woods and the chases.

Recently, Rob and I drove out to St Michael's Church to photograph the graves of Buscot's Robert Campbell and his wife Anne, who lie together on the left-hand side of the porch (see

© Rob Conolly

Buscot's Robert and Anne Campbell; at peace after financial failure and the disgrace of their daughter Florence

page 29). Perhaps it was felt they could rest more peacefully at Eaton Hastings than in Buscot churchyard, where the uneasy spirit of their daughter Florence hovered.

The Thames path wanders on to Radcot via Grafton Lock. According to a Saxon charter there was a stone bridge at Radcot by 958 and parts of its replacement date back to the twelfth century, making it the oldest bridge on the Thames. It was built by Cistercian monks from nearby Faringdon, which may be why its three Gothic arches are ribbed underneath like the roof of a cathedral. An empty niche in the downstream parapet was originally intended for a statue of the Virgin Mary. Prior to the First World War, the bridge was in danger of falling down but a spirited campaign by May Morris managed to save it. It is now bypassed by river traffic, which instead passes under a crossing built by the Thames Commissioners in 1787, after a new navigation channel was cut.

This important river crossing has been the scene of battles for centuries. In 1154 King Stephen fought Queen Matilda at a castle near Radcot and in the thirteenth century King John skirmished with his barons prior to the signing of the Magna Carta downstream at Runnymede. In 1387 the middle arch of the bridge was deliberately broken down by Henry Bolingbroke, son of John of Gaunt and later to become Henry IV. Henry wanted to prevent

Robert de Vere, Earl of Oxford, riding south to support Richard II in a dispute over the English crown. Henry's trap was only a partial success. Some of de Vere's men fell into the river and were stabbed to death but the Earl managed to struggle out of his armour and swim to safety.

The bridge was also the scene of Civil War skirmishes between Oliver Cromwell's Round-heads and King Charles I's Cavaliers. Cromwell had taken the nearby town of Faringdon and Royalist troops retreated to Elizabethan Faringdon House (since demolished), which stood behind the church. They received the following ultimatum from Cromwell, dated 29 April 1645:

> *To the Governor of the Garrison of Faringdon*
> *Sir*
> *I summon you to deliver into my hands the House wherein you are, and your ammunition with all things else there, together with your persons, to be disposed of as the parliament shall appoint. Which if you refuse to do, you are to expect the utmost extremity of war. I rest,*
>
> *Your servant*
> *Oliver Cromwell*

The Royalists ignored Cromwell's order and a battle ensued which almost destroyed the town. Local houses were demolished to establish clear lines of fire and the Parliamentarians tried to topple the church steeple onto Faringdon House. When their strategy failed, the damaged steeple was allowed to fall towards the township, inflicting even more damage. Somehow the King's men managed to hold out until a more honourable surrender could be negotiated but there is a truncated look about the church to this day, as the steeple was never rebuilt.

Faringdon received its first charter for a market from Henry III in 1218, so it is fitting that one of the first structures rebuilt after the Civil War was the pillared market hall. It has scarcely changed since it was completed in 1660 and locals still sit and chat under its shelter as they wait for the bus. The town is one of the most charming and friendly along the river, with a long history of hospitality. A pub called The Bell was built as a guesthouse for the abbey founded by the Cistercian monks, and later became a coaching inn. It still has a seventeenth-century chimney piece over an inglenook fireplace.

Across the square is The Crown. As its name suggests, this inn had strong Royalist connections during the Civil War and there is said to have been a tunnel connecting it to Faringdon House. Directly next door is a little cafe called The Sadlers. Upstairs, a secret door leading from The Crown has been uncovered. Rob and I sat beside it as we drank our coffee,

© Rob Conolly

Faringdon Church with its missing steeple; a casualty of the Civil War

imagining besieged Royalist soldiers slipping through to freedom after making their way to the inn via the tunnel. From 1635, post riders changed horses at The Crown in a courier service between London and Bath, and its landlords continued to serve as Faringdon's post-masters until 1898.

Back on the Thames Path by Radcot Bridge there is a view across to Folly Hill, where Queen Matilda's brother built a great wooden fortress in the twelfth century and where Cromwell later quartered his men. On the summit is an ornate tower, partly obscured by trees. This is Faringdon Folly, completed in 1935 by the eccentric composer and writer Lord Berners. He once put a notice on the wall of the folly warning: 'Members of the public committing suicide from this tower do so at their own risk.' The tower would have been far more bizarre if Berners' dying wish had been fulfilled: he had asked to be stuffed and seated at a grand piano on top of the folly. Berners lived at the current Faringdon House, surrounded by fantail pigeons which he dyed all the colours of the rainbow, to match his personality.

An earlier resident of Faringdon House was Henry James Pye, Poet Laureate to King George III. Pye's style was so florid that literary critic George Stevens satirized his birthday

Looking across Faringdon's Market Place to Sadler's Cafe, with its secret, 'Civil War' door

tribute to the King, with its allusions to 'vocal groves and the feathered choir', by comparing it to a choir of blackbirds, and cleverly punned on the poet's name in the familiar rhyme:

> *Sing a song of sixpence,*
> *A pocket full of rye;*
> *Four and twenty blackbirds,*
> *Baked in a pye.*
> *When the pye was opened,*
> *The birds began to sing;*
> *Was not that a dainty dish,*
> *To set before the king?*

Walking across the meadows between Radcot Lock and Rushley Lock, we filled our empty lunch boxes with field mushrooms. I was moved to tell Rob about an appreciative note Virginia Woolf once sent to Vita Sackville-West in response to a gift of mushrooms: 'they must have grown in a water meadow and been breathed on by cows'. I love the image of fungal spores stirring and swelling in the warmth of a cow's breath.

Rushley Lock is particularly beautiful, with its stone lock-keeper's cottage and old paddle and rymer weir. We photographed the cottage at dusk, its stonework warmed by the brilliant autumn colour of Virginia creeper and lamps glowing softly from within.

Having walked straight through from Cricklade, we arrived at Tadpole Bridge's Trout Inn tired and hungry, just as the doors opened at 6 p.m. Trout was not on the menu but there was tender loin of rabbit in a red wine glaze followed by a rib-sticking steamed pudding. We had booked accommodation at nearby Chimney Farm and our hostess Jean Kinch drove in to collect us. By ten o'clock we were sound asleep.

It was not until next morning that we met our fellow guests, two elderly sisters from Brisbane. They had been staying at the farm for several days; visiting local sights, walking the laneways and picking blackberries. Jean Kinch had obligingly turned the fruit into a pie and I am sure she would have fried our mushrooms for us if we had thought to ask. I am grateful to her for the following recipe, which combines blackberries and apples:

BLACKBERRY BUTTERSCOTCH CREAM

2 large cooking apples
450 g (1 lb) freshly picked blackberries
3 tablespoons clear honey
½ teaspoon cinnamon or ½ a cinnamon stick
150 ml (4 fl oz) double cream
150 ml (4 fl oz) yoghurt

TOPPING

75 ml (3 oz) unsalted butter
120 g (4 oz) coarse white breadcrumbs
30 g (1 oz) caster sugar

Peel and slice the apple and put with the rinsed blackberries. Add the honey and cinnamon and simmer over a low heat until the fruit is soft.

Remove cinnamon stick. Allow the fruit to cool a little and put into a glass serving bowl.

Whip the cream, adding the yoghurt spoonful by spoonful until thick. Keep to one side until topping is made.

To make the topping – melt the butter in a frying pan and add the breadcrumbs and caster sugar. Gently brown the breadcrumbs, stirring to prevent burning. Spread on a large plate to cool. Sprinkle some of the crumbs onto the fruit. Put the cream/yogurt mixture on top then add remaining crumbs as a final layer.

Chimney is a hamlet of only five houses. The reason it failed to thrive can be found in *Gardner's Directory of Oxfordshire*, published in 1852, which dismissed Chimney in just six words: 'generally inundated by water in winter'.

After breakfast the Brisbane sisters went off to visit nearby Blenheim Palace, birthplace of Winston Churchill. Rob and I were driven back to Tadpole Bridge by the ever-helpful Jean, to complete the second stage of our trek to Oxford. William Morris wrote a lovely description of the area around Tadpole when he rowed past on the way to Kelmscott in the summer of 1880:

> *One thing was very pleasant: they were hay-making on the flat flood-washed spits of ground and islets all about Tadpole; and the hay was gathered on punts and the like; odd stuff to look at, mostly sedge, but they told us it was the best stuff for milk ...*

Tadpole Bridge itself was built in the late eighteenth century. It carried a turnpike road to nearby Bampton, once dubbed Bampton-in-the-Bush because of its remote location. The town is noted for the gently eccentric art of Morris dancing, where men dance around with bells tied to their ankles. At Bampton's annual fair a jester bops people on the head with a pig's bladder and a sword bearer distributes 'lucky' slices from a plum cake impaled on his sword.

Downstream, the Shifford Lock 'cut' created an artificial island as it sliced past a winding, shallow section of the river that had long delayed and frustrated Thames bargemen. There is now little at Shifford to remind visitors that King Alfred held the first meeting of an English parliament here in 890, surrounded by 'many bishops, learned men, proud earls and awful knights'. What a satisfying occasion for the King after his battles with the Danes and that embarrassing cake-burning episode!

As with Eaton Hastings (see page 33), the settlement at Shifford was decimated by plague. We visited its isolated church but unfortunately found it locked. Afterwards we chatted to a dog walker who pointed out a field still known as Court Closet. He told us that many Roman artifacts had been found in the area. Perhaps it will be discovered that Alfred chose the site for his parliament because it was once a significant Roman settlement.

From Shifford the towpath continues its lonely route downstream to Newbridge. This stone crossing is 'new' only in the sense that it was established about fifty years after Radcot Bridge. It was built in the thirteenth century by Benedictine monks, who originally came from a monastery near Paris. There is a story that the monks added bull's blood to the mortar to give it extra strength. The stone was no doubt quarried at Taynton in the Cotswolds:

thousands of tons of Taynton stone were sent down the River Windrush, which enters the Thames at Newbridge. It was then barged downstream for use in landmark buildings such as the Oxford colleges and Windsor Castle. Following the Great Fire of London, Taynton stone was also used to rebuild St Paul's Cathedral.

Like Radcot, Newbridge was the scene of Civil War clashes, as mentioned in lines by John William Pitt:

> *This bridge has great antiquity, and thus belies its name,*
> *For like historic Radcot Bridge, it owes its present fame,*
> *To having been the scene of stormy battle long ago,*
> *When Charles I was England's King and Parliament his foe.*

Newbridge has twin inns: the Maybush and the Rose Revived. The Maybush evolved from the bridge's original toll-house, manned by a hermit appointed by the monks. As a pub it closed half an hour earlier than its competitor across the river and diehard drinkers were in the habit of slipping over the bridge for a final few 'revivers', which is how the Rose Revived got its name. Appropriately, the pub's sign shows a rose in a pint of ale.

The Thames Path follows the old drinking route over the bridge and along the Rose Revived's beautiful riverside garden; best enjoyed in early spring when the bulbs are out under the weeping willows but the summer hordes are still to emerge. It then rejoins the towpath and continues downstream to the footbridge of long-vanished Northmoor Weir, which has an eighteenth-century story romantic enough to inspire a Jane Austen novel. While fishing the river here, Oxford undergraduate Viscount Ashbrook met and fell in love with the daughter of the weir keeper, Betty Rudge. Despite their vastly different backgrounds the pair married and lived happily together until the viscount died twenty years later.

Beyond paddle-and-rymer Northmoor Lock, the Thames cuts a broad curve as it flows through the water meadows towards Bablock Hythe and Cumnor, a landscape made famous by Matthew Arnold in 'The Scholar-Gipsy' and little changed since he wrote the following lines:

> *Moor'd to the cool bank in the summer heats*
> *Mid wide grass meadows which the sunshine fills,*
> *And watch the warm green-muffled Cumnor Hills,*
> *And wonder if thou haunt'st their shy retreats*

While walking this section of the river, we passed several grim-faced fishermen. They complained they had not had a nibble all day but were after chub, a freshwater game fish. Thames fishermen are something of an enigma. To borrow from Winston Churchill, never have I seen so many anglers employing so much equipment for so little reward – unless those enormous keeper nets hold more than their owners are willing to let on.

There is talk of a bridge being built at Bablock Hythe, which has long been a Thames crossing point. The Romans created a ford here and from the year 904 there was a ferry, ultimately a vehicular service. It closed in 1986 but the publican at the Ferryman Inn now operates a foot ferry to the Cumnor bank in the summer months.

In John Galsworthy's novel *Over the River,* young Tony Croom walks down to the Thames at Bablock Hythe and throws himself into a hollow. Having recently returned from abroad, he breathes the early-morning scent of English grass and wild flowers and experiences an intense reconnection with his country:

> *Rabbits and bees and birds – nothing else as yet awake. He lay on his back staring at the grass and the bushes and the early sky, blue and lightly fleeced. Perhaps because he could see so little from that hollow all England seemed to be with him.*

Across the river a path from the ferry landing leads on to the village of Cumnor, otherwise reached by car via the A420 from Oxford. In the fourteenth century the monks of Abingdon Abbey built Cumnor Hall, which was the scene of a mysterious death in the sixteenth century.

On 8 September 1560, Amy Robsart was found dead from a broken neck at the foot of the stairs in her apartments at the hall, by then a private residence. Amy was the young wife of Lord Robert Dudley, a favourite of Queen Elizabeth I. The close relationship between Lord Robert and the Queen was said to have driven Amy to despair. Dudley's enemies fostered a rumour that his wife had been murdered, thereby freeing him to marry the Queen. De Quadra, the Spanish ambassador, went even further. He wrote a letter home after Amy died in which he inferred there had been a conspiracy involving Elizabeth herself: '… the Queen, on her return from hunting, told me that Lord Robert's wife was dead, or nearly so, and begged me to say nothing about it.' His words suggest Elizabeth had prior knowledge of a plot, as the hunting trip he referred to took place on 4 September, several days before Amy's fatal plunge down the Cumnor Hall stairs.

De Quadra's claim could merely have been salacious gossip as he was not noted for his integrity, but his letter highlights the intrigue and suspicion that surrounded the affair. During Amy's burial service, from which Dudley was tellingly absent, the priest made his own feelings clear by informing mourners she had been 'pitifully murdered'. Her body lies somewhere in the choir of the Church of St Mary the Virgin in Oxford.

Cumnor Hall was located immediately to the left of St Michael's Church. For centuries its towers stood as a poignant reminder of the tragedy, and in 1770 the poet Julius Mickle wrote 'The Ballad Of Cumnor Hall', which began:

Full many a traveler oft hath sigh'd
And pensive wept the Countess' fall,
As wand'ring onwards they've espied
The haunted towers of Cumnor Hall

Inspired by Mickle's poem, Sir Walter Scott created a sinister though highly fictionalized account of Amy's death in his novel *Kenilworth*.

Cumnor Hall was demolished in the early nineteenth century but by the churchyard path is some stonework thought to have been part of one of the manor's fireplaces. The church has a display of letters and photographs relating to Amy Robsart, and also a commanding, life-size statue of Elizabeth I. It is possible that this statue was commissioned by Robert Dudley himself as it was first recorded in the grounds of Dean Court, a house he owned within the parish.

The ghostly statue of Elizabeth I in Cumnor Church. Was she involved in the death of Amy Robsart?

In an interesting footnote to the story, modern medical science may have exonerated Lord Robert and the Queen. At the time of her death Amy Robsart was said to be suffering from what was described as 'a malady of the breast', most likely breast cancer. It is now known that advanced cancer can weaken surrounding bone structure, and that her fall could have been the result of a spontaneous fracture of the neck.

The community of Cumnor suffered a heavy loss of life during the Civil War, though not in battle. Charles I had made his headquarters at nearby Oxford and overcrowding during the long siege of the city led to what became known as camp fever, which spread to surrounding villages. In 1644 Cromwell's forces raided Cumnor for supplies and made off with St Michael's weathercock, to melt down for ammunition. Fortunately the church's greatest treasure was built thirty years later: a narrow, oak, spiral staircase leading to the bell tower. Dating from 1685, it twists around a central post made from a single tree.

It would be possible to remain on the south bank of the Thames and continue walking downriver to Pinkhill Lock via the towpath, which crossed to the Cumnor bank with the ferry. However, until there *is* a bridge at Bablock Hythe the official Thames Path not only holds to the north bank but temporarily leaves the riverside. When setting off, sensitive souls would be advised to avert their gaze from the caravan park and instead look forward to the mellow stone and thatched cottages of Stanton Harcourt.

The Harcourts are the only surviving family of the Norman Conquest in Oxfordshire. They lived in this village for 600 years before moving downstream to Nuneham Courtenay. All that remains of the original fifteenth-century manor house is its medieval kitchen and Pope's Tower, named for the poet and essayist Alexander Pope. Pope occupied the tower while translating Homer's *The Iliad* between 1717 and 1718. His specially designed chair survives, its leather padding allowing him to ease his twisted spine by sitting backwards and resting his arms as he wrote. Pope famously scratched a memorial of his stay at the manor on one of the tower's windows: 'In the year 1718 I Alexander Pope finished here the fifth volume of Homer.'

A beautiful chapel in the parish church remembers generations of the Harcourt family, including Sir Robert. As a Lancastrian, Robert Harcourt was Henry Tudor's standard bearer at Bosworth Field in 1485, when Henry defeated Richard III in the final battle of the War of the Roses. Beyond the churchyard is a duck pond, originally one of numerous 'stew ponds', stocked with fish to supplement the diet of villagers as well as Lord Harcourt's household. No doubt many plump carp were baked at the manor, which boasts the most complete medieval kitchen in England. The building's conical roof forms a unique chimney, with wooden shutters allowing smoke to escape by opening and closing according to the direction of the wind. Historian Dr Robert Plot (1645–96) described it as:

... so strangely unusual, that, by way of riddle, one may truly call it either a kitchen within a chimney, or a kitchen without one ... the fire being made against the walls.

During his stay at Stanton Harcourt, Alexander Pope wrote several epitaphs for twenty-five-year-old John Hewet and eighteen-year-old Sarah Drew, lovers who were killed by lightning in the summer of 1717 while helping with the harvest. Pope sent two versions to his friend Lady Mary Wortley Montague, who responded with slightly more cynical lines of her own. Lady Mary suggested that Sarah may have lived to become a beaten wife and John a cuckold swain, concluding:

Now they are happy in their doom,
FOR POPE HATH WROTE UPON THEIR TOMB

Perhaps Lady Mary's levity encouraged Pope to compose his own irreverent version:

Here lie two poor Lovers, who had the mishap
Although very chaste, to die of the Clap.

Enjoying a complementary self-serve snack

© Rob Conolly

Walking the towpath between Stanton Harcourt and Swinford Bridge, we came across a hedge with a bumper crop of blackberries. As we ate our fill, it occurred to us that prehistoric Britons may have picked far more exotic fruits from the riverbanks. In gravel deposits around Stanton Harcourt archeologists have found elephant tusk and the teeth of lions: 200,000-year-old fossils from a then-tropical Thames Valley.

We were discovering that ancient place names preserve history almost as well as fossils. The name Stanton means 'settlement near the stones'; a reference to a prehistoric stone circle located just south of the village and known as Devil's Quoits. Originally there were around thirty-five standing stones surrounded by a ditch, but many were purloined by locals. One was hauled off by an enterprising farmer in 1688 for use as a bridge. Perhaps he or his descendants feared retribution and decided to return it because there are said to be visible wheel ruts on one stone. Others were buried during gravel extraction and the site was further damaged during the Second World War, when it was levelled and used as an aerodrome. The 4,500-year-old circle has now been restored, raising fears in some quarters that there will be an 'invasion' of twenty-first-century Druids.

The next major river crossing is Swinford, the name indicating that pigs were once herded across to Eynsham on the opposite bank. This could only have occurred when the Thames was particularly low because before Swinford Bridge was built the ford was very dangerous. In the winter of 1764, the Methodist preacher John Wesley got a soaking when his horse stumbled on the flooded causeway

Once my mare lost both her fore feet, but she gave a spring and recovered the causeway, otherwise we must have taken a swim, for the water on either side was ten or twelve feet deep. However, after one or two plunges more, we got through ...

Wesley, who was returning home after preaching one of his first sermons, was already suffering from a painfully swollen face and gums. Clearly he should have ignored the Lord's call and stayed in bed.

George III also ended up wet through at Swinford, but was at least in a position to improve matters. He put pressure on the landowner, the Earl of Abingdon, to provide a bridge, which was completed in 1777. To cover expenses, the Earl was allowed to charge a tax-free toll and the bridge remains one of only two privately owned toll bridges on the Thames. Given the rate of inflation, it is amazing that motorists still pay only five pence. Pedestrians, postmen, and emergency vehicles cross for free.

Wytham Great Wood comes down to meet the river just a short walk downstream. This 600-acre (243-hectare) wildlife haven was bequeathed to Oxford University and for the last fifty years its population of small mammals and birds has been painstakingly monitored by volunteers.

The River Evenlode enters the Thames between Swinford Bridge and King's Lock, having risen below Moreton-in-Marsh and flowed through an idyllic Cotswold landscape. Hillaire Belloc captured its essence in verses from his poem, 'The Evenlode':

The tender Evenlode that makes
Her meadows hush to hear the sound
Of waters mingling in the brakes,
And binds my heart to English soil.
A lovely river, all alone,
She lingers in the hills and holds
A hundred little towns of stone,
Forgotten in the western wolds.

Beyond King's Lock, the Thames Path leads under a bypass bridge, then on towards the city of Oxford.

OXFORD

The Oxford boundary marker is an important milestone along the Thames Path. For downstream walkers it signals the end of what is sometimes referred to as the 'lonely Thames', where settlements are few and far between and often located some distance from the river. The iron post is dated 1886 and decorated with an ox, which I solemnly wreathed with golden ragwort. This was partly in gratitude for the kindly cattle that had allowed us to pass unmolested and partly as insurance against those we were yet to meet.

Ragwort was brought to the Physic Garden at Oxford during the seventeenth century, from the lava fields around Mount Etna. It was used as a cure for almost every ailment known to man, and dubbed 'staggerwort' because it was considered 'a certaine remedie to help the Staggers in horses'. Perhaps John Wesley should have dosed both himself and his horse with ragwort before attempting to cross the Thames at Swinford. Eventually the plant crept out of the Physic Garden and naturalized, its seeds distributed throughout the country via the undercarriage of trains during the mid nineteenth century.

In a meadow beyond the boundary marker are the remains of Godstow Abbey. Only crumbling walls and the ruins of a sixteenth-century chapel still stand as reminders of the romantic legend associated with the abbey. Godstow takes its name from 'God's Place'. A Benedictine nunnery was founded here in 1133 after Lady Launceline, widow of the nobleman Sir William Launceline, saw a shaft of light strike the ground on the site.

Godstow was the burial place of the beautiful Rosamund de Clifford, mistress of King Henry II between 1166 and 1176. According to legend, Henry hid his 'fair Rosamund' in a secret bower by his palace at Woodstock, locating their love nest at the centre of a maze which could only be penetrated by following a silver thread. But while Henry was away fighting in France his suspicious wife, Queen Eleanor of Aquitaine, is said to have slain the knight guarding the bower. She then followed the silver thread and discovered her husband's lover. Rosamund died mysteriously soon afterwards, supposedly poisoned by Eleanor. In the sixteenth century Thomas Delaney wrote a ballad called 'Fair Rosamund', in which the Queen proffers a cup of poison while making bitter reference to her rival's fine garments,

Queen Eleanor proffers poison to her rival, Fair Rosamund

which she suspected had been paid for by Henry:

'Cast off from thee those robes,' she said,
'That riche and costlye be;
And drinke thou up this deadlye draught,
Which I have brought to thee'

In an alternative version of the story Rosamund is stabbed by the Queen, and there is an appalling account of giant toads being allowed to suckle her breasts as she bleeds to death in a bath.

A grief-stricken Henry had Rosamund buried before the high altar at Godstow nunnery, as described in the final verse of Delaney's poem:

Her body then they did entomb,
When life was fled away,
At Godstowe, neare to Oxford towne,
As may be seene this day.

The body was later removed at the order of Bishop Hugh, who visited the diocese in 1191, two years after Henry's own death. The bishop was horrified to find nuns venerating the tomb and burning tapers around it. Reminding them that Rosamund's relationship with the King had been adulterous, he insisted she be buried 'out of the church with other common people', in order that 'other women, warned by her example, may refrain from unlawful love'. Fair Rosamund was reinterred in the monastery cemetery, by the nuns' chapter house.

Not everyone accepts that Eleanor was responsible for Rosamund's death. I was once approached in a Sydney library by a woman who noticed I was carrying a biography of the Queen. When I said I was researching the death of Rosamund de Clifford, she launched into such a spirited and informed defence of Eleanor that offering a contrary view was inconceivable.

In the late middle ages, Oxford undergraduates, inflamed by strong drink and dreams of Rosamund, would boast of getting up to all sorts of mischief with the Godstow nuns. (The stories were not generally believed as the nuns were running a highly disciplined finishing school, and considered very respectable.) At the Dissolution of the Monasteries in 1538, Godstow passed into the hands of Dr George Owen, Henry VIII's private physician. Dr Owen lived in part of the building but took stone from the cloisters to enlarge the abbey's twelfth-century hospice, just across the river at Wolvercote. It was during this period that Rosamund's tomb was destroyed.

The nunnery itself was almost completely levelled in the Civil War but its hospice evolved into the riverside Trout Inn. Fans of crime writer Colin Dexter might recognize it as one of Inspector Morse's watering holes. It is also mentioned in Evelyn Waugh's *Brideshead Revisited*. After Sebastian Flyte takes his friend Charles Ryder to visit Brideshead for the first time, the pair head back to their colleges at Oxford by car. Along the way Sebastian suggests:

> *'It's half past five. We'll get to Godstow in time for dinner, drink at the Trout, leave Hardcastle's motor-car, and walk back by the river. Wouldn't that be best?'*

The food on offer at the Trout has an international flavour these days but I am pleased to note that their pudding menu continues to feature old-fashioned favourites such as Apple and Blackcurrant Crumble and Summer Berry and Bilberry Eton Mess. I have provided a recipe for Eton Mess in a later chapter of this book (it's worth waiting for).

During the seventeenth century, Oxford scholars must have been regarded with some alarm by the residents of Wolvercote. In 1662 a group were caught stealing geese and one was placed in the stocks, dressed in his academic gown as added humiliation. He was rescued by around forty fellow students who proceeded to smash every window in the village. Their final act of revenge was to march back to Oxford with a stolen goose blatantly tied to the end of a long pole.

The international success of the movies based on J. R. R. Tolkien's trilogy *Lord of the Rings* has greatly increased the number of visitors to Wolvercote. Tolkien spent much of his life in Oxford. He and his wife Edith lie under Cornish granite in the Catholic section of the local cemetery. Their stone is engraved:

EDITH MARY TOLKIEN
LÚTHIEN, 1889-1971

JOHN RONALD REUEL TOLKIEN
BEREN, 1892-1973

Lúthien and Beren were the lovers in Tolkien's romantic novel, *The Silmarillion,* which was published after the author's death.

It was on the section of river between Godstow and Oxford that one of the world's best-loved children's books was conceived. On 4 July 1862 Charles Dodgson, a maths lecturer at Christ Church, went on a boating expedition with the three young daughters of Henry Liddell, dean of the college. The party left from Oxford's Folly Bridge and rowed upstream to a picnic spot near the abbey ruins. On the way, Dodgson (Lewis Carroll) entertained the little girls, Edith, Lorina and Alice, with some gloriously absurd nonsense made up as he went along. *Alice's Adventures in Wonderland* may never have appeared in print if Alice herself had not been so enchanted with the stories that she persuaded her friend to write them down.

The following summer a serious breach occurred in the friendship between Dodgson and the Liddells. His diary entry of 25 June 1863 recorded a further boating expedition with the children but after an accidental meeting six months later he wrote 'I held aloof from them as I have done all term'. Because of his intense affection for young girls there is a suggestion he may have behaved inappropriately towards Alice and her sisters. The truth will probably never be known because after his death in 1898 Dodgson's niece cut the pages covering 27 June to 29 June from the diary. Regardless of her motive, it should be remembered that not one of the many children the author befriended during his lifetime ever spoke a word against him.

A little way downstream is the village of Binsey and the Church of St Margaret, with its healing or 'treacle' well. St Margaret's Revd Prout was friendly with Charles Dodgson and sought his advice about restoration of the well, to which Dodgson replied humorously,

Tea's made, but where's the treacle sponge? No wonder Alice looks peeved!

'Leave well alone.' Ironically, it featured in *Alice in Wonderland,* thereby creating an unending stream of visitors. During the Mad Hatter's extraordinary tea party, the Dormouse launches into a story about three sisters, Elsie, Lacie and Tillie (Alice Liddell and her sisters Lorina and Edith), who lived at the bottom of a treacle well:

> *'What did they live on?' said Alice, who always took a great interest in questions of eating and drinking.*
> *'They lived on treacle,' said the Dormouse, after thinking a minute or two.*
> *'They couldn't have done that, you know,' Alice gently remarked; 'they'd have been ill.'*
> *'So they were,' said the Dormouse; 'Very ill.'*

In the following, very simple recipe for Treacle Sponge, the lighter golden syrup is used:

TREACLE SPONGE

250 g (8 oz) golden syrup
zest of a lemon, and the juice of half a lemon
5 tablespoons breadcrumbs
200 g (7 oz) softened butter
200 g (7 oz) golden caster sugar
3 eggs
200 g (7 oz self-raising flour)
5 tablespoons milk

Heat the oven to 180°C (350°F). Mix the syrup, lemon zest and juice and breadcrumbs and spread over the base of a baking dish. Beat the butter and sugar together until light and fluffy, then beat in the eggs one by one. Stir in the flour then the milk and spread over the base. Bake for 35-40 minutes until golden brown. Serve with custard and cream.

The Liddell children often walked to the village of Binsey with their governess, Miss Prickett, whose name surely destined her for life as a governess, if not a teacher of needle-work. Generations of Pricketts lived at Binsey and there are a number of old family graves in the churchyard. Miss Prickett was immortalized as the Red Queen in *Through the Looking Glass*, although Lewis Carroll once described the character as 'the concentrated essence of all governesses'.

Across the river is 350-acre (140 hectare) Port Meadow, held as common grazing land for a thousand years after being presented to the city by William the Conqueror. Horses and cattle still roam free, although in recent times they have faced the hazard of having their hooves cut by broken glass. Shards are left by people illegally digging up the meadow in search of intact Victorian bottles, now highly sought after by collectors.

Port Meadow has an association with yet another famous storyteller, Kenneth Grahame, whose only son, Alastair, was killed by a train here on Friday, 7 May 1920. The stories that became *Wind in the Willows* were originally written to entertain Alastair; a difficult child with very poor eyesight. At the time of his death he was an undergraduate at Oxford, but finding it hard to live up to his parents' expectations. After dining in hall, he uncharacteristically asked for a glass of port before setting off for a solitary walk across the meadow. His body was found on the railway line the following morning. The coronial inquest's finding of accidental death was viewed as a kindly interpretation of the evidence for the sake of his heartbroken parents. Evidence actually indicated suicide, as it appeared Alastair had intentionally placed himself on the train track. The manner of his death echoed strange behaviour he had displayed as a child, when he would lay down on the road if he heard a car coming.

The Thames Path crosses Medley footbridge at the end of Port Meadow but reverts to the south bank again via Osney Bridge. It is believed the monks of Osney Abbey altered the course of the river to power their water mill, and that the main channel once ran closer to the city. By the mid seventeenth century the walls of the abandoned abbey were starting to crumble and only the remarkable foresight of a young John Aubrey allows us any idea of what it looked like at the time. Despite the distractions of the Civil War, the seventeen-year-old undergraduate went to the trouble of having a prominent court artist make various drawings of the ruins, one of which appeared as an engraving in a contemporary encyclopedia of English monasteries. As Aubrey anticipated, the building was demolished soon after the drawings were completed.

Fortunately, Oxford has a wonderful memento of Osney Abbey. In the twelfth century, its seven-ton bell, Great Tom, was moved to Tom Tower at Christ Church. Each evening the bell chimes 101 times in memory of the college's 101 original members.

Walkers wishing to explore the heart of Oxford should follow the curve of the river as far as Folly Bridge, then turn left up St Aldate's. The name Folly Bridge remembers a building used as an observatory by Roger Bacon, a thirteenth-century friar. There is now a Victorian house on the site but the flavour of a folly remains, as the building is castellated and adorned with statues.

The city inspired Thomas Hardy's novel *Jude the Obscure,* in which it was renamed *Christminster.* It was here that the impoverished young Jude Fawley dreamed of one day living and studying:

'It is a city of light,' he said to himself.
'The tree of knowledge grows there,' he added a few steps further on.
'It is a place that teachers of men spring from and go to.
It is what you may call a castle, manned by scholarship and religion.'
After this figure he was silent a long while, till he added:
'It would just suit me.'

The depositary of knowledge Jude Fawley aspired to was Oxford's venerable Bodleian Library, founded by Thomas Bodley in 1598. No doubt Jude would have agreed with Charles Lamb's thoughts on the institution:

What a place to be in is an old library! It seems as though all the souls of all the writers that have bequeathed their labors to these Bodleians were reposing here, as in some dormitory or middle state. I do not want to handle, to profane the leaves, their winding sheets.

The Bodleian is strictly for research and both Oliver Cromwell and Charles I were refused permission to borrow books. The most venerable reading room is the fifteenth-century Duke Humfrey Library, where I have been privileged to work after making an oral declaration that I would not (amongst other things) 'bring into the Library, or kindle therein, any fire or flame'. As the setting for the library at Hogwarts School of Magic, it was here that a book famously 'shouted' at Harry Potter. The old diaries I was consulting were considerably quieter, but nevertheless imparted a good many secrets.

My favourite Oxford institution is the Ashmolean Museum, founded in 1659 by Elias Ashmole. The collection was built around twelve carts of curiosities gathered by John Tradescant, gardener to Charles I. Tradescant travelled to distant places, bringing home exotic plants and anything else that took his fancy. Ashmole acquired the collection from the estate of John Tradescant Jnr, in somewhat dubious circumstances. He mercilessly harassed Tradescant's widow Hester, even moving in next door. It may be unfair to suggest that Elias's passion drove him to more desperate measures but he finally got his hands on the collection after Mrs Tradescant drowned mysteriously in her garden pond.

Elias Ashmole was not the first person with a passion for curiosities, or the ability to separate them from their owners. In 1576 the Earl of Leicester visited Oxford's New College and spotted their prized unicorn horn. To the horror of the Dons, the Earl demanded the horn as 'a gift' and his powerful position meant they were unable to refuse. As a compromise, a piece was broken off and presented to Leicester. The remainder is held in the college's Muniments Tower.

Some of the Ashmolean's early exhibits have also disappeared, including a two-inch corn removed from the toe of an Oxford wheelwright and a horn removed from the head of a woman called Mary Davies. However, it is still possible to see a mummified cat, the hat worn by Charles I's executioner and Guy Fawkes' lantern. But most wonderful of all is the priceless Saxon jewel found near King Alfred's fort at Athelney and inscribed *Alred mec heht gewyrcan* (Alfred ordered me to be made).

The Ashmolean became the first public museum in the country, irritating a German visitor, who complained 'even women are allowed up here for sixpence; they run here and there, grabbing at everything'. There is still a tendency for people to grab at the museum's exhibits. A few years ago someone tried to make off with the Alfred jewel, although I can't believe it was a woman.

The Ashmolean collection was originally housed in a purpose-built building in Broad Street, which opened in 1683, now the home of Oxford's Museum of the History of Science. In the basement of the museum is a blackboard on which Albert Einstein chalked his Theory of Relativity during a lecture in 1931. With my sad grasp of science and mathematics, simply looking at the equation would create a feeling of inadequacy. Perhaps this is why I am so in awe of the women who fought to be allowed to attend science lectures at Oxford during the Victorian era. Men came up with some bizarre reasons as to why they should be excluded. For example, there was a suggestion that excessive learning could reduce the female brain to jelly, and that male undergraduates would be disadvantaged because ladies' hats would obscure their view during laboratory demonstrations.

Degrees for women in any field were not granted until 1920 and although crime writer Dorothy Sayers qualified for a first-class degree between 1912 and 1915, she had to wait five years before she could graduate. Oxford now lists some very well-known women among its alumni, including 'Iron Lady' Margaret Thatcher and Helen Fielding, author of *Bridget Jones's Diary.* (It is difficult to imagine Bridget herself at Oxford but perhaps I am doing her a disservice.)

Not all Oxford's institutions are of an academic nature. Having read this far you will not be surprised to hear that one of my favourite haunts is the city's covered market. It opened on 1 November 1774, a century too late for undergraduate Edmund Verney, who was forced to take along a tuckbox when he went up to Oxford in 1685. Edmund's box of goodies included exotic fruits but also enough sugar to rot every tooth in his head:

Eighteen seville oranges, six malaga lemons, one lb of pick't Raisons, four Nuttmegs, three lb brown sugar, one lb white powdered sugar, one lb of brown sugar candy and ¼ lb of white sugar candy.

For those who visit the market (especially hungry walkers), I suggest buying some pork and veal suet puddings and serving them with traditional Oxford sauce:

OXFORD SAUCE

100 ml (3 fl oz) port
200 g (7 oz) redcurrant jelly
2 teaspoons wholegrain mustard
½ orange (juice and zest)
½ lemon (juice and zest)
2 cm (1 in) piece of grated, fresh root ginger

Place the port, redcurrant jelly and mustard in a saucepan and heat to a gentle simmer.
Add the orange and lemon juice and zest, and the ginger. Reduce the mixture to a sauce
consistency. Season with salt and freshly ground black pepper.

The sauce was created to accompany game, and is therefore ideal with a venison or wild boar terrine, on sale at one of the stalls.

The covered market was built with the object of removing messy food stalls from the city streets, particularly those of butchers who by 1791 occupied 'forty commodious shops' in the market. Much of Oxford's garbage had been ending up in the Thames and the River Cherwell, as the seventeenth-century 'water poet' John Taylor discovered. After escaping to Oxford from some undisclosed difficulty in London, Taylor found himself destitute and forced to take a job as river inspector. He was horrified at the state of the waterways:

Dead Hogges, Dogges, Cats, and well flayd Carrryon Horses,
Their noysom Corpses soyld the Water Courses;
Both swines and Stable dunge, Beasts guts and Garbage,
Street durt, with Gardners weeds and Rotten Herbage.

Taylor may well have put the beasts' guts to good use. He once sailed a brown-paper boat on the Thames for an incredible thirty-six hours, using pigs' bladders as flotation. Sadly, it was a long time before the river pollution improved, which may explain why he wrote an ode to ale, a drink he described as 'a repairer of a decaied colour in the face'.

In 1616 the pollution of the Thames prompted a Christ Church lawyer to pay for fresh water to be piped into Oxford from a reservoir outside the city. It flowed through lead pipes and hollow elm trunks and was dispensed via the richly decorated Carfax Conduit. There were two cisterns – one for 'town' and one for 'gown'.

Oxford has such a rich literary history that it is tempting for Thames Path walkers to spend a while in Broad Street's many bookshops before heading back to Folly Bridge and on to Iffley.

IFFLEY TO NUNEHAM COURTENAY

In 1911 a young girl fell into the river at Iffley Lock while cycling along the towpath at night. She was rescued by lock-keeper Percy Mellon and his son. The pair received various medals and certificates for their bravery, but there was a more practical reward from Oxford City Council: two armchairs and a purse of gold.

Until the 1950s this lock had a tollgate, with a charge of tuppence to cross the river. A walkway leads over the lock and up Mill Lane to Iffley village. Although Oxford has wandered out to meet Iffley, the village has retained its identity. The water mill burned down in 1908 but Grist Cottage survives, with one of the old millstones decorating its front garden. Further on, in Church Way, is the thatched parish hall, originally built as a grain barn.

A magnificent chestnut, planted in 1828, shades twelfth-century St Mary the Virgin Church, one of England's best examples of Romanesque architecture. The remarkable west door is decorated with four rows of zig-zag patterns and two of birds' heads and beaks. The design on the south door is even more creative, with centaurs, knights in battle, Samson and a lion and a merman. On the left side is the carved head of King Henry II. Inside, there are Norman arches carved with leaves and flowers, fantastic beasts and more intricate zig-zag patterns. Below the tower are four round painted shapes, where the bishop made crosses at the consecration of the church.

Rob and I were initially drawn to St Mary's by the story of a religious recluse called Annora, who lived in a cell attached to the church. She was born around 1180, the daughter of a powerful baron called William de Braose. William was outlawed after quarrelling with King John and subsequently his wife and eldest son starved to death while imprisoned in Windsor Castle. Annora herself was held at Bristol Castle but was eventually released. She later married, but was childless when her husband died in 1227. Alone and grief stricken, she withdrew to Iffley in 1232 and lived in isolation for the rest of her life. She was held in great respect, even by royalty. Records show that King Henry III supplied her with firewood and sent gifts such as sacks of grain and a robe.

The remarkable Norman carvings at the entrance to St Mary's church, Iffley

It is believed Annora's cell joined the church at a bricked-up door in the south wall of the chancel, and that the coffin-shaped stone lying in the churchyard below the blocked door formed part of her grave. The cell had a window to the outside world, from which Annora would have looked upon a gnarled yew tree just yards away. It is now 1,500 years old, predating the church and making the 1828 chestnut seem scarcely more than a seedling. Some years ago an Australian friend wandered into the churchyard early on a Sunday morning and noticed smoke pouring from the tree's hollow centre. The distressed vicar explained that vandals were responsible and was extremely grateful when our friend Alan put out the fire with a few bucketfuls of water.

River traffic increases markedly below Oxford, from canoes, dinghies and flower-bedecked narrow boats to expensive motorized cruisers. The greenhorn-cruiser owner is easily identified. Often newly retired, he is likely to be wearing a captain's outfit complete with gold buttons and heavily braided cap. He mans the tiller with intense concentration while his wife nervously anticipates the next lock. She has discovered that locks are places where things can go badly wrong.

Watching Toad's inept handling of a boat in *Wind in the Willows*, the Otter asked Ratty: 'Did I ever tell you that good story about Toad and the lock-keeper? It happened this way. Toad ...' A mayfly distracted the Otter before he could finish but a curious young reader wrote to Kenneth Grahame about it years later. The author replied with the following care-fully chosen words: 'I am afraid I must not tell you the story about Toad and the lock-keeper. The fact is they both lost their tempers, and said things they much regretted ...'

Back on the path, a footbridge crosses the Hinksey Stream as it enters the Thames beyond Iffley. There are still thatched and half-timbered cottages in the village of South Hinksey, owned by Abingdon Abbey in Saxon times. Beyond tiny Rose Isle and the delightfully named Fiddler's Elbow is Sandford. There was a corn mill here in the twelfth century, providing bread for local monks. In 1826 it was converted to a paper mill and was where the exami-nation papers of Oxford undergraduates were pulped: another depository of learning! Eventually the mill was demolished to make way for a housing estate. Thankfully, the water meadows between Iffley and Sandford are owned by the Oxford Preservation Society and will never be developed.

Sandford Lock is the deepest on the river. Water thunders over the weir, giving rise to the name Sandford Lasher. Jerome K. Jerome was all too correct when he wrote: 'The pool under Sandford Lasher, just behind the lock, is a place to drown yourself in.' An obelisk on the weir was erected in memory of several young men who did just that. John Beckly, a lock-keeper's son, accidentally drowned while removing fish from a trap, but the death of Oxford undergraduate Michael Llewelyn Davies in 1921 was less straightforward. Davies was the adored godson of J. M. Barrie, author of *Peter Pan*. He drowned in the weir with his best friend, Rupert Buxton. The possibility of a suicide pact arose after onlookers reported seeing

A topiary Captain Toad raises his boating cap at the Chelsea Flower Show

the boys calmly embracing in the water rather than struggling. Barrie was told the boys had been bathing but Michael was a non-swimmer and the suicide theory was further strengthened by rumours that the young men were involved in a homosexual relationship.

A mounting stone beside Sandford Lock is a memento of the horse ferry that plied the river from the thirteenth century. During the siege of Oxford, Parliamentary forces were able to use it to cross the Thames and attack an otherwise well-defended city. Since the demise of the ferry, horse riders have had to find an alternative route but pedestrians can cross the river via lock gates for a drink at the aptly named King's Arms pub.

Sandford Manor is now called Temple Farm. It is associated with a religious martyr called George Napier, whose mother was the daughter of Edmund Powell, Lord of Sandford Manor. George became a Jesuit priest and on 9 November 1610 his Catholicism led to him being hung, drawn and quartered at Oxford as a traitor. Sections of his body were displayed around the city but were later retrieved by his family and buried at Temple Farm. Only the head, which had been on public view outside Christ Church, was not recovered. It is said that on Christmas Eve a ghostly coach makes the journey from Sandford to Oxford in search of the missing head.

Still standing in the village below the church is sixteenth-century Sandford House. In 1767 the property was let to a Mr Sutton, who set up a clinic and began inoculating locals against smallpox. Sutton used a mysterious serum imported from Turkey. He swore it was effective, but it was claimed that he lost far more clients than he was willing to admit to. Thirty years later, Dr Edward Jenner produced immunity against smallpox by injecting people with a cowpox virus which, to the residents of Sandford, must have sounded even more alarming than Mr Sutton's Turkish serum. One can only hope they were brave enough to give the vaccination a go.

Rob and I were sauntering through the fields between Sandford and Radley when we were overtaken by a Thames Path 'bolter', trying to make it to the Flood Barrier at Greenwich in under ten days. Keen to chat but desperate not to lose time, he turned and ran backwards as he passed; not a wise move on a narrow towpath. Before we could shout a warning, he had stepped into the Thames, filling his boots to the brim. We could hear them squelching as he disappeared.

The boathouses at Radley belong to Radley College, now the largest landowner in the parish. It encompasses Radley Hall, an early eighteenth-century manor which was owned for many years by the Bowyer family. Around 1815, Sir George Bowyer spent a fortune trying to find coal on land he owned nearby, optimistically digging a channel to transport it to the Thames. Not a lump was discovered and to recoup expenses Sir George was forced to sell the contents of the hall. Valuable paintings and books went under the hammer but it was probably the loss of 3,000 bottles of high-quality wine that prompted him to decamp to Italy. Forty-five years later his body came back for burial in the family vault at Radley's St James the Great Church. However, while he was in Italy, Bowyer had become a Roman Catholic and to avoid controversy his burial took place under the cover of darkness.

Sir George should have forgotten about coal mining and spent his money excavating Barrow Hills, an early Bronze Age burial mound near Radley. Grave goods discovered here include a pair of gold ornaments used as earrings or as hair decorations. Dating from around 2000 BC, they represent the earliest gold ever found in Britain and are on display in the Ashmolean Museum.

One of the treasures in Radley's parish church is its Norman font, rescued from a farm shed in 1840. This church was fortified by the Royalists during the Civil War and when the Roundheads attacked, the north aisle and transept were destroyed, leaving the building slightly out of plumb. One of the Royalist officers who died in the battle is buried in an altar tomb in the churchyard. A carved canopy over the pulpit also has Civil War associations. It originally sat above the Speaker's chair at Westminster and was given to the church in 1653 by William Lenthall, who lived in neighbouring Besselsleigh. Lenthall had been Speaker of the House at the outbreak of war, and was dragged from the chair by Cromwell's troops at the end of the Long Parliament.

King Henry VII's portrait appears in one of the church's stained-glass windows. His connection with St James the Great is via the lovely old vicarage, dating from the late thirteenth century and used as a hunting lodge by Henry when the parish was owned by Abingdon Abbey. It was built using oak framing, filled with wattle and daub.

Each summer, native freshwater rushes are harvested at Radley. It is now the only place on the river where this tradition survives, although both rushes and willows were once gathered extensively along the Upper Thames (willow branches, or osiers, were used in basket making). Radley rushes are used to make chair seats and there are Thames rush seats in Salisbury Cathedral. The wooden punts hired out to tourists at Oxford were originally designed to gather lightweight rushes, a point worth remembering before lumbering aboard after a full English breakfast or a generous cream tea.

On the hill across the river from Lower Radley is the mansion Nuneham House, built in 1756 by the first Lord Harcourt. Some twenty years later his daughter Lady Nuneham had a vivid dream in which she saw her dead father stretched out on the kitchen table. She told the family about it at breakfast, down to the detail of hearing the clock strike four as she looked at the body. Later that morning her father went out to mark some trees on the estate, accompanied by his little dog, Hunter. He did not return and a farm worker, alerted by the dog barking, eventually found Lord Harcourt head down in a well, drowned in mud. He was carried back to Nuneham House and laid out on the kitchen table at exactly four o'clock.

There were those in the nearby village of Nuneham, however, who believed his death was pre-ordained. When Lord Harcourt was building his mansion, he realized that a huddle of rustic cottages would blot the classical landscape he wished to create. As lord of the manor, he simply relocated it. Displaced tenants called his drowning a judgment from God for also destroying the church where their ancestors were buried.

Nuneham House certainly impressed the French La Rochefoucauld brothers, who visited while on a tour of England in 1785. They wrote about its 30 acres (12 hectares) of terraces and mile-long walk along the river, laid out by the famous landscape artist Capability Brown. In the centre of the grounds was a separate pleasure garden, fenced by trellis and filled with flowers and rare trees. The enclosure was designed by the 'poet-gardener' William Mason, who added romantic touches such as inscribed verses and a grotto decorated with shells and fossils. In 1781 Capability Brown's work on the estate had inspired Poet Laureate William Whitehead to compose some humorous verses entitled 'On The Late Improvements At Nuneham, The Seat Of The Earl Of Harcourt'. In the poem, Mother Nature insists it was *she* who clothed the hills with trees and poured the Thames through the meadows at their feet. Capability Brown replies:

> *Who thinned, and who grouped, and who scattered those trees,*
> *Who bade the slopes fall with that delicate ease,*
> *Who cast them in shade, and who placed them in light,*
> *Who bade them divide, and who bade them unite?*

Brown put up a good argument, but Whitehouse allowed Mother Nature the last word:

> *The world's little malice will baulk his design:*
> *Each fault they call his, and each excellence mine.*

Much of Nuneham's original landscaping was destroyed during the Second World War but the Jacobean Carfax Conduit from the city of Oxford remains – a unique garden ornament which can be seen from the Thames Path. The estate is also home to Oxford University's Harcourt Arboretum. In addition to a vast collection of mature trees, the 80-acre (30 hectare) arboretum has a 12-acre (5 hectare) bluebell wood and a 35-acre (14 hectare) wild flower meadow. Admission is free, which must please Mother Nature.

ABINGDON TO EWELME

The spire of St Anne's Church is a welcome sight for those who make the 10-mile (16-km) hike from Oxford downstream to Abingdon. The Thames Path connects to the township through an arch of the fifteenth-century stone bridge (technically two bridges separated by Nag's Head Island). It is well worth climbing the steps up to Bridge Street and spending some time exploring what is England's oldest continually occupied settlement.

The town began as a trading base for early Britons and later there was a Roman settlement. In the late seventh century an important Benedictine abbey was established. The abbey dominated the community until the dissolution of the monasteries by Henry VIII. In the ninth century it came under attack by the Danes and was plundered for its gold and silver. One unique relic from the conflict was recovered from the Thames; the richly decorated Abingdon sword, thought to have belonged to a Saxon leader. Intricate silverwork on the sword includes the figure of a man, various animals and the symbols of the Apostles. It is another of the Ashmolean Museum's treasures.

Danish raids almost spelled the ruin of the abbey but by the middle of the tenth century it was flourishing again under the guidance of Abbot Ethwolde. During this time the monks dug a channel from the Thames, still in existence as the Abbey Stream. I love John Leland's description of the channel and its purpose: 'Ethelwolde ... caused a Gut to come out of Isis by force to serve and purge the officis of the abbay.' The hernia-like loop also boosted local trade as it allowed water craft to pass conveniently close to town. However, by 1632 its dangerous shallows inspired John Taylor's couplet:

At Abingdon the shoales are worse and worse,
That Swift Ditch seems to be the better course.

Swift Ditch was the original main stream of the Thames. Others agreed with Taylor's view and the ditch was reopened, serving as the main channel until 1790 when Abingdon Lock was created.

Abingdon was 'for the King' during the Civil War and it was here that Charles I farewelled his wife, Queen Henrietta Maria, after arranging her escape to France. King Charles is said to have held a council of war at his lodgings; a coaching inn built in 1554 called The Bell, which subsequently changed its name to The King's Head and Bell. The inn, located in East St Helen Street, behind seventeenth-century County Hall, has a second claim to fame as Handel is said to have composed his Water Music here. It must be said that absolute proof regarding the Handel connection has thus far proved elusive, probably saving the pub from becoming The George Frideric Handel and King's Head and Bell.

Abingdon's location on the Thames ensured its prosperity as a commercial centre until river transportation gave way to rail. The town was bypassed by the Great Western Railway in the 1840s and a branch line arrived too late to produce an economic revival. The only reminders of the town's great trading days are St Helens Wharf and the lavish homes of the rich merchants in East St Helen Street.

Jerome K. Jerome declared Abingdon to be 'desperately dull' but maybe this was because his visits failed to coincide with one of the town's festive occasions. For instance, there is the annual election of a 'mock mayor', held on the Saturday nearest 19 June by the residents of Ock Street. The mayor's staff of office is a set of mounted ox horns, giving a clue to the origin of the event. In 1700 there was a fair at which an ox was roasted and the meat distributed among the poor. A fight broke out between two groups over the trophy of the horns and the leader of the winning group was dubbed mayor. He also happened to be leader of the town's Morris dancers, which is why they too are eligible to vote. Seated in a flower-bedecked chair, the newly elected Mayor of Ock Street is carried around local pubs by the Morris men, whose affinity with pubs has led to what some refer to as the Morris dancer's curse – cirrhosis of the liver.

Abingdon's Michaelmas Fair is held in October. It was originally a hiring fair where labourers offered their services to new masters and entered into yearly bonds. A second, smaller fair held a week later is still known as the Runaway Fair because those unhappy with their lot would sneak back to town in the hope of finding a better position. Strangely enough, Amy Robsart had allowed her entire household staff to attend Abingdon Fair the day she plunged to her death down the staircase at Cumnor Hall in 1560 (see page 41). This raises the possibility of a premeditated suicide, or that someone with murderous intent reduced the risk of witnesses by convincing Amy to grant the servants a holiday.

In mid October there is also a large craft fair with an emphasis on Christmas gifts and decorations. It is held in the town's medieval abbey buildings. The abbey itself was demolished under the orders of Henry VIII and its stone taken downriver for other purposes, but several ancient buildings survive: the Exchequer, the Long Gallery, twelfth-century St Nicholas Church (where lay servants and pilgrims worshipped) and the Abbey Gate.

Downstream of Abingdon a footbridge takes the Thames Path over the old Swift Ditch, where it enters the river. Ahead, the path follows the Culham Cut, dug to slice a loop off the Thames in the early 1800s and give Abingdon's barges an easier passage. Halfway along the cut is another little bridge, where a left turn leads into the village of Culham. Its manor and cottages are arranged around a village green and there is a gabled dovecote, which once held several thousand nest boxes.

A right turn at the bridge leads over the weirs of Sutton Pools to Sutton Courtenay. This village sits in the curve of river isolated by the Culham Cut and can only be described as idyllic. However, Sutton Courtenay has seen its share of drama, and of difficult times. During the Civil War the vicar was a Parliamentarian who used the parish church to store gunpowder and ammunition. In 1643 the whole lot blew up, shattering the windows and damaging the twelfth-century tower.

In 1835 the village was singled out for criticism by the Poor Law commissioners. Whenever relief funds ran out, the local overseer would simply post a notice on the church door asking for more. His requests were met without question and according to the commissioners, such easy access to pauper relief affected the morality of the parish. To illustrate their point they reported that in the previous five years, four men were hanged and nine transported for long periods, and this from a population of only 830. They also noted that the overseer happened to be the village shopkeeper and that in one instance he charged a pauper four shillings for goods worth only one shilling and sixpence.

Literary pilgrims visit Sutton Courtenay in search of George Orwell, who lived in the village and is buried in the churchyard. However, I was more interested in the grave of Martha Pye. Martha died in 1822 at the amazing age of 117. When she was 100 she walked from Sutton Courtenay to Abingdon, a distance of 3 miles (5 km). History does not record whether she walked back home but I am sure she would have refused offers of a lift so I credit her with 6 miles (10 km). Of course, if she had conserved her energy she might have lived to 120.

Generally speaking, the Thames Path is well maintained but while walking this section in high summer Rob and I often had to wade through knee-high grass. Thank God there are no poisonous snakes in England, apart from the odd adder. The only real risk is from stinging nettles, and very conveniently a salve made from the plant's own juice provides an instant antidote. Young, tender nettle leaves can also be cooked and eaten as a vegetable and Samuel Pepys commented favourably on nettle porridge. Here is a recipe for baked nettle pudding, which sounds really tasty but I have yet to try:

NETTLE PUDDING

A few handfuls of young nettle leaves
Soft breadcrumbs
Cooked meat (pork/chicken)
300 ml (½ pint chicken stock)
Bacon

Cook the young nettle leaves in a little water for a few minutes, then drain.
Place a layer of soft breadcrumbs ½ in (1 cm) thick in the bottom of a greased baking dish.
Add the cooked nettles, then a layer of cooked meat (pork or ckicken).
Pour over ½ pint (300 ml) of chicken stock and top with a layer of bacon.
Bake at 180°C (350°F) for about half an hour. Serve with gravy.

In the unlikely event of being bitten by an adder, the ingredients for an ancient remedy would be easy to come by along the Thames. Mix crushed hazelnuts, rue, garlic and treacle, and wash it all down with beer. Swap the beer for milk and *voila!,* it becomes a cure for the bite of a mad dog.

Once again the Thames Path follows a cut (the Clifton Cut), bypassing a circuitous stretch of the river and the village of Long Wittenham. The name Wittenham comes from Witta, a Saxon chief who settled in the area in the fifth century. The parish church of St Mary's dates from the twelfth century and is well worth a visit. In the vestry is a recumbent effigy of Gilbert the Red, lord of the manor. It was thought that Gilbert died in the Holy Land in 1295, and that his heart was returned and interred beneath the effigy by his grieving wife. Recently the church was embarrassed to discover that although Gilbert *intended* to go on a crusade, he never actually got around to it. I wonder if this is what prompted his wife to cut him down to size? His effigy is only 3 ft (1 m) long.

During the Civil War the church's lead font was hidden in a wooden case filled with rubbish, to prevent it being melted down for bullets by Cromwell's army. It was rediscovered in 1839 and the protective wood made into a small table which still sits inside the church. On the left-hand side of the church porch two sundials (one for summer, one for winter) have been scratched into the stonework. They date from 1300 and kept time for the sexton, who would ring a bell at 9 a.m. to announce mass. To the right of the church is one of the most majestic copper beeches I have ever seen.

The village of Long Wittenham is just that: a long row of charming cottages and houses, including half-timbered Willingtons, which has the remains of the village cock-pit in its grounds. Rob and I once stopped to admire roses tumbling over the picket fence of a cottage and walked away with handfuls of raspberries, a gift of the property's generous gardener. I have always believed the only improvement you can make to fresh raspberries is to add cream, but a Marlow friend later shared a recipe for baked raspberry pie which changed my mind. The filling is simply raspberries layered with caster sugar, about half a cup of sugar to 1 lb (500 g) fruit. A kitchen funnel is placed through a hole in the pastry lid and just before the cooking time is up the pie is removed from the oven. A cup of cream is heated to boiling point and two egg yolks are whisked in. The mixture is then carefully poured into the funnel and the pie baked for a final few minutes.

Long Wittenham is home to the Pendon Museum, founded by a young Australian called Roye England, who arrived in the UK in 1925 and was horrified to see traditional cottages disappearing and thatch being replaced by asbestos tiles. He devoted the rest of his life to preserving the past by reproducing English villages in miniature. Roye died in 1995 but his work continues through a team of talented volunteers.

The museum also contains several miniature railway systems. In one room the lights are turned out and the Great Western Express makes a magical overnight journey, stopping at a lamp-lit village station then heading west across Isambard Brunel's timber viaduct. Each carriage has a full complement of inch-high 1930s passengers. Despite their size, the figures have incredibly detailed costumes.

Upstairs, the museum's main exhibit is a work in progress: a vast country landscape where each building has been modelled on an existing structure and where the interiors of cottages have been faithfully reproduced. Apparently there were a few slip-ups and one elderly lady was quick to point out that the tiny desk spike in her cottage should have been full of receipts, not unpaid bills. Originally Roye England made his miniature thatched roofs from human hair but these days plumbers' hemp is preferred. I loved the highly individual cottage gardens and was amused to hear that Roye collected whiskers from his cat to use as hollyhock stems.

Beyond the Clifton Cut, the towpath returns to the riverbank and leads on to the village of Clifton Hampden. The bridge here was built in 1864 to replace a ferry service. It was designed by Sir George Gilbert Scott. Clifton Hampden's adaptable ferryman not only baked the bricks for the new bridge but became its first toll keeper.

Gilbert Scott was also responsible for restoring the church, set on a rock spur high above the river. It is located on one of the country's mysterious 'ley lines', thought to have aligned prehistoric sacred sites. Little remains of the church's medieval structure, but pillars in the south wall and the picina have been dated to the time of King Stephen (1135–54). There is also a twelfth-century stone carving of a boar hunt, which survived through having been set into the porch with its face to the wall.

On the south side of the churchyard close to the church is a cross marking the grave of William Dyke. William has a unique place in English history, having fired the first shot in the Battle of Waterloo, albeit by accident, when he was cleaning his musket. Local legend has it that he was demoted over the incident and had his sword taken from him, but that it was later returned to him by none other than the Duke of Wellington. According to the church notes, it is still in the possession of a local family. The majestic Cedar of Lebanon in the churchyard was grown from a seed brought back by vicar John Lomax Gibbs in 1864.

There is an intriguing ghost story concerning a house at Clifton Hampden. During the eighteenth century, the Courtiers was the home of a Captain Fletcher and his twenty-nine-year-old wife Sarah. The Captain was a true ladies' man with the proverbial girl in every port. Worse still, Sarah discovered he was also having an affair with a local girl and planning a bigamous marriage. After a terrible row, the unrepentant Captain went off to his ship and a humiliated Sarah returned to the Courtiers where she hanged herself from their four-poster bed. She was buried in Dorchester Abbey church below a memorial stating that she was a young woman 'whose artless Beauty, innocence of Mind and gentle Manners, once obtained for her the Love and Esteem of all who knew her. But when Nerves were too delicately spun to bear the rude Shakes and Joltings which we meet with in this transitory World, Nature gave way; she sunk and died a Martyr to Excessive Sensibility'.

I suspect Captain Fletcher may have written these euphemistic words himself, which could explain why his wife's spirit still haunts The Courtiers. She is probably doing her best to let people know that she did *not* sink and die due to excessive sensibility – she leapt from her lonely marriage bed and broke her neck!

Clifton Hampden is famous for its timber-framed thatched cottages which provide the perfect models for the Pendon Museum's miniature landscape. Just across the bridge, the low-thatched, low-beamed Barley Mow pub captured the imagination of Jerome K. Jerome on his boating trip and has been attracting literary pilgrims ever since.

A sweeping curve of the river runs between Clifton Hampden and Little Wittenham, by Day's Lock. The village nestles under the ancient Wittenham Clumps. In medieval times these mounds were dubbed Mother Dunch's Buttocks, after the presumably large wife of the local squire. The nearest is Round Hill and beyond is Castle Hill, an Iron Age fort ringed by massive earthworks. In 1844, Joseph Tubbs stood on Castle Hill looking out on a view steeped in English history. He wrote a poem describing the changes wrought on the landscape by Celts, Romans … and Danes:

Around this hill the ruthless Danes intrenched,
And these fair plains with glory slaughter drench'd.

The poem was inscribed by Tubb on a beech tree, which has since died. The lines are now recorded at the site on a plaque.

Inside St Peter's Church is a marble and alabaster monument to Walter Dunch and his wife. The figures have the most delicately carved Elizabethan ruffs and have remained intact, perhaps because Mother Dunch was Oliver Cromwell's auntie.

© Rob Conolly

My serene expression changed to one of terror when a bull actually appeared!

Crowds flock to Little Wittenham from around the world to take part in the annual Pooh Sticks competition. The event has been held at Little Wittenham Bridge near Day's Lock since 1983 although after the river froze in 1997 the date was moved from January to March. Pooh Sticks was invented by the A. A. Milne character Pooh Bear, who watched a fir cone float under the bridge in Kent's Ashdown Forest. Pooh and his friends dropped sticks over the bridge to see whose would emerge first. Piglet famously threw in a large grey stick and thought he had won when Eeyore the donkey floated past. For many years there was a permanent Pooh Sticks stall at Day's Lock but these days you have to forage for your own.

Walking by the lock, Rob and I came across a rusty sign nailed to a tree reading 'BEWARE OF BULL. AVOID COWS WITH YOUNG CALVES'. I had my photograph taken beside it, hoping to fool friends into believing we were undertaking a dangerous expedition. Despite my initial fear of cows, it did not occur to me that the warning was current until a large bull suddenly appeared from a copse of trees. He was followed by his many sons, all bellowing with adolescent aggression. Clearly my ragwort offering at the Oxford boundary marker was about to be put to the test. Faced with the choice of strolling across the field feigning nonchalance or running like hell, we chose the latter ... our boots scarcely touching the ground. At least we had been warned, unlike the rambler who ended up on his back after blithely opening an old gate marked PULL … the P having originally been a B.

On this occasion I need not have panicked. The Day's Lock bulls were a beef breed; far less aggressive than dairy breeds such as Jerseys. For this reason it is illegal for farmers to place dairy-breed bulls over the age of ten months in fields along the path. In fact, they are banned from any field in the country with a public right of way. To be fair, Jersey *cows* have sweet temperaments. More importantly, remembering those Long Wittenham raspberries, they produce the most sublime cream.

We had only walked another half mile when we came upon another threat to my equanimity – hundreds of geese. Again my fears were unfounded; they were docile Canada geese and we passed without so much as a peck at our legs. When the flock took to the air, the sound of their wings beating was amazing. Canada geese pose a greater threat to planes than to humans, sometimes flying into jet engines. They were introduced to Britain by Charles II, who imported a few dozen in the 1660s. Their numbers have since increased to around 70,000.

A path from the footbridge at Day's Lock leads over the fields to Dorchester-on-Thames, which is actually on the River Thame (a tributary of the Thames). The path emerges at Bridge End, and a tiny, triangular green surrounded by a jumble of cottages. Constructed in all manner of styles and materials, they have an unselfconscious charm, with gardens of self-seeded forget-me-nots, rampant clematis and old lilac trees. On our initial Thames Path walk, we met an elderly lady by the green who was searching for her cat. She had lived in timber-framed Plum Cottage for over fifty years, and kindly invited us in. Her garden ran down to the River Thames, but had become an almost impenetrable wilderness of vines, gnarled fruit trees, raspberry canes and old-fashioned roses. She had a boat moored on the river but had not set eyes on it for years and thought it might have sunk. As we left she presented me with a spray of fragrant white roses. I was happy to be able to return the favour by spotting her lost cat, asleep at the back door in a lavender bush. When we visited Bridge End a couple of years later, the old lady had gone, and Plum Cottage's jungle had been tamed.

The town's abbey church was built around 1140. Its brewery evolved into the galleried George Hotel in the High Street, a popular coaching inn during the eighteenth century. Nearby, the much loved Abbey Tearooms are housed in what was once the abbey guesthouse. The tearooms are staffed by volunteers who provide an array of home-made cakes. As the tables are communal, a visit can be compared to having afternoon tea with a group of distant cousins, while being waited on by kindly aunts. Customers are trusted to tot up their own bill. The long-term future of the enterprise seems assured as we recently enjoyed a chocolate slice made by a ten-year-old girl.

For many years the tearooms were run by Lettice Godfrey, who gave me the recipe for Elderflower Cake, a local specialty. However, according to Lettice, the most popular item on the menu at the time was Dorset Gooseberry Cake. I wonder whether tourists ordered it in the mistaken belief they were in the Dorchester of Thomas Hardy's Wessex rather than Dorchester-on-Thames? A book of the teashop's recipes has now been compiled. No prizes for the title: *Heavenly Cakes.*

Sadly, Lettice died in 2005, aged eighty-nine. Outside is a seat, carved with her name.

ABBEY TEAROOM ELDERFLOWER CAKE

120 g (4 oz) softened butter
120 g (4 oz) caster sugar
4 medium eggs
120 g (4 oz) self-raising flour
150 ml (4 fl oz) elderflower cordial essence
grated rind of 1 lemon

Preheat oven to 160°C (325°F). Cream the butter and sugar, then beat in the eggs. Sift the flour and fold in with a metal spoon and two tablespoons of the cordial. Pour into a greased and lined 500 g (1 lb) loaf tin. Bake for 50 minutes.

While the cake is still warm, drizzle the remaining cordial over the top and sprinkle with the lemon rind.

Instead of a grimacing gargoyle, a stone corbel on the face of the abbey's tower depicts a smiling, middle-aged woman. The corbel is a unique, twentieth-century tribute to the late Edith Stedman, of Boston, USA. Miss Stedman first visited Dorchester in 1953 and loved the abbey church so much that she returned annually to raise money for the restoration of its magnificent Tree of Jesse window.

In the Oxford Public Library I found a copy of Edith's charming memoir: *A Yankee in an English Village.* Describing her first glimpse of the corbel in 1977, she wrote: 'Heaven help me, there was my mug grinning down at me in place of an eight hundred year old monk whom the Vicar said had lost face. I rescued the old dear as he was being carted off and he rests peacefully by my English door step.'

The abbey has recently undergone a £5 million restoration. During initial excavations a tiny gold coin was found. It was minted for the Celtic King Cunobelin and is decorated with an ear of wheat on one side and a stylized horse on the other. Replicas of the coin were sold to fund the restoration so it might be said that Cunobelin took over where Edith Stedman left off. Perhaps he too will end up as a corbel. Excavations also revealed an Anglo-Saxon well and several male skeletons, including one thought to be that of a twelfth-century abbot.

Rob and I never leave Dorchester without gazing wistfully at estate agents' windows.

© Rob Conolly

Surely Dorchester Abbey has the most unusual corbel in the country

Many people dream of retiring here, to a thatched cottage with an inglenook fireplace and rustic oak beams. Sadly, property prices are high and we invariably wander off trying to convince ourselves that thatch would catch fire … or attract rats.

In a secluded curve of the Thames between Dorchester and Shillingford, we came across a pair of swans and two cygnets foraging under the willows. They looked so sweet that we walked down to take a photo but unfortunately we had expended our luck on bulls and geese. As the camera clicked, the male shot out of the water and chased us up the bank, hissing like a snake. We took off like a pair of frightened rabbits. It does not pay to upset swans, as Jerome K. Jerome's friend Harris discovered to his cost in *Three Men in a Boat*. Left on his own one night while George and Jerome walked into Henley-on-Thames, he greeted their return with a dramatic story of fending off twenty angry swans for four hours. When an incredulous George asked, 'How many swans did you say there were?', a battle-weary Harris upped the number to thirty-two. Next morning he denied everything and his friends put the incident down to an alcohol-induced nightmare. It is more likely that he erased it from his memory, unable to cope with the horror.

Swans once graced the dining tables of manor houses, though more for show than for the tenderness of their flesh. They were skinned with the feathers intact then reassembled to create a spectacular centrepiece. However, when the eighteenth-century country parson and diarist James Woodforde ate roast swan accompanied by a sauce of currant jelly, he recorded a very positive comment: 'I never eat a bit of a Swan before, and I think it good eating with sweet sauce. The Swan was killed three weeks before it was eat and yet not the least bad taste in it.' In 1874 Queen Victoria's youngest son, Prince Leopold, sent a swan to his Oxford tutor for Christmas dinner, but there is no mention of how the gift was received.

The Thames Path has to leave the river at the site of the former Keen Edge Ferry, running beside the busy main road into Shillingford. Happily, it turns back to the Thames via Wharf Road, where there is a magical sight in spring. A wisteria stretches along a row of cottages and a barn for a distance of about 165 ft (50 m). The riverside at Shillingford is a delight at any time of year, with a bench under a willow overlooking a thatched boathouse. According to flood levels marked on a nearby house, the river reached way above Rob's head during the winter of 1809.

Downstream is three-arched Shillingford Bridge and, across the river, the exclusive Shillingford Bridge Hotel. Ahead is the village of Benson, originally known as Bensington and mentioned as early as AD 571, in the Anglo-Saxon Chronicles. The parish church of St Helen's dates back to the twelfth century. Owing to some confusion over Roman numerals, the church clock informs locals that it is eleven o'clock twice every twelve hours, but never nine o'clock. There is an airbase nearby and during the Second World War the clock featured in an intercepted enemy message. When decoded it read that the Luftwaffe were planning to bomb the airfield by the church with two number elevens on its clock. Benson's main tourist attraction is its bicycle museum, and on the first Sunday of July (not commencing at nine o'clock, one hopes) there is a rally of antique bicycles. Entrants arrive from as far afield as the US and many add to the colour of the occasion by wearing appropriate period costume.

Just beyond Benson is Ewelme, one of the most beautiful villages in England. It is actually several miles from the Thames, but Jerome K. Jerome gives me licence to include it by being buried in St Mary's churchyard. I cannot resist a brief word about Jerome here, even though his excursion on the river ended downstream at Pangbourne. He was born Jerome Klapka Jerome (son of Jerome Clapp Jerome!) and had set out to compile a serious gazetteer of riverside villages. Fortunately *Three Men in a Boat* bubbled to the surface instead.

Ewelme's most famous inhabitant was Alice Chaucer, granddaughter of the poet Geoffrey Chaucer. In 1430 Alice married William de la Pole, 1st Duke of Suffolk. Their palace, long since vanished, was visited frequently by Henry VIII and later by Elizabeth I. Construction of St Mary's commenced soon after the couple married and was complete circa 1450, when

© Rob Conolly

Pilgrims must lie on the floor to view the lowest level of Alice Chaucer's tomb in St Mary's church, Ewelme

the Duke died. The church has unusual brick battlements and chequerboard walls of stone and flint.

In the fifteenth century John Leland wrote:

Ewelme paroche curche a cumly and new peace of work standing on an hill was lately made by William Duke of Southfolk and Alice his wife. William was slayn and Alice supervivid, and after was byried yn the paroche church of Ewelme on the south side of the high altare in a rich tumbe of alabaster …

The 'rich tumbe' was erected by Alice's son after her death in 1475. Eight wooden angels crown the elaborate alabaster canopy above her triple-tiered tomb. The figure of the Duchess as a vowess adorns the top tier. On her left forearm is the Garter of St George, which she was given permission to wear in 1432. Interestingly, Queen Victoria once inspected the effigy to establish exactly where the Garter should be worn by Ladies of the Order. The middle tier of the tomb contains the Duchess's remains. Below is a carved representation of the Duchess in death; her emaciated body wrapped in a shroud. Only by lying flat on the floor is it possible to see frescoes decorating the compartment's ceiling. A copy is provided for the convenience of visitors.

In the chancel is an elaborate monument to Colonel Francis Martyn, who died in 1682 aged seventy-four. Colonel Martyn is almost as worthy of attention as the Duchess. He fought on the side of the Roundheads during the Civil War but was also loyal to his village of Ewelme, saving the treasures of St Mary's by refusing entry to his own troops.

Through a door at the south side of the chancel, steps lead down to an architectural gem: a tiny courtyard surrounded by perfectly preserved fifteenth-century almshouses. They were built with funds provided by Alice Chaucer to house impoverished men, and are still lived in by elderly residents. The village school was also provided by the Duchess, and has been attended by the children of Ewelme ever since.

Ewelme Brook runs the length of the village on its way to the Thames and in spring the banks are covered in daffodils. The Chiltern Society is restoring the brook's medieval water-cress beds, which ceased as a commercial enterprise in 1988. The cress originally grew wild, thriving in water filtered through the chalk of the Chiltern Hills. Forget cucumber as a sand-wich filler and try peppery watercress with cold roast beef and mustard.

WALLINGFORD TO MOULSFORD

Below Benson and neighbouring Ewelme is the riverside town of Wallingford. Approaching from the towpath, the unusual open-work spire of St Peter's Church appears on the skyline. It was designed by the eighteenth-century architect Sir Robert Taylor, who also designed Harleyford Manor. It was paid for by the prominent Wallingford citizen Justice William Blackstone (1723–80).

Blackstone's *Commentaries on the Laws of England* had a strong influence on the English legal system and even helped shape the American Declaration of Independence. He is buried in a family vault at St Peter's but has another, more unique memorial in Wallingford: a bend in a road. The last twenty years of Blackstone's life were spent at his riverside house, Castle Priory, in Thames Street. When the judge wanted to extend his garden, the roadway was deliberately curved to accommodate him.

As the name Wallingford suggests, a shallow crossing point on the Thames led to a Roman settlement. Between 1067 and 1071, following the Norman Conquest, Robert D'Oyley built a motte-and-bailey castle. His daughter married a supporter of Empress Matilda, who fought her cousin Stephen for the English throne and made a dramatic mid-winter escape from Oxford Castle. Dressed in white to blend with the snow, she crossed the Thames at Abingdon and fled to the safety of Wallingford Castle.

A wooden bridge already existed at Wallingford when the castle was built. By the thirteenth century it had been replaced by a solid stone structure. The town was a Royalist stronghold during the Civil War and when the King's men were forced to retreat to the castle they protected themselves by cutting the bridge in four places and inserting wooden draw-bridges. Judging from the 1646 surrender terms, their withdrawal must have been a dramatic affair. The governor and the officers of the garrison had to march out of town with their horses and weaponry, accompanied by flying colours, trumpets sounding and drums beating. They also had to promise never to bear arms against Parliament again. Oliver Cromwell later had the castle dismantled stone by stone.

Twenty years after the war, the bridge defended the town against another enemy: plague.

In 1665 the disease was raging in London and sentries were posted to prevent travellers carrying infection into the town. It appears the strategy worked because Wallingford did not suffer nearly as badly as it had in 1349, during the Black Death. The drawbridges remained until the mid eighteenth century. Wallingford is now a quiet backwater but the bridge still strides across the water meadows in seventeen arched 'steps'.

Before leaving town we called at a twelfth-century coaching inn called the George Hotel, to investigate the story of an ill-fated Civil War romance. Royalist soldiers were billeted in the town and inevitably there were tensions, particularly in matters of the heart. In 1626, landlord Francis Smith's daughter fell in love with Sergeant John Hobson. Hobson was murdered by a local rival and the girl locked herself in her bedroom where she went mad with grief. The plaster around the room's fireplace has a pattern of black teardrops, said to have been painted with soot from the fire, mixed with the girl's tears. The receptionist at the George took us upstairs to show us the plasterwork, now preserved under glass. Guests can still spend the night in the room if the idea of a ghost doesn't faze them. Apparently the landlord's daughter has been known to appear in silhouette, still weeping.

Original oak beams survive in the George, particularly in the Royalist and Tavern Bars. Adding to the atmosphere, the bars have sealed entrances to secret passages which once led to the town hall.

Across Wallingford Bridge a footpath leads under the arches and along the northern riverbank. It veers off through fields and a farmyard to St Mary's Church, in the tiny hamlet of Newnham Murren. The name Murren derives from Richard Moren, lord of the manor in 1261. St Mary's is now redundant and is not always accessible, but Rob and I were lucky enough to find two elderly villagers preparing for one of four annual services.

Unlike Wallingford with its drawbridge, Newnham Murren was defenceless when the plague arrived. One of the church workers told us the village fell into decline after people fleeing London brought the disease with them. I sensed a lingering resentment and remembered reading that country people believed they could smell plague in hawthorn blossom generations after the epidemic had passed. The Sars virus was causing concern at the time and I wondered whether he perceived a new threat

The old chap cheered up when I said we had come to see the church's memento of the Civil War. As his companion quietly arranged flowers, he showed us the brass wall plate damaged during the siege of Wallingford. The bullet-pierced plate is in memory of Letitia Barnarde, who died in 1593: 'A woman of the greatest modesty, faithful to her husbands [she survived three] good to the poor and loved by her neighbours.' She is shown kneeling in prayer with her four children. Because electricity was never installed at St Mary's, evening services are candle-lit, and must be very moving occasions.

To complete the next section of the river, between Cholsey and Pangbourne, we drove out to Pangbourne from Harleyford then took the train to Cholsey. Walking the Thames Path is generally a relaxing experience, but Pangbourne railway station has very narrow platforms and after an express train hurtled through to London we almost had to peel ourselves from the wall like old posters.

From Cholsey station we walked to St Mary's churchyard to find the grave of Dame Agatha Christie. In 1934 the author and her second husband, the archaeologist Max Mallowan, purchased Winterbrook House, a riverside property between Wallingford and Cholsey. They regularly attended Cholsey Church and when Miss Christie died at Winterbrook in 1976, she was buried at St Mary's. Her grave is by the wall in the right-hand corner of the churchyard. Before her death she instructed her family in writing: 'Put on my Slate: Sleep after Toyle, Port after Stormie Seas, Ease after Warre, Death after Life, Doth greatly please.' The words are from Edmund Spenser's *The Faerie Queene.* Dame Agatha's impressive headstone had to be lifted over the churchyard wall with a crane. Within twelve

© Rob Conolly

Agatha Christie's grave at Cholsey, with a strange Christmas offering from a fan months the widowed Max Mallowan married fellow archeologist Barbara Parker, who is also buried at St Mary's, at a discreet distance from her famous predecessor. It was just after Christmas when we visited the churchyard to photograph Miss Christie's grave and someone had left a festively wrapped gift: one of the author's own novels (unfortunately the title now escapes me). I had visions of finding an accompanying note or an inscription confessing that the book had inspired a real-life murder, but there was absolutely nothing to explain the offering.

In 1990, to mark the centenary of Dame Agatha's birth, twenty-five trees were planted in the churchyard. Oddly enough, two much older trees growing in the rectory garden are associated with a crime, though not one of Miss Christie's murders. In the eighteenth century the local vicar, a Revd Cottle, married and honeymooned in Lebanon. Returning home, his new bride smuggled two tiny Cedars of Lebanon out of the country in her parasol.

Agatha Christie adored food and was an enthusiastic cook. Having grown up in Devon, it is not surprising she developed a taste for dairy products. As an elderly woman she described as 'super' a birthday dinner which included a main course of hot lobster à la crème followed by a dessert of blackberries and cream. Strictly teetotal, she then drank half a cup of straight cream while her guests toasted her in champagne. Appropriately, a cup of cream is used in a dish called Mystery Potatoes, which Dame Agatha is said to have invented during the Second World War.

AGATHA CHRISTIE'S MYSTERY POTATOES

2 large baking potatoes
1 cup cream
1 tin anchovies
salt and pepper

Bake the potatoes until tender. Halve them and scoop out the flesh. Mash the flesh with the cream and seasonings. Add the finely chopped anchovies and mix well. Refill the potato cases with the mixture and bake in a hot oven until the tops are nicely browned.

Agatha Christie guarded her privacy so fiercely that locals seldom saw her. An American fan once summoned the nerve to telephone Winterbrook House from a phone box across the road but needless to say she was not invited in and the entrance gates to the property were hastily locked.

Instead of a towpath wandering along the riverbank from Cholsey to Moulsford, the Thames Path runs beside the busy A329. The footpath is alarmingly narrow and whenever a truck roared past we were forced to violate the privacy of robins, nesting in the hawthorn hedges.

Moulsford may be assaulted by twentieth-century transport but it also has the mystique of buried treasure. Coins and jewellery from Roman and Saxon times have been found in the area and in 1960 a farmer unearthed a heavy gold necklace from the Bronze Age, known as the Moulsford Torque. Exquisitely fashioned from four bands of gold, it no doubt belonged to someone of great consequence. Under the English law of treasure trove, finds of deliberately hidden gold or silver belong to the Crown but the gold torque was judged to be a casual loss, so it was 'finders keepers'. The necklace was later sold to Reading Museum.

On the outskirts of the village a lane leads to the sanctuary of St John the Baptist Church, where I thanked God for sparing our lives. Parts of this little church date back to the twelfth century and the bells in the quaint belfry are 400 years old. According to the church notes, Thomas Benet left the odd sum of three and fourpence to the chapel in 1547. Rob disappeared as I was reading this whimsical snippet aloud and when I found him in the churchyard he said, 'I escaped to avoid your corny old joke about three and fourpence.'

Needless to say I launched forth: 'Oh, you mean the one about the soldier sending the radio message during the war?' He walked away, but by then I was in full flight: '... and the message said, "Send reinforcements, we're going to advance," but it got all muddled up and came out, "Send three and fourpence, WE'RE GOING TO A DANCE!"' I had to shout the last bit because he had his ears blocked.

Our attention was suddenly diverted by movement in a small heap of earth between two graves. A mole was snuffling just below the surface and we waited for ages hoping it might accidentally pop its head out. We left disappointed but I have since been told that if you want to catch a mole you should stand absolutely still, wait for a major shift in the soil, then thrust both hands in and grab it.

On rare occasions a careless mole does blunder into the daylight. Valentine Ackland, life-long companion of writer Sylvia Townsend Warner, came upon one in the couple's vegetable garden:

> *I was picking green peas into a colander and saw the earth near my feet heaving, and a mole emerged, and I caught it instantly, in the colander, and carried it in to Sylvia, who was writing in her room, and set it down beside the typewriter on her table.*

According to Kenneth Grahame's widow Elspeth, the mole her husband immortalized as Ratty's diffident friend in *Wind in the Willows* was captured in similar circumstances, though with a less charming outcome. While dressing for dinner one evening, Grahame saw a mole and a robin fighting over a worm. He rushed out and captured the mole, intending to show it to his son Alastair next morning. For safekeeping he put it in a turf-lined box, secured the lid with a heavy weight, and sat it on the grand piano. However, the mole managed to shoulder its way out overnight and was heading for the back door when the housekeeper

It's not often that a mole emerges into the daylight. He seems amused by his surroundings!

spotted it. I regret to say she mistook it for a rat and dealt it a fatal blow with her broom. This was a sad case of mistaken identity but moles often have a price on their heads due to their ability to shift twice their own weight in soil every minute. They drive serious lawn growers to distraction but despite some unspeakable methods of eradication, most people agree that only two things really work: cementing the garden or moving house.

In early summer Moulsford's Beetle and Wedge Boathouse is a heavenly place to spend time. Roses form scented arbours in the garden and clamber over lattice by the riverbank. The Beetle and Wedge appeared as the Potwell Inn in H. G. Wells's *The History of Mr Polly*. I warmed to Mr Polly immediately when I discovered he had food on his mind as he approached via the towpath: '"Provinder," he whispered, drawing near to the Inn. "Cold sirloin for choice. And nut-brown brew and wheaten bread."' He got exactly what he was after, and a bit of cheese besides. George Bernard Shaw used to stay at this pub too, and liked to row on the river. Both Mr Polly and I would agree with Shaw's comment: 'There is no love sincerer than the love of food.'

The fishing season was well underway as we walked downstream from the pub and anglers had set themselves up along the riverbanks. One young group had pitched their tent right across the towpath, presumably so they could throw in a line from their sleeping bags. It was well past noon but the boys were barely awake. They looked pathetically fragile and apologized profusely as we picked our way around empty beer cans, half drunk mugs of tea, and guy ropes strung with wet socks. Further along, a more elderly angler explained he was fishing for giant carp but catching small roach. He said it was a depressing analogy of his life, but we thought he looked unusually chirpy for a Thames fisherman. He was the only one we had met who had caught anything at all, which probably accounted for his good humour.

Downriver by Cleeve Lock there is another famous pub: the Old Leatherne Bottel Inn. Alongside is a brick well fed by an underground spring. The water here was once collected and sold as a cure for a uniquely British affliction known as melancholy dumps (local fishermen no doubt provided a ready market). During damp summers the disease can still reach epidemic proportions and is capable of bringing down the most resolutely cheerful soul.

STREATLEY TO TILEHURST

There was nothing depressing about the weather when we walked past Cleeve Lock en route to riverside Goring. Field poppies and buttercups were waving in the sunshine and hazelnuts were swelling in the hedgerows. Humans could survive quite nicely under an English hedgerow. Dinner might consist of hazelnut bread, buttered steamed nettles and fat-hen pancakes, with blackberries and wild strawberries to follow. After a glass or two of elderberry wine you could nod off, protected from intruders by the dagger-like thorns of hawthorn. Of course we're talking high-density row housing. Every 1,000 yards of hedgerow is inhabited by an average of thirty-four nesting pairs of nineteen different bird species. Never mind, the stress of communal living could be relieved by nibbling the hedgerow herb St John's wort, which some argue is better than pills (or even Cleeve spring water) in treating depression.

Rob and I had another reason for feeling cheerful as we approached the twin towns of Streatley and Goring. A friend had told us there was a store at Streatley famous for its selection of English cheeses, and that in neighbouring Goring we would find an internationally renowned bakery. There has always been a healthy rivalry between these two settlements, which lie on opposite sides of the Thames. In the early nineteenth century Streatley was the more important village, by dint of being on the turnpike road leading to Reading. The Bull Inn at Streatley was the post house. However, when the Great Western Railway arrived, the station was built at Goring and the residents of Streatley had to slink across the bridge to catch the train. I doubt if they minded because while Goring grew by leaps and bounds, Streatley became rather select and superior.

Two ancient pathways, the Ridgeway and the Icknield Way, forded the shallow Thames at Goring. The Romans crossed via a causeway and subsequently a ferry operated. In July 1674 there was a tragic accident when a ferry passed too close to the weir and overturned. It was returning to Streatley after the Goring Fair with seventy-four people on board. Only fourteen survived.

To our dismay we discovered Streatley's cheese shop had closed its doors, the owner

© Rob Conolly

A colourful canal boat passes through Goring Lock

having succumbed to the lure of ripe Camembert and retired to France. We were unable to find Goring's bread shop either, but loved its timeless 'Groceries and Provisions' store. Sloping floorboards are covered in faded linoleum and staff wear traditional, striped aprons. This could well be the store Walter de la Mare had in mind when he wrote the following nonsense verse:

> *There was an old grocer of Goring*
> *Had a butter assistant named Green,*
> *Who sank through a hole in the flooring*
> *And never was afterwards seen.*

Hard by Goring's shopping centre, beside the lane leading to the car park, is an old-fashioned vegetable garden where sweet peas clamber up stakes between lettuce plants and runner beans. In the lane itself is a little shop honest enough to describe its goods as second-hand rather than antique. For the huge sum of £4 I bought two small etchings for the entrance hall at Harleyford; one of a hare sitting in a field and the other of geese by a river.

The town's oldest pub is the Catherine Wheel, in Station Street. It is thought to date back to Elizabethan times, when what is now Station Street was the main road. Another old pub is the Miller of Mansfield, which is associated with a story about King Henry II. Without revealing his identity, Henry called at this pub after being separated from the royal hunting party. The miller's wife served a dish she cryptically referred to as 'Lightfoot Pie', but after one mouthful Henry knew he was eating venison – in fact his own venison, as all deer were owned by the Crown. When questioned, the miller blithely admitted he had a couple more carcasses in the loft, adding, 'What the King doesn't know won't hurt him.' Poaching could have cost the miller his life, but his generous hospitality and the King's good humour saved his neck.

Goring's Church of St Thomas of Canterbury was built in the late eleventh century. An adjoining priory was later established by Augustinian nuns. It was dissolved in 1536, when only a prioress and three nuns remained. In 1303 the priory was visited by a wealthy woman known as Isabella of Kent. Unfortunately Isabella caught the eye of a rapacious character called William of Huntersull. Whether William was after Isabella's virtue or her fortune (or both) is unclear but he pursued her through the church and captured her in the tower. He and his twenty-one cohorts also attacked the chaplain during the fray and were later excommunicated. Isabella not only survived but brought a successful civil action against the men.

Preserved above the west door of the church is a bell which may have pealed in celebration of Isabella's deliverance. It was cast around 1290 and is one of the oldest inscribed bells in England. It rang out for the next 600 years.

A native plant known as butterbur thrives in marshy ground below the bridge by the Goring bank. Its soft, circular leaves grow to almost 3 ft (1 m) in diameter. The name butterbur comes from the old country practice of wrapping the wet leaves around butter to prevent it melting in hot weather. They are also useful on riverside picnics as makeshift tablecloths or sunshades. On a more romantic note, butterbur could be used if a young woman wished to 'see' her future husband. The seeds of the plant were strewn on the grass as the girl chanted:

I sow, I sow!
Then, my own dear,
Come here, come here,
And mow and mow!

Miraculously her future husband would appear, mowing with a phantom scythe. The method was said to be infallible. Whether the girl could alter her fate if she disliked like what she saw is another question.

We stopped for lunch at Goring's Riverside Tearoom and awarded their homemade carrot cake a rare ten out of ten. It was moist and open textured, seeded with currants and slathered in tangy lemon butter. I tried to wheedle the recipe from the cafe's owner but she refused, fearing it might fall into the hands of rival teashops. She told us she had once worked at the town's famous bread shop, which, like the Streatley cheese shop, had closed its doors. Never mind – with a mouthful of her carrot cake I was beyond caring.

Steps opposite the tearooms lead back to the Thames and on to the Goring Gap, carved by the river through the chalky Chiltern Hills during the Ice Age. The Great Western railway line crosses the river via one of Isambard Brunel's famous bridges and soon afterwards the Thames Path begins to climb – up into the woods of the Chilterns. Occasionally there are views south to the Berkshire Downs which form the other side of the valley.

The Downs were the setting for Richard Adams' bestselling novel *Watership Down,* the engaging story of a community of rabbits and their battle for survival. I re-read the book after we walked through the Chilterns but regretted not having doing so before we started out on the path back in Gloucestershire. It provides a unique view of the English countryside from, as writer Monica Dickens put it, 'the ground-level detail of a rabbit's eye and ear and nose'.

Across the river at Lower Basildon is Beale Park, a wildlife centre featuring deer and exotic birds. There is also a steam train and, appropriate for a Thames-side park, a willow maze. On higher ground, with expansive views over the Thames, is the National Trust property, Basildon Park. The house on the estate was built in the late eighteenth century by Sir Francis Sykes, who made his fortune with the East India Company trading in spices, sugar and tea. It was virtually derelict when it was rescued and restored in the 1950s by Lord and Lady Iliffe.

This very grand home has retained its cosy, 1950s ambience and will forever be the country house I imagine when reading an Agatha Christie novel. I half expected to find a body slumped over the desk in the library. Perhaps Dame Agatha occasionally popped down from Wallingford with her notebook. The dining table is set for dinner, ready for a deadly dose of arsenic in a glass of port. Upstairs there are inter-connecting bedrooms; so convenient for those illicit nocturnal encounters. Below stairs, the servants' bells are intact. The spell may be broken in the visitors' restaurant but the food is excellent. Produce grown on the estate is used whenever possible and the cakes are all home-made. Their wonderful apple and walnut cake was so light I almost had to hold it down with a fork between mouthfuls.

Back on the north bank, the Thames Path leaves the river and continues on and up through the Chiltern Hills. This was the most appropriate section of the walk for me to sing the old Peter Dawson song my mother used to belt out in her Tasmanian kitchen:

High in the hills, down in the dales,
Happy and fancy-free,
Old Father Thames keeps rolling along,
Down to the mighty sea.

After the rare experience of exerting more than minimal energy, we were soon heading down to the river again at Whitbridge, with its attractive, white-painted iron bridge. Motorists pay a ten pence toll to cross but, as at Swinford, pedestrians are not charged for the stroll across to neighbouring Pangbourne.

In 1924, Kenneth and Elspeth Grahame came to live by the riverside here at a house called Church Cottage. After the tragedy of their son Alastair's death (see page 53) they sold their home at Blewbury in Oxfordshire and spent a long period in Italy before returning to England and settling at Pangbourne. My initial image of them enjoying ham pie and summer pudding under the willows was somewhat wide of the mark. They were considered quite eccentric, especially Elspeth, who liked to practise her continental bartering skills on local shopkeepers. Perhaps trying to recapture the flavour of their Italian experience, the Grahames existed largely on bread, cheese, sausages and wine. They did dine outdoors when weather permitted, but on the back doorstep from a paper bag rather than from a wicker hamper by the river. Kenneth Grahame died in 1932 and is buried in Oxford's Holywell Cemetery. His cousin Anthony Hope composed the perfect epitaph for the creator of *Wind in the Willows*: 'To the beautiful memory of Kenneth Grahame, husband of Elspeth and father of Alastair, who passed the river on the 6th of July, 1932, leaving childhood and literature through him the more blest for all time.'

In 1910 the acerbic Charles Harper wrote a book called *Thames Valley Villages,* in which he complained about the appearance of 'detestable villas'. He could have been referring to Pangbourne's seven villas, which were commissioned at the turn of the century for the department store owner, D. H. Evans. Locals joked that there was one for each of his mistresses and that he visited them on separate days of the week. The snobbish Mr Harper also disliked campers and boaters. He claimed they were changing the nature of riverside shops, which according to him were now displaying 'tinned everything, festering in the sun … cheap camp kettles, spirit stoves, tin enamelled cups and saucers, and the like utensils, hammocks and lounge chairs'. Quaint old riverside establishments were being tarted up, giving Harper more cause for complaint: 'Swiss and German waiters, clothed in deplorable reach-me-down dress-suits and English of the Whitechapel-atte-Bowe variety have replaced the neat-handed – heavy-footed – Phyllises.'

It was at Pangbourne that Jerome K. Jerome and his friends abandoned their boating journey, defeated by rain, grime and the lack of decent food. Somewhat guiltily they caught the train back to London, ending the day with a fine French supper. As Jerome explained:

For about ten days we seemed to have been living, more or less, on nothing but cold meat, cake, and bread and jam. It had been a simple, a nutritious diet; but there had been nothing exciting about it, and the odour of Burgundy, and the smell of French sauces, and the sight of clean napkins and long loaves, knocked as a very welcome visitor at the door of our inner man.

The trio raised their glasses to Old Father Thames, but Harris added: 'Here's a toast to three men well out of a boat!'

The river now sweeps in a curve towards Mapledurham. Halfway around, on the north bank, is the Tudor mansion Hardwick House where, as Jerome K. Jerome informed his readers, Charles I once played bowls on the riverside lawn. Hardwick House was owned by the Lybbe family for generations and the diaries of Mrs Philip Lybbe Powys (1755–1809) provide a wonderful account of English upper-class life. There are descriptions of balls, card parties and shopping trips to London but also insights into eighteenth-century medical care. After her son was involved in a coach accident, Mrs Lybbe Powys revealed he was put on a restricted diet and 'blooded' every three or four days for several weeks. It's a wonder his body's natural recuperative powers were not fatally suppressed.

© Rob Conolly

A helping hand for a fellow
Thames traveller near
Mapledurham Lock

Approaching Mapledurham Lock through the golden glow of buttercups, we came across a little plastic duckling lying bottom up on the towpath, his beak embedded in the dirt. Somehow he had strayed from the river during a charity race. I cleaned him up and sent him on his way. Who knows, someone might have been camped out downstream waiting for duckling number 248 to cross the finish line. A sign at the lock states that from here it is just 78½ miles (126 km) to London. It is entirely possible that the duckling might have swam on, beating us to the Flood Barrier at Greenwich.

Across the river stands Mapledurham House, St Margaret's Church, and the old corn mill. In his *Portrait of the Thames* published in 1967, J. H. B. Peel wrote of seeing an area between the church and mill marked out with string as the possible site for a car park. He hoped this would never eventuate, commenting: 'If people wish to visit the place, let them leave their vehicle on the main road, and benefit themselves and Mapledurham by walking a mile down-hill through woods.' Needless to say, there is now a very large car park by the fifteenth-century mill. On a more positive note, it was sensitively restored in 1977 and is now the only working mill on the river. The waterwheel is made of elm and the shaft of oak. Visitors can climb up and watch the millstones in action, then buy a bag of freshly ground wholewheat flour downstairs.

Elizabethan Mapledurham House was the home of the Blount family for 500 years. There is a portrait in the house of Sir Charles Blount, who became a casualty of the Civil War when he was killed during the siege of Oxford. The Blounts were devout Catholics, and at a period when it was dangerous to practise their faith they wanted to let fellow Catholics know that Mapledurham House was a safe refuge. Their secret signal can still be seen at the back of the house: a pattern of oyster shells decorating the gable of a window. In 1797, when it *was* safe to worship, the Blounts built a private chapel featuring ornate, Gothic plasterwork.

In John Galsworthy's *The Forsyte Saga*, Soames Forsyte built a riverside house at Mapledurham. It was here that Soames's French wife Annette gave birth to their daughter Fleur.

The Thames Path veers away from the water again at neighbouring Purley, thanks to an eighteenth-century landowner who refused to allow the towpath to cross his property. In the days of barges, whenever the towpath reached an impasse men had to pole their heavy craft through or send the harnessed towing horses to the opposite bank on pontoons. The Roebuck Ferry cottage is a legacy of Purley's pontoons. It took bargemen hours to circumvent the short stretch of 'out of bounds' territory here.

After a silence of thirty years, the bells at Purley's St Mary's Church were rehung in time to herald the new millennium. Church bells rang out in towns and villages all along the Thames on New Year's Day 2000, as part of a nationwide celebratory peal. I was sorry Rob and I were not in England to hear it but the lure of fireworks on Sydney Harbour proved too great.

An upstream walker stopped to chat with us on the towpath and told us that in 1808 the painter J. M. W. Turner had written a poem in his sketchbook while fishing in the Thames at Purley. I managed to track the poem down and found it included lines about a village boy floating a paper boat into the river:

Where the deep gullys which his fathers cart
Made in their progress to the mart
Full to the brim deluged by rain
They prove to him a channel to the main
Guiding his vessel down the stream
The pangs of hunger vanish like a dream.

Turner loved fishing, but ago nized over whether to eat or release his catch.

The final south bank settlement before the Thames Path reaches the outskirts of Reading is Tilehurst, which derives from Tigel-Hurst, meaning 'tile wood'. Tiles were made here from Saxon times, using Thames-Valley clay.

Reading to Shiplake

On the north bank of the river, the tower of Caversham Church comes into view, followed by Caversham Bridge. In November 1642, Charles I marched to Reading from his base at Oxford intending to set up a Royalist outpost. Locals were given one day to strengthen Caversham Bridge so that it could support the King's troops. The arrival of the army put great pressure on a community of only 500. Reading's tailors were commanded to produce 1,000 uniforms and the demand for food and fuel was immense. Charles returned to Oxford within a month but left behind a garrison of 2,000 soldiers to be housed and fed. When the Parliamentarians advanced on the garrison, cannons were positioned at strategic locations, including one on the steeple of Caversham Church. The gun was shot down by enemy fire and the steeple collapsed.

Like Dorchester, Reading actually sits on a tributary of the Thames, in this case the River Kennet. At Kennet Mouth it is possible to explore an 1810 towpath running beside the Kennet and Avon Canal. Thames Path walkers who get carried away and forget to turn back could end up 87 miles (140 km) away in Bristol.

Reading is often dubbed 'Dreading' by its disaffected youth and Jerome K. Jerome must have shared their view as he famously wrote, 'One does not linger in the neighbourhood of Reading.' Rob and I linger in it surprisingly often; not because we love the place or are detained against our will, like Oscar Wilde at Reading Gaol, but because we cannot find our way out. Do bored teenagers amuse themselves by removing and swapping street signs?

Reading was little more than a village in the eighteenth century, but the story of Stephen Duck suggests it had already developed the ability to confound travellers. Duck was a plough-boy poet from Wiltshire, and in 1729 his verses on the wonders of nature brought him to the attention of Queen Caroline. He was summoned to Windsor Castle, where he became royal librarian and married the Queen's housekeeper. Duck began to write sophisticated poetry to match his lifestyle but it was rejected by the public. In 1756, he set off for his old home in Wiltshire hoping to find inspiration in his childhood surroundings. Sadly, he got no further than Reading where, either from depression or the inability to find the road leading west, he drowned himself in a stream behind the Black Horse Inn.

It appears even Reading's own inhabitants find it difficult to get a handle on the town. On our first visit we asked a young waiter for directions to the abbey ruins. He looked astonished and replied: 'I didn't know we had an abbey!' Fortunately a lady at the next table overheard and put us on the right track. She also told us where to find the museum, Reading Gaol, the post office and the lion statue in Forbury Gardens. I tried to persuade her to spend the day with us but she was on her lunch break from a local bank.

The Forbury Gardens' lion has become famous for having its legs in the wrong position. There was really no excuse for the error because the artist visited London Zoo to study his subject and in some aspects the anatomical detail is astonishing. However, there would be no fear of being eaten if the lion came to life because it would fall flat on its face.

Reading has an infamous culinary history. During the Second World War, food shortages prompted a national survey in which 8,000 workers were asked what foods they considered most necessary for their health. All seven representatives from Reading answered 'tea and chips'. With the strange logic of government departments, the Ministry of Food then chose the town to trial exotic dietary supplements, including cormorants' eggs and dried Chinese peas. As might be expected, the foods did not go down well, although officials were heartened by a positive response to an imported fish called snoek. Mind you, it was never determined whether Reading had overcome its prejudice against the unfamiliar or taken to snoek because it was nutritionally deficient.

Appropriately enough, the town became renowned for the production of beer and biscuits. Its biscuit company Huntley & Palmers was established in 1822 and became a household name throughout Britain. Conveniently, Mr Huntley's son was an innovative ironmonger who developed an airtight container allowing biscuits to be sent all over the country. The foundry also manufactured boilers, which were exported filled with biscuits, arguably becoming the world's first shipping containers. The business closed in 1977 but Reading Museum displays 300 decorative biscuit tins; a very popular exhibit despite competing with a full-sized copy of the Bayeux Tapestry. The tins are collectors' items, although the most sought-after design is neither the oldest or rarest. In the late 1970s a disgruntled employee painted an idyllic garden party but hid lewd images in the flowerbeds and wrote the word 'shit' on a tiny jam jar label. This design brings hundreds of pounds at auction. One of the company's luxury biscuits lines was Ratafias, which are very simple to make:

RATAFIAS

2 egg whites
150 g (5 oz) superfine caster sugar
120 g (4 oz) ground almonds
2 teaspoons ground rice

Grease a baking sheet and set oven to 160°C (325°F). Whisk the egg whites until frothy. Stir in the sugar, ground almonds and ground rice. Beat with a wooden spoon until thick and white. Drop tiny heaps, 2 cm (¾ in) in diameter, onto the baking paper allowing room for them to expand. Bake for 10-12 minutes until the palest fawn. Cool on a wire rack.

I know of only one recipe specific to Reading and as you may guess it is not a cormorant egg omelette or a soup made from dried Chinese peas. It is a rich, eighteenth-century cake flavoured with a good splash of alcohol. It could be made using the leftover egg yolks from the Ratafias.

READING SWEET CAKE

185 g (6 oz) softened butter
120 g (4 oz) caster sugar
3 eggs plus 2 extra egg yolks, beaten together
250 g (8 oz) flour
3 tablespoons brandy
3 tablespoons sherry
sifted icing sugar

Set oven to 180°C (350°F). Butter and line a 20 cm (8 in) round cake tin. Cream the butter and sugar then beat in the beaten eggs. Add the flour a little at a time, beating well after each addition. Mix together the brandy and sherry and stir in gradually. Turn into the prepared tin and bake for approximately one hour. Allow the cake to cool then dust with icing sugar.

Just before the Great Western Railway opened, a freak accident took the life of a Reading man called Henry West. He was working on the new station when a gust of wind picked up the section of roof he was standing on. The poor fellow was taken on a terrifying 'magic carpet' ride before eventually plummeting to his death. Henry is remembered on a memorial board in St Laurence's churchyard.

There is another, very touching burial site in Reading. In the London Road Cemetery is the grave of an Aboriginal boy whose short life reflects the harsh treatment indigenous Australians received after white settlement. In 1846, fighting broke out between a group of squatters and the Wotjobaluk people, on the banks of the Wimmera River in Victoria. Afterwards, a boy of about six was found huddled against his dead mother, who had been shot through the heart. The child was taken away by one of the settlers, reputedly the same man who had killed his mother. He was treated as a servant until he ran away, finding his way to Melbourne where he was befriended by an Anglican missionary from Reading, Septimus Chase.

In 1851 the boy was taken to England by the well-meaning Mr Chase and christened William Wimmera. Unfortunately the damp English climate had a terrible effect on his health

© Rob Conolly

Far from his tribe, Aboriginal boy William Wimmera was buried at Reading in 1852

and although plans were made to return him to Australia he died in Reading in March 1852. Long afterwards it was discovered that the boy's father and brothers had survived the battle at Wimmera River, but no efforts had been made to find them.

Later in the century a number of much younger children died in Reading in equally tragic circumstances. A middle-aged resident called Mrs Amelia Dyer was hanged in 1896 for infanticide. Dyer took in babies from unmarried mothers then strangled them using dress-maker's tape. She parcelled the bodies with brown paper and string before throwing them into the Thames. Meanwhile, the unsuspecting mothers continued to pay Mrs Dyer until she eventually informed them their infants had died of natural causes. It was Dyer's penny-pinching habit of recycling paper that proved her downfall. When a dead child was pulled from the river by a bargeman, police deciphered one of her previous addresses on the wrapping. It had been written in indelible ink. Further evidence came from a neighbour who had innocently supplied string for the parcels. Mrs Dyer confessed during questioning and as the river was being searched for more bodies she told police: 'You'll know mine by the tape around their necks.' Seven bodies were recovered but since Mrs Dyer had been in business for over twenty years the true number of her tiny victims scarcely bears thinking about.

The young waiter we met at Reading might be forgiven his ignorance about the abbey because there is not a lot of it left. It was founded early in the twelfth century by Henry I, who was buried there with great ceremony in 1135 after dying in France from 'a surfeit of stewed lampreys'. Only parts of him ended up at Reading; his bowels, brain, heart, eyes and tongue were buried at Rouen. The rest was embalmed, sewn into a bull's hide, then taken across the channel and up the Thames to the abbey.

Reading Abbey's main claim to fame is a musical composition set down by the monks in 1240. It is generally accepted as being the first song in the English language. The lyrics appear on a plaque at the abbey in Old English. The following is a more modern translation:

> *Summer is a-comin' in,*
> *Loud sing cuckoo!*
> *Groweth seed, and bloweth mead,*
> *And springeth the wood anew-*
> *Sing cuckoo!*

Children particularly like the second verse which includes the lines:

> *Bullock starteth, buck farteth*
> *Merry sing cuckoo!*

In 1539 Henry VIII suppressed the abbey and the last abbot was sentenced to death at a court held above the arch of the abbey's inner gateway. The plan was that he should be hung until nearly dead then drawn and quartered. Mercifully the hangman miscalculated and the abbot was already dead when he was cut down.

I realize that I have done little to counter Jerome's advice not to linger in Reading, having begun with a story of suicide, moved on to serial murder and ended with a public hanging. Perhaps I should point out that thousands of young people flock to the town each August for the country's oldest music festival.

There is a wetlands nature reserve bordering the Thames on the outskirts of town. I found it hard to resist the urge to pick the wild flowers, but refrained and simply tried to avoid crushing them under my boots. In 1594 Edmund Spenser wrote of nymphs he called 'daughters of the flood' gathering wild flowers by the Thames:

> Of every sort, which in that meadow grew
> They gathered some; the Violet pallid blew,
> The little Dazie, that at evening closes,
> The virgin Lillie, and the Primrose trew

Sixteenth-century nymphs did not have to worry about breaking the Country Code and could no doubt trip lightly through the flowers without bruising a petal. Thankfully all the flowers Spenser mentions, and many others, can still be found along the river. Even a list of their names reads like a poem: kingcups, Queen Anne's lace, loosestrife, ladies smock, meadowsweet and trailing tansy. The lily Spenser refers to could be the Loddon Lily, which flowers in this area during May and June. It looks like a giant snowdrop and is not really a lily at all. The name comes from the River Loddon, which enters the Thames downstream by Shiplake Lock.

But before Shiplake comes Sonning Lock, also known for flowers due to its lovingly tended garden beds. From 1845 until 1885 the keeper here was Mr James Sadler, a poet and rose grower whose efforts to beautify his surroundings were remarked upon favourably by Charles Dickens. Sadler was also a beekeeper, credited with having invented the Berkshire ornamental hive. I like to imagine him brewing mead during quiet times, the honey-based liquor flavoured (as was common) with fragrant rose petals. Mr Sadler celebrated many Thames towns and villages in verse, but closest to his heart was Sonning (pronounced 'Sunning'):

Is there a spot more lovely than the rest,
By art improved, by nature truly blest?
A noble river at its base running
It is a little village known as Sonning.

The original settlement grew up around the site of a medieval bishops' palace; held by the bishops of Salisbury from the eleventh century until 1574, when it was surrendered to Elizabeth I in exchange for other property. Her Majesty visited so infrequently that the palace fell into ruin and disappeared, though much of its stone was incorporated in the walls of local homes.

Walkers can make their way to the village via peaceful St Andrew's churchyard, where the dead now rest more easily than in Victorian times. Grave-robbing was common in those days, supplying the medical profession with corpses for their experiments. The story goes that a certain doctor from Reading would keep Sonning's vicar chatting over dinner while his partners in crime removed bodies next door.

A memorial arch in the south wall of the churchyard was built from bricks collected from homes bombed in London's East End during the Blitz. The north wall was once the boundary between the church and the sprawling residence of the deans of Salisbury. Replacing the old deanery is a house called Deanery Gardens, designed by Sir Edwin Lutyens in 1901 for Edward Hudson, founder of *Country Life*. The house has a weather vane depicting a dean preaching to empty pews – prophetic considering today's dwindling congregations. The garden of the property was designed by Gertrude Jekyll and incorporates the deanery's original walled garden. Incidentally, the Australian garden designer Edna Walling was strongly influenced by both Jekyll and Hudson's informal approach to house and garden design. Her stone cottage in Victoria was called Sonning, after this lovely Berkshire village.

Next door to the church is the Bull Inn, with wisteria climbing over its black and white timbers. It was probably built as a guesthouse for the bishop's palace. Another old pub at Sonning inspired a verse that appeared in *Punch* magazine a hundred years ago:

Lets land at the lawn of the cheery White Hart
Now gay with the glamour of June;
For here we can lunch to the music of trees
In sight of the swift river running.
Offcuts of cold beef and a pure Cheddar cheese,
And a tankard of bitter, at Sonning.

The thirteenth-century White Hart evolved into the Great House at Sonning Hotel, once the home of 1950s playwright Terence Rattigan, who wrote *The Winslow Boy*. The lawn still runs down to the Thames although lunch is now more likely to consist of smoked salmon and a glass or two of French champagne than cold beef and bitter.

There is a story that highwayman Dick Turpin's aunt lived at Sonning, in a cottage with an underground stable. Dick is supposed to have hidden his mare Black Bess in the stable before slipping across the river into Oxfordshire after robbing a coach on the Bath Road. Well, it might be true. The cottage has been incorporated into a larger house called, naturally enough, Turpins.

It was not known until relatively recently that the beautiful ceiling of the Chapel Royal at Hampton Court Palace was carved at Sonning and sent down to Hampton Court by barge. A man called George Heath had spent his retirement researching the history of the palace and on the side of an old document describing the ceiling he found a note other historians had overlooked: 'Wrought at Sonning.'

The Thames Path crosses to the north bank of the river at Sonning via a beautiful but busy bridge, built in 1772. Hump-backed, it has eleven red-brick arches of varying widths. Sonning village is now heartbreakingly assaulted by traffic. Whenever I visit, I think of Bea Miles, an eccentric Sydney woman notorious for kicking taxis. It would give me great satisfaction to follow Bea's example at Sonning, although I would also target tourist buses and Range Rovers.

Just across the bridge is a weir stream that once powered eighteenth-century Sonning Mill. There was a mill on this site at the time of the Domesday survey and during the Civil War it provided much-needed flour for the garrison at Reading. Sonning Mill has been converted into a very popular theatre/restaurant, worth visiting for its magical setting alone.

There was not a Range Rover or a bus to be seen when we walked from Sonning to Shiplake. We passed several small islands or aits, including Buck Ait, named for the woven eel traps (or bucks) that formed weirs all long the Thames until the late nineteenth century, presenting a hazard to navigation.

The towpath stays well away from roads and built-up areas as it wanders down to the boat-houses of prestigious Shiplake College. At this point, a footpath leads to the village via a chalk bluff.

After a long and problematical courtship, forty-one-year-old Alfred Lord Tennyson married Emily Sellwood at Shiplake's St Peter and St Paul's Church on 13 June 1850. Edward Lear wrote that Emily exceeded the combined virtues of fifteen angels, several hundred ordinary women, many philosophers, a heap of truly wise and kind mothers, three or four minor prophets and a lot of doctors and school-mistresses. Essayist Thomas Carlyle described her more prosaically: 'A freckly round-faced woman, rather tallish and without shape, a slight lisp too.' Perhaps the last word should go to Tennyson, who suffered from depression and emotional instability: 'The peace of God came into my life before the altar when I married her.'

" Eel Bucks" on the Thames.

Trapping eels, once plentiful all along the Thames

On the outskirts of Shiplake is Keep Lane, scene of a freakish double fatality in 1839. Charles Stonor Esquire was watching trees being cut on his property at nearby Binfield Heath when he stepped in front of a falling tree and was critically injured. His groom left on horseback to call a doctor from Reading but Stonor died before help arrived. The butler, who was also present, immediately rode towards Reading to let everyone know it was too late. However, in a dreadful twist of fate he collided at full gallop with the returning groom in Keep Lane. He later died from his injuries.

The town of Wargrave sits just across the river from Shiplake Lock in Berkshire and has had to cope with its own dramas. Its church, St Mary's, has a Norman tower topped with Tudor brick but the rest of the building is twentieth century because on Whitsunday 1914 a group of Suffragettes burned it to the ground. They were said to be furious at the vicar's refusal to remove the word 'obey' from the marriage service, although St Mary's may only have become a target after the Suffragettes alighted at the wrong train station. An alternative theory was that they were originally heading for Shiplake, intending to burn the home of a judge notorious for giving harsh sentences to their equally militant sisters.

Buried in Wargrave Cemetery is the eighteenth-century author Thomas Day, who believed that every person could be improved by kindness. To test his theory he took a penniless orphan under his wing, gently grooming her in the hope she might make him a suitable wife. His plan backfired when she fell in love with his best friend. Worse was to come when Day tried his softly-softly approach on a horse. He refused to have the animal broken in and eventually it threw him and kicked him to death.

Back in Oxfordshire, the Thames Path veers away from the river beyond Shiplake to connect two ferry sites, as it did at Purley. Just before rejoining the towpath at Bolney Ferry, it follows a road behind several riverfront estates, including the impressive Thames Side Court. In the early 1990s an extensive miniature railway system was installed in this property's 8-acre (3-hectare) grounds. Tracks can be seen running past a sunken garden and formal rose beds, through signalled intersections and finally into a head-high, multi-storeyed railway station.

The meadows between Shiplake and Henley form one of the loveliest sections of the Thames Path, especially when the river is bathed in late-afternoon sunshine. Walking here in early October, Rob and I came upon a scene straight from the pages of Hudson's *Country Life.* Against a background of golden woodland, a young man was rowing gently downstream in a traditional wooden slipper boat. Under a fringed awning, his lady friend reclined in a wicker chair, sipping wine and trailing a languid hand in the river. I was reminded of an old rhyming couplet:

Ring out the bells from every steeple,
It makes no difference to boating people.

At nearby Marsh Lock an elevated towing path was built across the weir to bypass a mill that once powered a brass foundry. There was also a flour mill on the opposite bank. The long wooden walkway now takes the Thames Path into very posh Henley.

HeNLeY TO HURLeY

There could be no better place to begin a visit to Henley-on-Thames than the new River and Rowing Museum, located on Mill Meadows just beyond Marsh Lock. This state-of-the-art museum encompasses the entire social history of the town. Its greatest treasure is a large oil painting by the seventeenth-century artist Jan Siberechts. The picture is a detailed representation of Henley as seen from Wargrave Road in 1698. It provides a rare opportunity to see how a flash lock operated. Four men are shown laboriously turning a winch as a loaded barge is hauled over the lock at Marsh Mills.

Naturally there is an emphasis at the museum on Henley's Royal Regatta, which achieved royal status when Queen Victoria's consort Prince Albert became patron in 1851. Initially, manual labourers were not allowed to compete in the rowing races as it was deemed they would have an unfair advantage over 'gentlemen'. One young man banned from the Diamond Sculls under those rules was Jack Kelly, the father of Princess Grace.

Australian visitors to the museum should not miss a display of silver cups presented to Stuart (Sam) Mackenzie, a poultry farmer's son from Sydney who won the Diamond Sculls a record six consecutive times (1957–62). Sam's response to the constant jibe 'How do you sex chickens?' was 'You rattle 'em!', which was exactly what he did to his rivals. On one occasion he meandered along the course chatting to bystanders before putting on a last-minute spurt to win the race. 'Very bad form,' the old buffers muttered, but I doubt if Sam cared.

The riverbanks around Henley are prime picnic sites during the regatta, held during the first week of July. Approaching Thames Path walkers are diverted by eagle-eyed stewards, but if one wore a big hat and distracted attention from one's boots it might just be possible to sneak past. Hats and hemlines create a lot of angst at the regatta. Hemlines must be no more than 2 in (5 cm) above the knee and there is often debate over what constitutes a hat. A giant silk rose may fail the test while three small goose feathers are given the nod. One woman invited at short notice borrowed a broad-brimmed hat, which fitted perfectly when she arrived but slid down her forehead as her freshly set hair collapsed. By lunchtime the river had completely vanished from her view. However, after downing half a dozen glasses of Pimms she regained her composure, climbing onto a chair and giving a running commentary of several races, convinced she could see quite clearly.

HENLEY HAT RAISER

Combine the following:
1 part gin
3 parts Pimms
5 parts chilled dry ginger ale
dash of Cointreau

Garnish with:
slice of lemon
slice of cucumber
sprig of fresh mint

Along with Wimbledon and Ascot, the Henley Regatta is regarded as one of the highlights of the English social season. However, there are those who see it as an elitist gathering of 'hooray Henrys'. In 1985 a group called Class Wars protested by walking along the banks kicking Fortnum & Mason picnic hampers into the river.

As evening falls during regatta week, the black-tie Henley Festival transforms the riverside into a scene straight from the Edwardian era. Ladies in evening gowns stroll and chat and young men in dinner jackets arrive in traditional wooden boats. One almost expects to see a slightly tipsy Sebastian Flyte enjoying a glass of pink champagne and a plover's egg. Sculptures are exhibited on the lawns and my favourite remains a superbly crafted silver stile: surely the perfect memento for a Thames Path walker. Patrons wine and dine in marquees before wandering down to hear musicians perform on a floating stage.

The town's annual May fair is held on Mill Meadow. It is a far more relaxed event, with families sprawled on the grass scoffing doughnuts and toffee apples instead of nibbling smoked-salmon canapés. We were once entertained by some endearingly inept marching girls. As they clipped each other's heels and collided on turns, ripples of amusement spread through the crowd. Soon, everyone had deserted the Rotary Club's chocolate wheel in favour of placing bets on baton falls.

Beside Henley Bridge is the Angel Hotel, where water birds congregate to be fed by diners at the Angel's outdoor tables. At regatta time it all becomes too much for the stately swans and officials remove them to a refuge centre at Egham. Before the centre existed, the swans were simply transported further downstream. In a book called *The Story of Cookham,* written by Robin and Valerie Boole, there is a photo of about thirty unrestrained swans sitting quietly on the back of a truck while being driven from Henley to Cookham. No doubt some of Henley's human residents would like to be evacuated as well but they have to cope as best they can, along with the ducks and coots.

Coots would make wonderful cartoon characters. They have disproportionately large feet which are segmented, like branches of Zygo cactus. Their babies are adorable: sweet and cheeky, with bald red heads. Perhaps tripping over its feet on the towpath sours a young coot's temperament because the chicks grow into extremely bad-tempered adults, flapping and flying at each other at the slightest provocation. Their nests are messy piles of sticks and discarded ice-cream wrappers, plonked anywhere. Sometimes they build on narrow pontoons at Henley, forcing boat owners to leap over clutches of eggs, not an easy task when carrying a picnic basket and a couple of magnums of champagne.

In 1976 a diver found an Iron Age sword buried in silt under Henley Bridge, still in its decorated bronze scabbard. Evidence of even earlier human presence was discovered when a 250,000-year-old Stone Age axe was picked up in a nearby field.

On the outskirts of Henley is Greys Court, a fortified house which passed to the Knolly family in 1518. The house was associated with one of the greatest court scandals in English history. In 1615 the poet Sir Thomas Overbury died at the Tower of London in suspicious circumstances. Two years later the Earl of Somerset and his wife Frances, who was William Knolly's sister-in-law, were found guilty of his murder. Overbury had violently opposed his friend Somerset's relationship with Frances, particularly as she was already married when the Earl became infatuated with her. Pressure from high places orchestrated by Somerset led to Sir Thomas being sent to the tower, where Frances arranged to have him sent arsenic-laced tarts and jellies.

QUINCE JELLY

(Guaranteed absolutely innocuous!)
Rub 3 or 4 quinces with a cloth to remove fuzz. Cut into large pieces. Do not bother to skin or core the fruit. Place in a deep saucepan. Cover with water and cook with the lid on until tender (2–3 hours). Strain through a fine sieve, but avoid forcing the pulp through or the jelly will be clouded. Add enough cups of oven-warmed sugar to equal the volume of the liquid. Stir in until the sugar dissolves. Return to the saucepan and bring to the boil. Simmer uncovered until a little of the mixture will set in a saucer. Allow to cool for five minutes before pouring into sterilized jars.

After suffering weeks of agony, Overbury was said to have been finished off with a poison-filled enema. Long aware of his fate, he had already written his own epitaph which began:

The span of my days measure'd here I rest,
That is, my body, but my soule his guest
Is hence ascended, wither, neither time,
Nor faith, nor hope, but only love can clime.

At her trial, Frances, by then the Countess of Somerset, pleaded guilty. Four accomplices were executed but Frances and the Earl were reprieved. The pair were confined at Greys Court and later pardoned. During the trial the chief justice was moved to comment that of all felonies, murder was the most horrible, of all murders, poisoning the most detestable, and of all poisonings, that causing a lingering death the most cruel. Having expressed such views, one wonders whether he considered confinement at a relative's country house adequate punishment. The public made their feelings clear with a series of derogatory rhymes. Somerset's various titles inspired the following:

Lord Thomas Overbury, victim of arsenic-filled tarts and jellies

A page, a Knight, a Viscount and an Earl
All four were married to one lustful girl
A match well made, for she was likewise four
A wife, a witch, a murderess and a whore.

Only one tower remains from Greys Court's medieval courtyard. The property is surrounded by an informal garden featuring wisteria, peony roses, espaliered fruit trees and an ornamental vegetable garden. There is also a well house with an intact Tudor donkey wheel. A donkey paced inside the giant wheel drawing water from a depth of 200 ft (60m). The well remained in operation until 1912.

Thames Path walkers leave Henley via the town bridge, crossing into Berkshire to follow the regatta course to its starting point at Temple Island. The tiny temple houses the statue of a naked lady and was built as a decorative fishing lodge to enhance the view from nearby Fawley Court.

Fawley Court was home to Henley's lords of the manor for centuries. It was designed by

Christopher Wren and built between 1684 and1690 for William Freeman, who had substantial interests in West Indian sugar plantations. William of Orange reputedly stayed at the house on his way to London to accept the throne in 1688. For a long time a circular mound in the deer park was thought to be a prehistoric burial mound but in the 1930s it was opened and an eighteenth-century time capsule was found. A Latin inscription had been engraved on a piece of glass:

> *In the year of our Lord 1731 John Freeman of Fawley Esq. has raised up this mass mound, having buried in it a medley of pieces of glass, of vessels of pottery and other household utensils, so that if perchance at sometime, curious posterity should examine this old rubbish, it may find something to give pleasure, and profit since some arts are dying out.*

The collection is on display at Henley's River and Rowing Museum and it certainly gave me pleasure, Mr Freeman.

Fawley Court also has a view across the Thames to the hamlet of Remenham, which had achieved village status before plague virtually wiped out the population in the seventeenth century. Only the church and a few houses remain. From the Thames Path a laneway leads to the church, one of very few along the Thames Path which is locked and appears to have no local 'key holder'. Never mind, the churchyard is a lovely place to visit, especially in May when pink hawthorn and wisteria form the romantic backdrop for a weathered stone angel. A few weeks later the south door of the church is surrounded by heavenly scented climbing roses.

Lying in the churchyard with just a glimpse of the river he served for many years is Caleb Gould, keeper of downstream Hambleden Lock from 1777 until his death in 1836. Caleb baked bread to sell to bargemen and other users of the river. He was somewhat eccentric, dressing in a long, silver-buttoned coat and sustaining himself on a nightly supper of onion porridge. Apparently the diet was good for him because he lived to be ninety-two. If his no-nonsense epitaph seems well suited to a man who lived on onion porridge, it is because he chose it himself:

> *The World's a jest*
> *And all things show it,*
> *I thought so once;*
> *And now I know it.*

By contrast, Caleb had a touching verse engraved on his wife Sarah's headstone. It begins:

Lo! Where this silent stone now weeps,
A friend, a wife, a mother sleeps.

Sarah died in 1813, predeceasing Caleb by over twenty years.

I took a young Australian friend to see Caleb and Sarah's graves, but she was more inter-ested in a nearby memorial to Misses Sally and Julia Stapleton, who also died in the nineteenth century. Considering the lowly status of unmarried women in Victorian times, Clare thought it unnecessarily cruel that 'Spinster' was writ so large below their names. I told her to remember the lady who used her last breath to croak: 'Put "Miss" on my grave if you like, but I haven't missed as much as people think!' The old girl was definitely ahead of her time!

Regrettably the lock-keeper at Hambleden has not followed Caleb Gould's example of bread baking, but an ice-cream van does a roaring trade, especially on bank holidays. Hambleden's weatherboard mill and its white-water weirs have drawn tourists for genera-tions. The mill ceased operation in 1955 and is now an exclusive residential complex. In summer, locals stroll out from Henley to watch tiny runabouts jostle for position at the lock with expensive cruisers. One day Rob and I were standing with a crowd of onlookers as a 40-ft (12-m) launch went through. Two silver cups mounted beside its polished wooden steering wheel prompted the man beside me to quip: 'Oh look, that wanker's won Poser of the Year twice running!'

A footbridge crosses Hambleden Weir to the hamlet of Mill End. When a Roman-British villa was excavated here in 1911, the graves of hundreds of infants were discovered. Some experts have suggested the babies' deaths could have been the result of an early exercise in population control.

In a valley of beech trees a mile or so north of the mill is Hambleden itself, a quintessential English village with brick and flint cottages, a manor house, church and pub, grouped around a communal water pump under a giant chestnut. Hambleden often becomes a film set and one local told me she was so busy identifying villagers in the film version of a Joanna Trol-lope novel that she completely lost the thread of the story. Cars present the main problem for makers of period films, but villagers can earn a few quid by agreeing to park out of sight.

One Christmas we attended a carols-by-candlelight service at Hambleden's St Mary's Church. A fur-clad Lady Hambleden read the lesson and at the end of the service the congre-gation stood in respectful silence as she made her exit. I half expected the vicar to give the old benediction: 'God bless the squire and his relations, and keep us in our proper stations.' Despite my love of history and tradition, my colonial blood stirred with a vague sense of rebellion. However, I later attended an open day at the manor, where Lady Hambleden chatted to all and sundry with a warmth that completely disarmed me.

St Mary's has a document chest that belonged to the Earl of Cardigan, who was born in

Hambleden. This man has a lot to answer for. During the Crimean War he led the disastrous Charge of the Light Brigade, in which 673 men rode out to confront the Russian cavalry, with only 198 returning. The Earl took to wearing an innovative but now all-too-familiar knitted garment, fastened at the front for convenience. The cardigan, as it became known, may have looked fine on a cavalry officer but is now often worn by elderly men, whose stomachs would be restrained more adequately by chainmail than 8-ply wool. Some also blame Lord Cardigan for the balaclava, a woollen helmet originally worn by soldiers at Crimea but later adopted by sufferers of earache … and armed robbers.

The Thames Path leaves the riverside beyond Hambleden Lock at the site of Aston Ferry. It turns up Ferry Lane, where chickens scrabble among the cottages. At the top of the hill is the delightfully named Flowerpot Inn, a famous anglers' haunt with a beer garden full of old apple trees.

In early summer a right turn at the rear of the pub provides a landscape that is pure Van Gogh; a large pond is fringed with trees and surrounded by the brilliant yellow of flowering canola. Footpaths create an abstract design through the crop down to the banks of the river. A hundred years earlier an American couple called Pennell travelled down the Thames and were impressed by very different scenery at the Flowerpot. In their book *The Stream of Pleasure*, published in 1891, they wrote of beautiful old elms and fields of poppies. Sadly, the elms succumbed to Dutch elm disease, and the poppy fields to broad-acre crops.

To continue in a downstream direction it is necessary to backtrack and turn left towards red-bricked Culham Court, which dates from 1770. I have been unable to discover who built it, but when a gentleman called West owned the property King George III was an overnight guest. Taking his duties as royal host very seriously, Mr West arranged for a relay of horsemen to deliver freshly baked breakfast rolls from London, a distance of some 30 miles (48 km). The rolls were from Gunter's, the royal purveyors who owned a fashionable shop in Berkeley Square. They arrived still warm, having been wrapped in flannel, but it is hard to impress a king. Apparently the royal guest's only comment was a slightly underwhelmed, 'Oh, I'm glad you deal with Gunter, West.'

There is no record of what Mr West served the King for dinner but after less than rapturous praise for his London rolls, he may have opted for the more homely dish of Berkshire Jugged Beef. At least Culham Farm could have provided the basic ingredient and George III was noted for his interest in agriculture.

BERKSHIRE JUGGED BEEF

750 g (½ lb) braising steak
2 onions stuck with cloves
4 sticks celery (chopped)
120 g (4 oz) mushrooms (chopped)
300 ml (10 fl oz) red wine
2 tablespoons redcurrant jelly
2 tablespoons chopped parsley
salt
black pepper

Lay cubed braising steak in a deep earthenware casserole with the clove studded onions, chopped celery and mushrooms. Season with salt and pepper. Pour in the red wine and redcurrant jelly. Cover tightly with foil and put on the lid. Cook for 2½–3 hours at 150°C (300°F). Garnish with the chopped parsley.

Back by the river, at Frogmill Farm we paused beside a pock-marked field of sheep where scarcely a blade of grass separated hundreds of molehills. Sleepy newborn lambs lay in tangled heaps in the sunshine and it occurred to me that a mole could pop up anywhere and warm its damp nose on lambswool. The eccentric nineteenth-century Oxford geologist William Buckland cooked and ate a mole but said it tasted truly horrible; and this from a man who had tried everything from bluebottles to mice fried in batter. On the other hand, lamb's ears were once considered a delicacy; stewed in stock until tender then served on a bed of sorrel with butter and nutmeg.

Directly across the river on the north bank, now Buckinghamshire instead of Oxfordshire, is the village of Medmenham, and Medmenham Abbey. Long since a private residence, the abbey sits by the Thames surrounded by sweeping lawns. There are stern warnings for any boater cheeky enough to drive a peg into the perfect turf and tie up for the night.

Very little remains of the original Cistercian abbey. An Elizabethan manor was built on its ruins and in the eighteenth century the property was bought by Sir Francis Dashwood, who added a cloister and a folly tower. Dashwood also added more than a hint of scandal when he established what became known as the Hell Fire Club. There were two prerequisites for membership: having visited Italy and having been gloriously drunk. The club's motto was 'Do as you choose' and the aristocratic members chose to do some outrageous things. There were stories of sexual orgies at masked balls and obscene pagan rites.

In a contemporary satire called *The Adventures of a Guinea* by Charles Johnstone, a golden guinea becomes part of its owner's gambling stake at a Hell Fire dinner where 'In the course of the evening I often went the circuit of the whole company round, and at length was carried home by a new master'. Some of the goings on were too torrid for the guinea to relate but he concluded: 'They continued at it till about six in the morning, when they retired for the night.'

Medmenham's church is dedicated to St Peter and St Paul. It now has three bells but it seems there were originally four. In 1717, Dr Thomas Hearne wrote:

> *There is a tradition at Medmenham that there were in the Norman Conquest four bells in the Parish Church and that in the Reigne of Richard the first, he being taken prisoner at his Returne from the Holy Lande one of the Bells was sold to pay his Ransome.*

Standing high on a cliff beside Medmenham is Danesfield House, a close neighbour to Harleyford. The castellated house was built from chalk rock, which was mined locally. The par-three twelfth hole on Harleyford's golf course actually finishes in one of the old chalk pits, and has a cliff of white chalk rising behind the green. Danesfield House is now a luxury hotel but was built as a private home for a soap manufacturer around 1900. However, the name Danesfield has much older associations. Historians believe the invading Danes set up camp here on their way to fight King Alfred's Anglo-Saxons, further west. The house played a significant role during the Second World War as the base for a joint intelligence unit involving eight allied nations. The main activity of the unit was the interpretation of aerial photographs of enemy military sites.

Caravans are a bit of an eyesore by the river as the Thames Path continues along the Berkshire bank towards Hurley. There are also bungalows which began life as mobile homes, though nowadays it would be difficult to budge them with a stick of dynamite. I suspect their owners have been quietly anchoring them to the earth over many years, sneaking out at night to mortar in another brick.

A charming reference to upcoming Harleyford was made by a passenger identified only as C. W. P., during a boat trip from Oxford to Maidenhead on the steam launch *Swallow*, in 1877. Harleyford was then owned by Sir William Clayton. Approaching Hurley Weir, C. W. P. looked across to the Buckinghamshire bank and wrote:

> *And now it is time to look up at the woods belonging to Sir William Clayton, and we see a kind of summer house or wigwam. Possibly something of a lovery. And soon we sight the windlass. Hurley Lock is generally much infested by landscape painters, but they do not bite. Through this, we find ourselves at Harleyford, where once the owner put on his boots and gave us very good tea made of champagne which we drank by pints out of silver mugs.*

Traditional wooden boats are still crafted at Hurley

Still in Berkshire, walkers can choose between two routes to Hurley village from the lock. One leads under a flowering cherry to a quiet backwater; originally a mill pond but for many years home to Peter Freebody's unique boatyard. Mouldering boat hulls surround a line of weatherboard buildings that sag ever closer to the water. Warped iron roofing is thatched by spider webs and inch-high flowering lichen. However, behind this 'Miss Havisham' facade is a superbly equipped workshop where skilled craftsmen produce traditional wooden river vessels, from tiny skiffs to romantic Victorian pleasure boats. No one minds if bypassers quietly step inside for a look. The saying goes that if you have to ask how much it costs to build a Freebody boat you cannot afford one. In our climate of rapid social change it is amazing to think that Peter Freebody's ancestor John was a bargeman at Hurley in 1642, and that the family lived and worked by the Thames for generations before that.

The track continues to the village and the site of seventeenth-century Ladye Place, built for Lord Richard Lovelace, who sailed with Sir Francis Drake and made his fortune plundering the Spanish galleons. In 1688 Lord John Lovelace met with political allies in the crypt at Ladye Place and hatched a successful plot to overthrow the Catholic-sympathizing James II and put William III (better known as William of Orange) on the throne. After what was dubbed the Glorious Revolution, William ruled jointly with his wife Mary, who happened to be James II's eldest surviving daughter.

The following recipe dates from the accession of William of Orange to the English throne:

KING WILLIAM CREAM

3 egg whites
2 lemons
6 tablespoons sugar
1–2 teaspoons orange flower or rose water

Squeeze the lemons and mix their juice with the sugar and orange flower or rose water. Put this mixture into a pan and heat until the sugar has melted. Remove from the heat and allow to cool. Beat the egg whites until stiff and fold them into the lemon mixture. Cook on a low heat, stirring continuously until the pudding becomes thick. Eat warm or cold.

Ladye Place was demolished in 1837 but its historic crypt survives. It was built on the ruins of Hurley's eleventh-century Benedictine priory. According to ancient documents, Edward the Confessor's wife Edith was buried at the priory, although no trace has been found of her tomb. One person who did his best to find it was Colonel River-Moore, who lived in Hurley House, dower house to Ladye Place. The Colonel spent from 1924 to 1944 on an obsessive search. Sightings of a ghostly grey lady increased during the period, so perhaps he got close enough to disturb Queen Edith's spirit.

A gentleman called Laurence Hancock purchased a rebuilt Ladye Place in 1903. In 1911 he wrote a small book called *Hurley and Ladye Place*. Hancock not only mentioned the crypt, but a secret tunnel with a possible connection to Harleyford:

While levelling the lawn to the south of the crypt many skulls and quantities of human bones were found in 1910. Also in the previous year a secret passage in a good state of repair leading direct to the Thames was exposed. We are of the opinion that this passage extends under the river to the grounds of Harleyford, the seat of Sir Wm. Clayton, and thence turns sharply at right angles in the direction of Medmenham Abbey. It is, at all events, certain that there is a cavern under the lawn at Harleyford large enough to hold a coach and four, with indications of a passage leading towards Medmenham.

Goodness me. I am tempted to take up a shovel!

Nearby is a house I would sell my soul to own, a converted tithe barn with a thirteenth-century dovecote in its garden. Both buildings originally belonged to the priory. The circular dovecote held 750 nestboxes and still has its potence: a revolving ladder used to collect eggs and young birds, called squabs.

Each summer Hurley holds a traditional fete centred around the Church of St Mary the Virgin, once the chapel for the priory. ('Ladye' in Ladye Place refers to the Virgin Mary.) The church's deep medieval font was designed for the total submersion of babies. Perhaps the idea was that baptism could be combined with a swimming lesson, lest a wandering infant should fall into the Thames. Nevertheless, Hurley mothers must have breathed a collective sigh of relief when a shallow lining was installed in 1852.

On Sunday mornings during winter the sound of St Mary's bells floats across the river to Harleyford. I love the sound, but the following rhyme was obviously written by someone who lived a little too close to church bells for comfort:

> *Ye rascally ringers, inveterate foes*
> *Disturbers of those who are fond of repose,*
> *I wish for the peace and quiet of these lands,*
> *That ye had round your necks what ye pull with your hands!*

Further on is Hurley's Ye Olde Bell hotel. Built in 1135, it claims to be the country's oldest. Like many ancient inns it began as a guesthouse for the priory and its bell was rung to announce the arrival of visitors.

Amid great excitement on 18 October 1974, Queen Elizabeth arrived in Hurley by car then took the footpath from the village to the lock, where she boarded a steamer for a trip down to Runnymede. The Queen planted an oak tree on Hurley Lock Island to commemorate the journey, or as a plaque states more regally, 'the occasion of her river progress'. Oaks grow slowly but forty years on the tree has reached a considerable size.

The half-mile walk between Hurley and Temple Lock is a delight at any time of year but particularly so in spring, when the horse chestnuts are in flower. Their blooms resemble miniature candelabras and are composed of perhaps a hundred rosettes. Although they appear creamy white from a distance, each tiny flower is splashed at the centre with crimson. Below canopies of new foliage the buttressed roots are covered in fine, almost luminous green moss; a legacy of the mists that shroud the river in autumn. Willows dip into the water and majestic beech trees feature prominently, especially across the river in Buckinghamshire. The name Buckinghamshire actually derives from *buche,* the German word for beech. At nearby High Wycombe the timber provided the basis of a thriving cottage industry in chair making, and beech wood is still prized for furniture. The trees had many other uses. Pigs were fattened on beech nuts and the leaves were used to flavour a gin-based liqueur.

There is a small tea garden at Temple Lock and, always welcome on the path, a loo. In summer, queues form along a fence line where estimated waiting times are signposted to

© Rob Conolly

Ye Olde Bell, Hurley, built in 1135 as a guesthouse to the Benedictine priory

reassure the desperate: i.e., 'THREE FLUSHES TO GO'.

Temple Mill Island was named for the Knights Templar, who established nearby Bisham Abbey in 1139. In the early eighteenth century the mill powered a copper foundry. It produced cladding for the hulls of ships, although when Daniel Defoe visited in 1722 after completing *Robinson Crusoe,* it was brass kettles and cooking pans that caught his eye. A century later copper had given way to the making of brown paper, an industry that continued until 1969. The island is now home to an exclusive residential and marina complex.

Just beyond Temple Lock there are views across the river to Harleyford Manor. It is thought the name Harleyford derives from *Hurley ford*, and that early man crossed the river here to collect flints. In 894 the Saxon Chronicles reported that the Danes forded the river at 'Herlei' as they marched towards Gloucester. The river is crossed more easily today thanks to a 150 ft (46 m) arched wooden footbridge. It opened in 1989 as one of the final links in the Thames Path, replacing a ferry that ceased operation in 1953. Before it was built, residents on the Harleyford Estate had to either follow the example of the Danes, or walk a mile downstream to Marlow Bridge. It is impossible to cross the footbridge without pausing to enjoy the idyllic view back towards Temple. The riverbanks are lined with boats from Harleyford Marina and there are usually swans and mallards foraging under the willows.

Harleyford is reached from the Thames Path via a private road, where the hedgerows are full of elder. I love the old saying that an English summer has not arrived until the elderflower blooms, and that it ends when the berries are ripe. John Evelyn lauded the plant's curative powers:

> *If the medicinal properties of its leaves, bark and berries were fully known, I cannot tell what our countryman could ail for which he might not fetch a remedy from every hedge, either for sickness or wounds.*

There is an ancient country recipe in which the flowerheads are held by the stalk and dipped into a thin batter before being deep fried then dusted with sugar before serving. During the Second World War, the Ministry of Food issued a recipe for elderberry and apple jam, both fruits being widely available at a time of strict rationing. Mind you, 6 kg (12 lb) of sugar might have been a bit more difficult to get hold of!

ELDERBERRY AND APPLE JAM

3 kg (6 lb) elderberries
3 kg (6 lb) sliced apples
6 kg (12 lb) sugar

Make a pulp of the apples by boiling in water until soft and passing through a coarse sieve to remove any seeds or cores. The elderberries should also be stewed for half an hour to soften them. Combine the apple pulp, berries and sugar and return to the heat to boil until thick.

HARLEYFORD TO MEDMENHAM

The history of Harleyford dates back to a riverside rights transfer between Geoffrey and William de Harleyford in 1288. The estate changed hands many times and records show that in the sixteenth century it sold for 800 silver marks, one mark being worth two thirds of one pound sterling. In the contract of sale it was described as:

> … the manor of Harleyford with appurtenances and of 20 messuages, 1000 acres of land, 200 acres of meadow, 200 acres of pasture, 100 acres of wood and 40s. rent in Harleyford, Medmenham and Little Marlow.

In 1586, when Roman Catholicism was being severely repressed, Harleyford Manor was the setting for a political and religious intrigue rivalling the plot at Hurley's Ladye Place (see page 111). It was then owned by Richard Bold, who hosted a secret eight-day conference at which it was decided that missionary priests would be based in the houses of practising Catholics, despite the fact that priests were being executed as traitors and that harbouring them could incur the death penalty. Morning sessions at the conference were spent in prayer and the afternoons in planning missionary action. The gathering was attended by Jesuit priests and representatives of well-known Catholic families. It concluded without incident, but it is indicative of the dangers faced by priests that just three months later Richard Bold's chaplain, Father Richard Dibdale, was arrested and executed at Tyburn.

There must be something in the water flowing between Hurley and Harleyford that encourages insurrection because a century later another owner of the estate was causing trouble. It had passed into the hands of Sir Miles Hobart, MP for Marlow. Sir Miles was in the House of Commons when resolutions opposed by King Charles I were being debated. The King tried to dissolve parliament but the MP for Marlow thwarted him by locking the doors of the House against the royal messenger:

The Members, apprehending an abrupt Diffolution, Sir Miles Hobart ftept to the Door and lock't it and Meffiers Holles, Valentine, Hayman and others, held the Speaker Finch in the Chair. The King hearing of this Heat in the Houfe, fent for the Serjeant of Arms, commanding him to bring away the Mace; But the Serjeant was lock'd in. The King then fent for Maxwell, the Uther of the Black Rod, to Diffolve the Parliement; But neither he nor his meffage would be admitted. (Free Parliaments: or an Argument on their Constitution; Proving Some of their Powers to be Independent. London, MDCCXXXI)

The resolutions were duly passed but afterwards Sir Miles was arrested and imprisoned in the tower. His spontaneous move against the monarch is remembered whenever the House of Commons is summoned to the House of Lords for the Queen's Speech. As her messenger the Black Rod approaches, the doors are initially barred, just as they were against the messenger of Charles I.

© Rob Conolly

Sir Robert Clayton, whose fortune funded the construction of Harleyford Manor

A unique monument to Sir Miles in Marlow's All Saints' Church depicts the dramatic circumstances of his death in 1632, shortly after his release from the Tower, when his four-horse coach ran away down London's Holborn Hill after losing a rear wheel. There was a lengthy dispute over his will and Richard Lovelace of Hurley's Ladye Place was quick to take advantage of the situation. The old buccaneer treated Harleyford Manor as if it were a disabled Spanish galleon marooned in the Thames. He marched 'aboard', took up residence, and began claiming all the income from the estate. Lovelace was eventually removed but no doubt he returned to Ladye Place with a few more chests of gold.

In 1735 the wealthy Clayton family acquired Harleyford. It was Sir William Clayton, 1st Baronet and another MP for Marlow, who built the present manor house. The Clayton family fortune had been inherited from Sir Robert Clayton, Lord Mayor of London in 1679. Two imposing statues of Sir Robert Clayton in his ceremonial robes still stand in the grounds of the estate.

The Victorian era produced a suitably sentimental story involving Colonel William Clayton. The Colonel owned a black charger called Skirmisher which he rode during campaigns in Spain, Portugal and the Netherlands. When the horse was twenty-four years old it was fatally wounded in the advance on Paris following the Battle of Waterloo. Sir William was so fond of Skirmisher that he had the body returned for burial at Marlow. A tablet commemorating the horse remains in the walled garden at Harleyford, inscribed with verses written by Colonel Clayton.

There were two earlier manor houses at Harleyford. The first was deliberately burnt to the ground in the 1580s and the second fell into ruin and was demolished. The current building was completed in 1755. It was designed by the fashionable architect Sir Robert Taylor, and constructed around a central domed hall with a top-lit, cantilevered staircase. It features a number of unusually shaped rooms: oval bedrooms, a semi-circular drawing room and a library opening into a large bay. Over an arch in the house are the words: 'Remember! In waiting for a late guest, insult is offered to the punctual ones.' Guests who happened to be *very* late for a Harleyford dinner might have found the elegant dining room deserted. When the house was built, the tradition of serving dessert in a separate area was continued. At Harleyford, 'banquetting stuffe' was taken up to the roof terrace and eaten while enjoying the view over the Hurley backwaters.

Among many notable figures to visit Harleyford Manor in later years were Emperor Napoleon III of France and the flamboyant British prime minister Benjamin Disraeli. Writer Kenneth Grahame was a guest in 1908, prompting a belief that the house was the inspiration for Toad Hall in *Wind in the Willows.* It certainly fits Grahame's description of Toad's home: 'a handsome, dignified old house of mellowed red brick, with well-kept lawns reaching down to the water's edge.'

It is many years since the house was a private residence. After serving for a period as the

© Rob Conolly

The roof terrace of Harleyford Manor provides a wonderful view towards Hurley Weir

clubhouse for Harleyford Marina, it is now divided into out-of-town office space. By the twentieth century the estate had reduced in size to 160 acres (65 hectares). In 1954 it was purchased by the Folley family, who eventually developed Harleyford golf course (now owned by club members) and a residential estate. The project was completed under extremely stringent guidelines, particularly as the estate's park was designed by the eighteenth-century landscape gardener Capability Brown. The character of the park was preserved when the golf course was designed, with natural hazards used in place of sand bunkers. An eighteenth-century folly known as the Temple of Friendship stands beside what is now the fifteenth fairway. The temple has an underground chamber, once used as a makeshift mortuary when the river flooded and the roads to Marlow were impassable.

Hundreds of historic trees were retained, both on the course and around the lodges. Additional hawthorn hedges and areas of native woodland were planted to enhance what had long been a haven for birds and wildlife. In recent years colonies of endangered red kites have been established in the area and can be spotted soaring above the golf course. For a romantic such as myself, the estate was impossible to resist and in 1996 we bought one of the two-storey lodges.

A few years ago, during what had been an unusually mild autumn, we woke to the season's first hard frost. Although it was very cold the sun was shining and I took my morning coffee onto the deck. There was not the slightest breath of wind but suddenly my view of the river was obliterated by a shower of leaves from a sycamore. Within seconds the lawn had turned from green to gold. As I walked back to the kitchen, I noticed the leaves of chestnut and beech at the rear of the house were in similar freefall. The trees had succumbed to the cold snap en masse. Weeks later at a Christmas party, I met someone who had shared the same magical experience while walking in woodland near his own home, downstream at Cookham.

Autumn also means Guy Fawkes night. Some years ago my friend Yvonne came out from London to attend a communal bonfire in the sheep paddock. Before the fireworks began everyone warmed up on hot soup, followed by spit-roasted pork served with crackling and apple sauce. Yvonne is a self-confessed pyromaniac and after the little ones went home and the safety fence came down, she was in her element. We watched her dancing around the fire like a leprechaun, tossing on dead boughs twice her size as showers of sparks fizzed in her hair.

Fireworks soon make way for Christmas fare in local shops. One frosty mid-December morning we heard music floating up the river and walked onto the upstairs balcony to see a steam boat approaching from Marlow with a group of carol singers on board. The boat made a slow turn in front of the manor house as the carollers sang 'Hark The Herald Angels Sing'; an unforgettable start to the festive season. Our first Christmas at Harleyford turned out to be one of the coldest on record and almost snap-froze our guests, who had flown in from Sydney and Morocco. Large sections of the river actually did freeze. We took bread down to feed hungry wildfowl and watched in amusement as ducks made three-point landings on the ice then slid the final metres towards us on their bottoms. On a more serious note, swans had to be rescued when they went to sleep in the shallows and woke with their legs imprisoned in ice. Describing a similar freeze forty years earlier, J. H. B. Peel wrote:

> A swan collapses on the ice, like a tipsy ballerina past her prime, showing withered shins.

Neighbours had warned us to pick holly for the house before the wood pigeons gobbled all the ripe berries. The pigeons blunder out of the trees with crops so full they can hardly fly, and despite my love of birds I find myself imagining their plump breasts simmering in wine and herbs. It would be unseasonably cruel to shoot them, but I sometimes hope a couple might collapse providentially at my feet. They would made a great starter for Christmas dinner, garnished with any sprigs of holly they may have overlooked.

WOOD PIGEON BRAISED IN BRANDY

2 wood pigeons (available pre-prepared from any game butcher)
120 g (4 oz) streaky bacon, cut into 2½ cm (1 inch) pieces
8 black olives
4 tablespoons dry sherry
2 tablespoons olive oil
1 large onion, chopped
300 ml (10 fl oz) chicken stock
2 tablespoons brandy
2 tablespoons plain flour
salt and pepper

Halve the olives and marinade in the sherry for a couple of hours. Sauté the pigeons in olive oil until brown and place in a casserole. Sauté the onion and bacon in the same oil then add to the casserole. Stir the flour into the pan fat slowly, then add the chicken stock, stirring continuously until the sauce thickens. Add the brandy, sherry and olives and season with salt and pepper. Pour the sauce over the pigeons and cook at 170°C (325°F) for about 1½ hours.

Winter provides its own beauty on the estate, especially after heavy frosts or the occasional fall of snow. On damp days, mist drifts up from the river until you feel you could reach out and catch a stray wisp in your fingers.

When spring arrives the manor house is framed by two giant copper beeches growing on the opposite bank. Their new foliage is the colour of stewed plums; a wonderful contrast to the varying greens of beech, sycamore, oak and chestnut. Blackbirds begin to defend their territory and blue tits start to investigate nest boxes on surrounding trees. Robin redbreasts prefer to nest lower to the ground, in the hawthorn hedge. We once watched a pair of robins conduct a touching courtship. The female had a hunched back, prompting a neighbour to dub her Quasimodo. Despite her affliction she had attracted a suitor. At dusk she would sit on our balcony rail while he wooed her with worms, gently placing them in her open beak. After we returned to Australia that summer, Quasimodo became so tame she would hop into our neighbour's kitchen for breakfast.

There are several lovely walks around the estate, including one leading to Medmenham via Hurley Weir. A public footpath runs beside the golf-club driving range then through a woodland glade before disappearing into a 'secret' tunnel about 64 yd (70 m) long and pitch black. Having read too many Agatha Christie novels, I often feel a shiver of alarm midway through, imagining being struck down by a rogue golfer armed with a niblick. At the other end a steep

© Rob Conolly

A winter view of the Thames and Harleyford Manor

section of path leads down to the river. Chalk from the cliffs here was used to build Medmenham Abbey (see page 109). By the bank a few metres further on is a unique piece of Thames history: the last flash-lock winch on the river. I am sure this is the windlass referred to by C. W. P. as he steamed towards Hurley Lock en route to Maidenhead (see page 110). It ceased operation in 1780 and when we first arrived at Harleyford only the great capston remained, within a circular depression worn by the feet of men who laboriously hauled boats over Hurley Weir. A narrow channel leading to the river once held the towing ropes.

The winch has been sensitively restored by Harleyford's nearest neighbour, a public-spirited American software company. In 1986 the company's UK subsidiary purchased Wittington House and grounds as their headquarters. The house was built in 1898 by Hudson Kearley, who made his fortune in the tea trade. As MP for Devonport he became Minister of Food in the First World War and chairman of the Port of London Authority. The 110-acre (45-hectare) estate is being restored with the help of photographs found in old issues of *Country Life* and an employee who decided she preferred horticulture to computers! Clippings from the yew hedges are collected for use in cancer research and honey from beehives is sold to raise money for charity. Fruit is harvested and served in the staff canteen. Beyond

© Rob Conolly

The last flash-lock winch on the Thames, by Hurley Weir

the old winch, the thundering waters of the weir provides great sport for canoeists.

The path finally emerges onto Henley Road a few hundred yards before the Dog and Badger pub, which dates from around 1390. Regrettably, constant road widening has left the pub so close to passing traffic that if a window was open in the lounge bar a speeding truck would blow the froth off a pint. The Dog and Badger has a colourful history. Sitting on one of the ceiling beams is a Civil War cannon ball, found in a wall during renovation work. There is also a story that King Charles II's mistress Nell Gwyn sold her wares here, although I'm not sure if we're talking about oranges! I was amused to read that Nell used to refer to the King as Charles III, because she had already had two lovers called Charles. Nell was by no means the first or last of the King's mistresses either and perhaps the pub should put a Charles II omelette on the menu. The dish was jokingly described as being made by whisking several swan's eggs with a gilded willow twig then serving it over hot strumpets! Balancing its history of illicit love, until the end of the nineteenth century marriage banns were read at the Dog and Badger before being posted across the road at the church.

Medmenham's Bockmer Manor was home to a noble family called Borlase. When Lady Alice Borlase died in 1683 she left a miscellany of remedies and recipes which was expanded upon by succeeding generations. After finding its way to the United States, the manuscript was published in 1998 as *Ladie Borlase's Receiptes Book* (edited by David Schoonover). It contains recipes and remedies dating from 1665 to 1822.

Mr Halfords Glyster for Childrens fitts

Take a quarter of a Pint of Chicken Broth, put to it a spoonful of syrup of violets, half a spoonfull of juice of Rue & half a tea Spoonfull of tincture of Castor Mixt. To be administered in the fitt.

I like to imagine Lady Alice serving her syllabubs, comfits and marchpane (marzipan) to guests from Harleyford Manor and Ladye Place.

Just outside Medmenham a copse of woodland on a hillside presents a landscape of the sort that must have inspired Jack Kerouac to write of 'brain trees growing out of Shakespeare's fields, and dreaming meadows full of lamb dots'. By mid May the hawthorn hedges are in flower and on the northern side of the road about 2 miles (3 km) from Henley is a glorious bluebell wood, crisscrossed with public walking trails. Bluebells are not simply decorative. Their sap was once used to fix flights to arrows and the bulbs produced starch for book printing and for stiffening the collars and cuffs of the gentry. There is now a fear that these delicate little natives are hybridizing with their more robust Spanish cousins.

BISHAM TO CLIVEDEN

Downriver from Harleyford on the Berkshire bank is Bisham Abbey, granted to the Knights Templar in the thirteenth century. Bisham Grange was originally attached to the abbey and is now a highly desirable residential complex. The riverside lawns have a depression left from a moat, and there are regular checks to ensure residents have not taken the liberty of enlarging 'The Ditch' into fish ponds or swimming pools. I once attended a ladies luncheon at the Grange and as we strolled out onto the lawn, a herd of cattle came down to drink on the Buckinghamshire bank. They stood knee-deep under a thicket of flowering hawthorn in a scene so picturesque we wondered if our hostess had arranged it.

Unaccountably, Bisham is pronounced 'Bissum' by locals, establishing a sense of boundary as effective as a palisade – or a moat! Despite being very fond of Bisham I am not sure it has the right to feel too select. When Henry VIII granted Bisham Abbey to his fourth wife, Anne of Cleves, as part of their divorce settlement, she promptly swapped it with Sir Philip Hoby for a house in Kent.

Lady Elizabeth Hoby was a personal friend of Queen Elizabeth I, who lived at Bisham Abbey for three years during her exile from court in the reign of her half-sister Mary. In 1592 Queen Elizabeth returned to Bisham and stayed with the Hoby family for almost a week. It is just as well the royal visit did not take place the following year, as Lady Hoby became embroiled in an unseemly dispute with her neighbour from Hurley, Richard Lovelace. Lady Hoby had accused two of Lovelace's men of lewd behaviour and took it upon herself to have them placed in the stocks. Lovelace reacted by interfering with Lady Hoby's access to some goods she had stored at Windsor Castle. Not to be outdone, Lady Hoby then threatened Lovelace with court action. It all became very unpleasant as such quarrels are wont to do.

Lady Hoby had a reputation for dispensing rough justice. She was a great scholar who expected the same academic brilliance from her children and was angry and frustrated when her sickly young son William continually blotted his copybooks. Locals thought the boy may have been suffering from a brain tumour. One day, before leaving for the royal court at

Windsor, Lady Hoby allegedly beat William so severely that by the time she returned home he was dead. She was stricken with remorse and after her own death in 1604 her ghost could be seen wandering the abbey. According to most accounts she was trying to wash the guilt from her hands in a bowl of water, like Lady Macbeth.

In the nineteenth century the abbey was owned by the Vansittart family and Admiral Edward Vansittart had his own unnerving encounter with the ghost. Late one night in the library he felt a presence behind him and turned to face the spectre of Lady Hoby. Her portrait hung on the library wall, but when Vansittart looked past the ghost he saw only an empty frame.

During building repairs in 1840, books and papers belonging to the Hoby family were found under the dining-room floorboards. The material included a child's copy books heavily corrected in Lady Hoby's hand. Mrs Vansittart asked that they be left in place until her husband could see them but unfortunately they were removed by workmen and never seen again. A portrait of Lady Hoby still hangs in the abbey's Great Hall. The property is now home to one of five National Sports Centres. It once played host to the England football team, prompting some to suggest that William's mother had a lot more to wring her hands over.

© Shutterstock

The chalk tower of Bisham's All Saints' Church dates from Norman times

There are imposing memorials to the family in Bisham's All Saints Church, located a little further along the riverbank. The church has a Norman tower built of chalk, which itself can appear rather ghostly. According to folklore the heavy mists that sometimes envelop the towpath are associated with Lady Hoby and have been known to suck hapless walkers into the Thames. All Saints is prone to flooding and in 1894 the water reached the pulpit and lectern. Across the road is an old pub called The Bull Inn at Bisham, built around 1250 to provide accommodation for stonemasons working on All Saints. It now houses an upmarket restaurant.

Entering Marlow via the Buckinghamshire bank, the steeple of All Saints' Church rises beside the town's famous little suspension bridge designed by Tierney Clark in 1836. After the Second World War, traffic congestion prompted calls to replace the bridge with a multi-lane crossing but fortunately a bypass was built instead. During major repair work in 1964 it was discovered the bridge had been patched so often that its chains were straining under the weight of road material. Enough was removed to surface several miles of a new road.

On the opposite end of the bridge is the famous Compleat Angler hotel. Dining with a river view is never cheap, but in 1888 it was reported that a waiter and a diner at the hotel both flushed (the former with embarrassment and the latter with indignation) when a bill for three shillings was presented for tea with bread and jam. There was a more positive report on the hotel a few years later when an American with the wonderful name of Wellington Wack described its beds as 'fat and crisp and without the varicose lumps and flabby linen so common in all bedchambers from Bow to Belgravia'.

In 1880, dissention over the outcome of an election created a riot in Marlow's High Street, and soldiers were called in from Windsor Barracks to restore order. According to folklore, in the midst of the fray an inventive officer led his men to the local grocer's shop where he ordered them to fill their muskets with strawberry jam. The rioters ran off when the soldiers opened fire, thinking they were covered in blood. Exactly what sparked the initial trouble is unclear, but two of the greatest political rivals at this time were the Claytons of Harleyford for the Whigs and the Williams of Temple for the Tories. Both sides had previously been involved in illegally influencing voters.

Marlow has a number of literary associations. Jerome K. Jerome wrote chapters of *Three Men in a Boat* at The Two Brewers pub and Mary Shelley completed *Frankenstein* at a house in West Street while her husband Percy Shelley wrote *Revolt to Islam.* Much later, T. S. Eliot chose the same street when he moved from London to escape the bombing during the First World War. At nearby Little Marlow the thriller writer Edgar Wallace is buried.

In early December the festive street lights go up in Marlow and the Georgian bow windows along the High Street are decorated, resembling a scene from a traditional greetings card. The town centre is closed to traffic for a night-time street fair, with stalls selling toffee apples and cups of mulled wine. Perhaps it is only the wine cheering everyone up but

I have to disagree with Mr James Thorne who attended a fair at Marlow in 1847 and reported: 'The countrymen hereabouts are not of a mirthful cast, and their liveliness is of a very laborious character.'

If anything *does* make the residents of Marlow miserable, it is that the town lives in the shade of Henley and that wretched Royal Regatta. Marlow's own carnival has never reached the same heights, and suffered a severe blow when the rowing events relocated to Dorney Lake at Eton. However, there is some compensation in that Marlow's favourite son is the legendary rower Steve Redgrave, who won an historic fifth consecutive gold medal at the Sydney Olympics. Redgrave received a knighthood and there is a larger-than-life bronze statue of him in riverside Higginson Park. Perhaps, like Lord Nelson in Trafalgar Square, Sir Steve should be mounted on a very tall column; preferably high enough to cast a shadow on the rowing course at Henley.

© Rob Conolly

The bronze figure of the extraordinary Olympic rower Sir Steve Redgrave, Marlow's favourite son

The town tries to balance tradition with progress, with varying degrees of success. Thankfully, a projected high-rise development planned in the 1960s did not eventuate but inevitably the character of the town is changing. After trading for seventy years, Marlow's old-fashioned sweet shop was forced to close due to lack of custom. Having heard it was in trouble everyone rushed down to buy bull's eyes and citrus drops but it was too late and 'Sweet Talk' quietly disappeared.

Two weeks later the local paper ran a story on a fast-food restaurant's search for a site in the town centre. Locals were asked how they felt about the idea and there was a delightfully 'Marlovian' response from a shocked long-term resident: 'I went to a McDonald's once in Wycombe and I couldn't believe it – everyone was eating with their fingers. Hopefully they will give people knives and forks. I don't think people should eat with their fingers in a place like Marlow.'

The town's first experience with takeaway food has entered the realms of folklore. The landlady of the Two Brewers had the habit of setting her pies on a window ledge to cool. When they began to disappear, she blamed passing bargemen, and took her revenge by filling the next pie with drowned puppies. It duly vanished and for years the bargemen were plagued with the taunt: 'Who ate puppy-dog pies under Marlow Bridge?' The words subsequently formed the set piece of a firework display organized by a colourful character called Captain Marshall. Marshall was famous for strolling down the High Street accompanied by his pet leopard. The puppy-dog pie story also found its way into Edith Nesbit's novel, *The Railway Children*. At one point the children have an altercation with a bargeman, whose wife tells them not to worry:

> *'You mustn't take no notice of my Bill', said the woman; ''is bark's worse'n 'is bite. Some of the kids down Farley way is fair terrors. It was them put 'is back up calling out about who ate the puppy-pie under Marlow Bridge.'*
> *'Who did?' asked Phyllis.*
> *'I dunno', said the woman. 'Nobody don't know! But somehow, and I don't know the why nor the wherefore of it, them words is pisin to a bargeman ...'*

The Two Brewers features in another old Marlow tale. From the sixteenth century until Victorian times it was run by the Truss family. In 1897 lightning struck the spire of All Saints' Church and steeplejacks were called in to repair it. While the men were having their lunch, the Trusses' small daughter Mary quietly climbed a series of ladders to the top of the spire. She was brought down safely but shaken church officials blamed her parents for the incident and threatened them with eviction. However, little Mary's spirit of adventure won the hearts of the steeplejacks, who presented her with a gold watch.

The pub is located on a circuitous route known as Seven Corner Alley which still leads from Marlow Bridge to the lock. With no towpath, bargemen were forced to take their horses across the churchyard, past the pub, and through a maze of back streets to the river. The heavy barges were then hauled through manually, on long towlines. In the circumstances even a saint might have succumbed to the fragrance of a freshly baked pie.

The Thames Path continues past the site of Marlow Mill, which used to produce high-quality brass thimbles. On the opposite bank of the river is Quarry Wood; the mysterious Wild Wood in Kenneth Grahame's *Wind in the Willows*. Beech woods form an appropriately dramatic backdrop to a castellated house built right on the banks of the river. The Australian soprano Dame Nellie Melba was a frequent visitor to this house and when she was rehearsing on summer evenings, boaters would drift close to the bank to enjoy a free concert. In the summer of 1901 Melba rented a riverside property in the area, called Quarrywood Cottage. She obviously loved the Thames so perhaps it is appropriate that Peach Melba, created in her honour by legendary French chef Auguste Escoffier, was originally served in a swan carved from ice. It is scarcely necessary for me to provide a recipe as the classic dessert is simply poached peaches and vanilla ice cream topped with a raspberry coulis.

The next downstream village is Bourne End. Between 1929 and 1937 it was the home of children's writer Enid Blyton, who lived in a house called Old Thatch, near Coldmoorholme Lane. Bourne End almost certainly appears as riverside Peterswood in one of Enid Blyton's mystery series (the Five Find-Outers). Like Bourne End, the fictional Peterswood has a railway station and is described as being 3 miles (5 km) from Marlow. *The Magic Faraway Tree* was not written at Bourne End, but I like to think the story was inspired by a giant Buckinghamshire beech.

The novelist Rosamond Lehmann was also born here, in 1901. Her family lived in a river-side house called Fieldhead, close to Bourne End station. The Thames, which she described lyrically as 'wax skinned and reed pierced', became her playground. As a child, Rosie received piano lessons from William Spencer, the father of artist Stanley Spencer, who lived at nearby Cookham. Rosamond recalled Mr Spencer abandoning the music lessons and entertaining her with recitations of his own poetry. Her childhood at Bourne End was so idyllic that as an elderly woman she dreamed she had died and 'in paradise' watched her father stroll down to the river again at Fieldhead.

The Thames Path reverts to the Berkshire bank at Bourne End via a footpath attached to the railway bridge, but it is worth remaining in Buckinghamshire and carrying on to neigh-bouring Hedsor. The wharf here was an important loading point for 500 years, until it was bypassed by a lock, cut in 1830. Hedsor's Church of St Nicholas is full of interest. It is located on private property, but access by car is usually permitted and there is public access via a footpath. Volunteers open the church on Sunday afternoons in summer.

Saint Nicholas has always been associated with the 'magical' arrival of Christmas gifts, adding significance to what occurred at the church on Christmas Eve 2000. The Revd John

Sclater found a gift-wrapped wooden crucifix, left by an anonymous benefactor. A note attached read: 'Given in the spirit of St Nicholas.' The wooden cross was of white maple and the figure of Christ had been carved from old English oak. It was sculpted over a period of eight months by artist Colin Mantripp, who confirmed that the woman who commissioned it did not wish to be identified.

Hedsor Church had a close association with the Astors at nearby Cliveden. The actress and comedienne Joyce Grenfell was Nancy Astor's niece, and as a child she often attended Christmas services with the family. She wrote about the vicar's unusually deep voice, which she described as being a terrible 'giggle hazard'. Young Joyce and the Astor children imagined the vicar with two stomachs; an ordinary one plus an echo chamber. I am surprised she didn't mention Hedsor's unique water-powered organ, which by all accounts was an even more powerful 'giggle hazard' than the vicar's voice. Incidentally, when William Spencer was not reciting poetry to Rosamond Lehmann, he supplemented his income by filling in as Hedsor's organist.

The organ was designed in 1893 by Montagu Hepworth. Its twenty ranks of pipes required huge bellows and a water engine was installed to pump them. The engine was housed in a pit under the vestry and the water stored in a tank at Hedsor House. Whenever the organ was played at full volume, it needed auxiliary manpower. The verger (a Mr Quelch!) would run into the vestry and pump frantically. If the organist forgot to warn Mr Quelch in time, the whole system could collapse in the middle of a hymn. The church was candlelit and on one occasion a candelabra swung around and set fire to the organist's hair. I wonder whether it was Mr Spencer? During the Second World War there were no men around to stoke the boiler and in a hard frost the organ pipes froze and burst. The instrument was eventually dismantled and sold, but fortunately the beautifully decorated display pipes were retained.

In 1765, the English historian Nathaniel Hooke was buried in St Nicholas's churchyard, having spent an incredible thirty-nine years toiling over a history of Rome. Thank God he would never know that just a decade later his work would be overshadowed by Edward Gibbon's landmark *History of the Decline and Fall of the Roman Empire.* Alexander Pope's friend Lady Mary Montague may have stumbled upon the reason why Hooke was so slow to complete the book. In 1753 she visited him at his house in Cookham and could find no signs of authorship whatsoever. She wrote afterwards: 'I fear the fine ladies and fine prospects of Cookham divert his attention from the Roman History.'

The view from the churchyard extends over the Thames Valley to Cookham and Bourne End. On the opposite hill is Boston Folly, also known as Hedsor Towers and now a private house. It was built by the second Lord Boston. The first of its three towers was completed in 1793 to celebrate the return to sanity of King George III. In the circumstances, Lord Boston's building of a folly was appropriate because the King was as mad as a hatter again before very long.

Having crossed to the Berkshire bank at Bourne End, the Thames Path leads on to Cookham via the National Trust-owned water meadows that form 130-acre (50-hectare) Cock Marsh. A kingfisher and sandmartin reserve has been created here. Also worth mentioning is a nearby riverside pub that can be accessed only from the towpath. The Bounty proclaims itself to be located within The Independent Republic of Cock Marsh, where the laws of common sense apply. In keeping with this principle there is a sign to make foot sloggers weep with joy:

Hot Food, Tea, Coffee and Hot Chocolate
Muddy boots, dirty dogs, and children welcome
Walkers are welcome to just use our loos.

This earthly paradise has lots of riverside tables.

The busy village of Cookham is entered via Holy Trinity churchyard, the final resting place of Stanley Spencer. The artist painted himself and his Cookham friends and neighbours rising from their graves in a work titled 'The Resurrection'. On the south wall of the church is a tall, stained-glass window divided by moulded red bricks instead of stone. The brickwork dates from 1465 and is thought to be the earliest of its kind in England. Inside, the north chapel has a carved memorial to mariner Sir Isaac Pocock. He is depicted in the arms of an angel after dying from a heart attack whilst punting on the river at downstream Maidenhead:

SUDDENLY CALLED FROM THIS WORLD TO A BETTER STATE WHILST ON THE THAMES, NEAR HIS HOME, OCTOBER 8TH IN THE YEAR OF OUR LORD 1810.

A disused Wesleyan chapel in the village reopened in 1962 as a gallery for Stanley Spencer's work. Inside is the old pram he used for transporting his painting gear around the village. The gallery presents changing exhibitions of Spencer's work, as well as family photographs, letters and extracts from his diaries. My favourite exhibit is a photograph showing a small boy perching on a fence to inspect the artist at disconcertingly close range. Perhaps this incident prompted the sign on Spencer's pram: 'Please do not disturb the artist.' It is unlikely a small boy would pose much of a threat, although Spencer once commented:

I no more like people personally than I like dogs. When I meet them I am only apprehensive whether they will bite me, which is reasonable and sensible.

In 1937 Spencer made the less than sensible decision to divorce his wife Hilda and marry a woman called Patricia Preece. In Stanley's mind the divorce was simply a technicality as he really wanted two wives, and hoped he would be able to enjoy the sexual favours of both women. However, even if Hilda had agreed to Stanley's plan it was doomed to failure as Patricia Preece refused to sleep with her new husband and continued to live nearby in Cookham with her long-term companion, the artist Dorothy Hepworth. The wedding photo is a sight to behold, with Miss Hepworth glowering on one side of the bride and a diminutive Spencer on the other wearing his favourite felt hat … or was it an upturned pudding bowl?

In the interest of fair play I should point out that Patricia Preece insisted Stanley was responsible for the failure of their marriage. After the ceremony she and Dorothy Hepworth went down to Cornwall to begin the 'honeymoon', but Stanley stayed behind and spent the night with Hilda.

Spencer was knighted in 1959 and thought it would be nice to mark the occasion by painting something for the Queen Mother. He decided on a picture of several roses in a fish paste jar, which he took along to Buckingham Palace in a shopping bag. He was deflated when officials told him it would breach protocol to present a gift. However, when the Queen Mother heard about the painting she said she would love to accept it. Unfortunately Stanley had already given it to Mrs Barrett, owner of the Torquil Cafe in Cookham High Street. It was a kindly attempt by Stanley to cheer Mrs Barrett up, as dishwashing had got her down. Delighted with the gift, she promptly renamed her cafe 'The Two Roses'. The Barretts emigrated to Australia in the 1960s, so perhaps the little painting now hangs on the wall of an Australian milk bar. At the end of his life Stanley Spencer became rather unkempt and was sometimes heard to declare 'I am on the side of angels and dirt'.

Rob and I took a break from the path to picnic on the green at Cookham, breathing the scent of lilac and honeysuckle. As we ate I remembered the story of a Cookham ferryman who fell into the river while preparing a bacon supper. In January 1893 he arrived home very late and went to an outhouse to find a frying pan. Days later his body was dredged from the Thames. The fly of his trousers was open, suggesting he may have fallen in while adding to the flow of the river. There are a few lessons in this sad tale, not the least being to store one's cooking utensils close at hand.

Cookham is at the centre of the annual swan-upping ceremony on the Thames, which begins at Sunbury-on-Thames and ends five days later at Abingdon. The cygnets are given a health check and have their beaks nicked as a sign of ownership; one nick for those belonging to the ancient Dyers Company, two for the Vinters. All unmarked swans belong to the Queen. The birds have long been associated with royalty. Travelling down the Thames between 1584 and 1585, Lupold von Wedel wrote:

I again stepped into my boat, sailing down the river thirty miles towards London, where I arrived at twelve o'clock. All the time the river was full of tame swans, who have nests and breed on small islands formed by the river. They are exclusively used for the Queen's table, and it is on pain of death forbidden to meddle with them.

Even stealing the eggs attracted a gaol term of a year and a day, which may be why they were able to breed so prolifically. One traveller described seeing 'a snowfall of swans' on the Thames. Perhaps it was the sight of so many that prompted the poet Michael Drayton to suggest they could form a guard of honour when Elizabeth I made one of her processions along the river:

Range all thy swannes, faire
Thames, together on a ranke,

And place them duly one by one
Upon thy stately banke

The swans may not have co-operated, but spectacular pageants and courtly masques were often organized along the riverbanks to entertain the Queen.

Below Cookham village the Thames separates into several channels, and the path wanders away from them through open fields and woodland. It returns in spectacular fashion opposite the Cliveden estate. The famous beech woods below the house are absolutely superb in autumn when their foliage is reflected in the river. By the way, Cliveden is pronounced 'Clivden', just as Bicester contracts to 'Bister', Worcester to 'Wooster', etc. One American tourist lost patience with the English correcting him over place names and retaliated by saying he came from Niffles. When people said they had never heard of it he snapped: 'I'm not surprised, because you English always mispronounce it as Niagara Falls.'

A whiff of scandal has surrounded the Cliveden Estate since the days of its first owner, George Villiers, the 2nd Duke of Buckingham. In 1668 the Duke fought a duel with the Earl of Shewsbury over Lady Shrewsbury. The countess had become Buckingham's mistress two years earlier. Described bluntly by Samuel Pepys as 'a whore', Lady Shrewsbury was said to have stood by disguised as a page, while cheering on her lover. Her husband was run through from breast to shoulder, and died of his wounds. The duel is remembered at Cliveden in the Duke's garden, where stones are set into a tablet in the shape of a rapier.

When American millionaire William Waldorf Astor bought Cliveden in 1893, bad behaviour from the public prompted him to enclose the grounds within brick walls. Day-trippers from London had been leaving their rubbish behind them, but were incensed by what they saw as Astor's high-handed action and cheekily nicknamed him 'Walled–Off Astor'. I was intrigued to hear that the Astors installed a miniature railway line in the basement of the house to ferry food to dumb waiters, and hence to the dining tables. It is no longer in use but apparently parts of the system are still in place.

Cliveden passed to Astor's son and his daughter-in-law Nancy Astor, who became the first woman to enter Parliament. She was not welcomed into this male bastion of power and her prickly relationship with Winston Churchill resulted in the following exchange:

> *'Winston, if I was married to you I would poison your coffee.'*
> *'Nancy, if I was your husband, I would drink it!'*

Nancy Astor led the racy 'Cliveden Set' in the 1930s, but the estate is also associated with the swinging sixties and another Member of Parliament, John Profumo. War Minister Profumo dallied in one of Cliveden's riverside cottages with a showgirl called Christine Keeler. Unfortunately for the minister, Miss Keeler was also spending time with a Russian naval attaché and in 1963 the resulting scandal caused more fall-out than a nuclear bomb.

The Profumo affair was extremely damaging for the Astors. Another girl involved in the scandal was Mandy Rice-Davies, who claimed to have had an affair with Nancy's son, Bill. When Lord Astor protested his innocence, Miss Rice-Davies famously responded: 'Well, he would, wouldn't he?' Her quip made its way into the *Oxford Dictionary of Quotations*. Newspapers were hidden in an effort to protect a frail and aging Nancy, but inevitably she found out. The old lady must have been particularly annoyed by allegations of improper behaviour around Cliveden's swimming pool, having always insisted they did not need one. She thought the family should have been happy to swim in the Thames, as her own generation had done.

Two years later, on 10 and 11 May 1965, Cliveden stood in for Buckingham Palace when the Beatles arrived to film scenes for their hit movie *Help!* The boys were smoking quite a bit of pot at the time and Paul McCartney later confessed that they showed up slightly stoned and hoped they would muddle through:

> *I remember one time at Cliveden we were filming the Buckingham Palace scene where we were all supposed to have our hands up. It was after lunch, which was fatal because someone might have brought out a glass of wine as well. We were all a bit merry and all had our backs to the camera and the giggles set in. All we had to do was turn around and look amazed or something. But every time we would turn round to the camera there were tears streaming down our faces.*

During breaks the Fab Four competed in relay races on the lawns against the film crew. Congratulated on winning and asked, 'Have you ever done this before?' Paul gave an engagingly muddled response: 'Not since school. Done a bit since … I haven't done any since, I mean. I've done some now, you know.'

Maidenhead to Eton

From Cliveden the towpath leads on to Maidenhead and Boulter's Lock, which was in its heyday during the Victorian and Edwardian eras. On Ascot Sunday as many as a thousand boats would pass through the lock. At times the river is almost as busy today but power boats are not as picturesque as punts and parasols, so old prints of Boulter's are very popular. They present a rosy view of the public enjoying themselves, but loutish behaviour was as much a problem then as now. Affected by alcohol and the midday sun, young men sometimes disgraced themselves by throwing food into passing boats and making indelicate remarks to young ladies. One gentleman told a Maidenhead court that when he remonstrated with some youths after being pelted with grape skins they shouted: 'Who the f… are you? Have you f…... bought the river?' The taunt has echoed down the generations and is often heard at crowded locks on bank holidays.

Contributing to a book called *The Royal River: The Thames from Source to Sea*, Godfrey Wordsworth Turner wrote witheringly of steam launches and their passengers, who were mostly those infamous day-trippers from London:

To rush, screaming on, with their hands in their pockets, and no motion of their own is the height of bliss to such people, and this is the enjoyment a steam launch affords.

Set into the footpath near Boulter's Lock is a plaque bearing this 2002 tribute to the river by contemporary poet Ian Miles:

Old Father Thames goes gliding by:
As ripples run he winks his eye
At Cotswold cows & Oxford dons;
Nodding to Windsor's royal swans,
He bears our nation's liquid crown
By lock & weir to London town.

May all that know and love his banks
Pause here awhile to offer thanks.

Maidenhead prospered as an important staging post on the road to Oxford. By the eighteenth century ninety stagecoaches a day were arriving. The threat from highwaymen prompted many lone travellers to head for the town at nightfall, although this held its own dangers. Scrubland known as Maidenhead Thicket was a notoriously dangerous place. Records of Hurley Church show that in the late sixteenth century vicars were granted £50 a year to cover the risk of robbery in the area. Ostlers from Maidenhead's inns would sometimes rob a guest at night then have the nerve to offer sympathy as they saddled their victim's horse the next morning.

One of Maidenhead's inns, The Greyhound, played a poignant role in history. Charles I was allowed to visit his children here while he was imprisoned at Caversham Park, prior to his execution. The King was welcomed by the local people, who strewed flowers before him. The inn burned down in 1735 but a plaque on the NatWest Bank records the event.

Directly across the river is Taplow, and the rather surprising sight of a paper mill, which ceased operation in 2006 after operating since the early nineteenth century. In 1086 the Domesday Book recorded a flour mill on the site, which had provided flour to the Roman legions. Not surprisingly there are plans afoot to redevelop the mill into a residential complex. The Thames Path crosses to Taplow at Maidenhead Bridge, built in 1777. In 2002, divers located the remains of the town's medieval wooden crossing, first mentioned in 1254. A row of oak piles was found to extend from Bridge Gardens to the slipway beside Skindles Hotel, just upstream of the present bridge. Samples of the timber were sent to a laboratory in Oxford and dated to the mid fifteenth century.

A plaque on the bridge thanks people from around the world for providing assistance during the disastrous floods of March 1947. The river was a mile wide just outside town, after rising 8 ft (2.5 m). In flooded Bridge Street, a disoriented cow blundered into Mr Loosley's grocer's shop and managed to get its horn caught in the bacon saw. A thousand residents were evacuated from the town but others remained stranded in their homes, supplied with hot food by boat. The meal was a stoic British offering of stew, mashed potatoes and boiled pudding.

There was still a strong military presence in the area following the Second World War and army personnel assisted in rescue work – though not without drama. When a detachment of Scots Guards unwisely stepped aboard a line of punts in unison, the boats promptly capsized and sank. Downstream at Datchet, craft which had taken part in the evacuation of Dunkirk were used to rescue families. Floods remain an annual threat, although the situation has been improved by the recent completion of a flood relief-channel, running from Maidenhead to Windsor.

In 1633 Maidenhead Bridge was the centre of a bitter dispute over parish boundaries between Maidenhead (Berkshire) and Taplow (Buckinghamshire). Fishing rights were at issue, as Maidenhead had claimed the entire width of the river. Giving evidence for Taplow, a parishioner claimed that twenty years earlier he had watched the Sheriff of Berkshire halt in the middle of the bridge and transfer twelve convicts being transported to London into the custody of the Sheriff of Buckinghamshire. This was clear evidence, he argued, of an official 'boundary'. The point was also made that when homeless women gave birth under the arches on the Taplow bank, their babies were christened at Taplow, not Maidenhead, and that the infants were buried in Taplow churchyard when they died, as they all too often did.

The old churchyard lies above the river beside the Victorian splendour of Taplow Court. Among the crumbling headstones is a far more ancient monument – the sixth-century round barrow of the Saxon chief, Taeppa. His skeleton was removed from the mound in 1883 along with a cache of grave goods which included a golden buckle set with garnets, bronze and silver mounted drinking horns, luminous green glass tumblers and a pair of gilt bronze clasps. The treasures are now on display in the British Museum.

For many years Taplow Court was the home of William Henry Grenfell, who later became Lord Desborough and was Chairman of the Thames Conservancy for a record thirty-two years. Accomplished in athletics and cricket, Grenfell also excelled on the river. He was the Thames punting champion for three years running, and a member of the Oxford rowing team which beat Cambridge by ten lengths in 1878. He once sculled the river from London to Oxford in twenty-two hours. Lord Desborough's commitment to community service can be judged by the fact that at one point he was serving on 115 different committees. He was also instrumental in organizing the 1908 Olympics, awarded to London after the original host city, Rome, dropped out in the wake of the devastating eruption of Mount Vesuvius on 7 April 1906.

Perhaps the lingering memory of Taeppa's treasure is responsible for the popularity of the giant Taplow boot sale, which creates dreadful traffic jams along the busy A4. In adjoining fields, treasure hunters shuffle past rows of stalls trying to spot that seemingly worthless old pot that will turn out to be priceless on the *Antiques Roadshow*. Haggling is intense but unfailingly good humoured. I love car-boot sales and have also been a stall holder here, offloading my own collection of worthless old pots in order to start hunting again.

A short walk along the towpath is Brunel's railway bridge, with its intriguing 'sounding arch', where a sharp clap of the hands resounds like a volley of gunfire. When Rob and I first visited we noticed a nearby house that had clearly stood empty for years, the occupants presumably having been driven out by the claps and shouts of enthusiastic echo testers. By the way, you will never hear the echo of ducks under the sounding arch; for some reason their quacks just don't come back.

When Brunel completed the bridge in 1839, critics claimed its brick span of 128 ft

An express train crosses Brunel's famous railway bridge at Maidenhead 170 years after its completion

(39 m), the world's widest and flattest, would not support the locomotives of the Great Western Railway. Some of the scaffolding was left in place 'just in case'. Looking at the bridge, it is easy to understand their concern but Brunel would be happy to know that over 170 years later, it is still safely carrying express trains.

J. M. W. Turner's 1844 painting of the bridge, 'Rain, Steam and Speed – The Great Western Railway', hangs in the National Gallery. When the picture was exhibited for the first time, it struck a chord with a woman who had crossed the bridge in the same compartment as Turner the previous year. She remembered the artist opening a window and leaning into the storm to imprint the scene on his memory. The word 'speed' in the title is said to refer to a hare, running for its life along the tracks – but despite inspecting the picture closely enough to raise the suspicion of gallery staff, I have never been able to distinguish anything even vaguely resembling a hare.

The Thames Path follows the Buckinghamshire bank to Bray Lock. The village of Bray is known for its vicar, who regularly changed his religion to suit the political climate:

And this is the law, that I'll maintain,
Unto my dying day, Sir,
That whatsoever King shall reign,
I'll be the Vicar of Bray, Sir.

The village is almost as well known for a restaurant called The Fat Duck, where celebrity chef Heston Blumenthal serves his highly innovative food. As I write, the £180-a-head tasting menu (a three-and-a-half hour, twelve-course experience) includes Blumenthal's signature Snail Porridge and a dish called Mad Hatter's Tea Party (*c.* 1850), described as Mock Turtle Soup with a Pocket Watch Toast Sandwich. Nearby in Ferry Lane is the equally exclusive Waterside Inn, the restaurant owned by French *père et fils,* Michel and Alain Roux (head chef and patron). It was here that Prince Andrew and Sarah Ferguson lunched after announcing their very civilized separation. Bray has an earlier royal connection, as Prince Andrew's great-great-grandfather Edward VII leased a riverside house in the village for his mistress Lillie Langtry.

Like Maidenhead, Bray is prone to flooding. During the 1947 floods some residents adapted to the situation by leaving their front door open and tying a boat up at the foot of the stairs.

Beyond Bray Lock is a section of the river known as Dorney Reach and half a mile back from the river stands Dorney Court. This ornate Tudor manor house has been owned for generations by the Palmer family, with one member suffering notable misfortune in affairs of the heart. In 1661, Roger Palmer's beautiful young wife, Barbara Villiers, became the mistress of Charles II. Around this time Barbara gave birth to her daughter Anne and, needless to say, there were rumours about her parentage. A Palmer descendant either had a strong view on the subject or a sense of humour, because an ancient row of lineage charts at the house shows Lady Anne's coat of arms topped with a gold crown. Roger was heartbroken over his wife's affair with the King and ran away to sea.

A few years later England's first pineapple was produced at Dorney Court. It was grown outside rather than in a hothouse, which may be why it took three years to ripen. Poor Roger lost out again because Dorney's head gardener presented the fruit to King Charles, who no doubt shared it with Barbara.

As with many old houses, Dorney Court has its own spooky story. During the Civil War, the Palmer family hid a cache of jewels which was apparently never recovered. In 1800, when Lord Palmer was burning some old papers, the heat of the fire produced the outline of print on a blank page. Before the document caught fire, he was able to make out the words: 'There is great treasure buried in or about Cabb's Fort.' Unfortunately the clue proved useless because Lord Palmer had never heard of Cabb's Fort and neither had anyone else. No subsequent reference to the jewels has come to light, although there is always a chance they may turn up at Taplow boot sale.

Rob and I visited Dorney Court on a Bank Holiday Monday. It is still very much a family home, and our guide let slip that one of the young Palmer boys had cycled home from Eton for the weekend but returned to school as soon as he heard we were coming. I felt quite guilty, especially when we all trooped through his bedroom. During the Second World War, the family filled Dorney Court with their Irish relatives rather than have it requisitioned by the army. They also took in a number of young evacuees and when one woman returned on a nostalgic visit she recalled the house being so full that a bed was made up for her in an airing cupboard.

In the Great Hall is the oldest piece of furniture in the house: a medieval dining table carved from a single oak trunk. The newest piece is a 1990s coffee table incorporating the famous pineapple motif. It was produced by the company owned by Princess Margaret's son, Lord Linley, which specializes in hand-carved furniture. The table was purchased with the proceeds of an insurance claim, after burglars stole a quantity of antique china.

Oddly enough, it was on nearby Dorney Reach that a titanic struggle to open a tin of pineapple took place in *Three Men in a Boat*. Was this coincidence, I wonder, or did Jerome place the event here as a little joke? When the trio finally gave up and threw the battered tin into the river, Jerome described himself as 'worn out and sick at heart', an emotional state Roger Palmer would certainly have identified with. Perhaps the boys should have taken along a box of Mrs Beeton's preserved pineapple slices. The only barrier between picnicker and pineapple in her recipe being waxed paper.

MRS BEETON'S PINEAPPLE CHIPS

Ingredients – Pineapples, sugar to taste. Mode – Pare and slice the fruit thinly. Put it in dishes, and strew over it plenty of pounded sugar. Keep it in a hot closet [Dorney Court's airing cupboard might do!] *or a slow oven, 8 or 10 days, and turn the fruit every day until dry, then put the slices of pine on tins and place them in a quick oven for 10 minutes. Let them cool, and store in dry boxes with paper between each layer. Time – 8–10 days. Seasonable – foreign pines, in July and August.*

The Victorians loved picnics on or beside the river and as their families were large, so were their al fresco meals. Mrs Beeton gave advice on catering for parties of forty, recommending vast quantities of puddings and cakes. Her list of *THINGS NOT TO BE FORGOTTEN AT A PICNIC* included three corkscrews – not excessive considering the list of beverages she suggested:

3 dozen quart bottles of ale, packed in hampers; ginger-beer, soda-water, and lemonade, of each 2 dozen bottles; 6 bottles of sherry, 6 bottles of claret, champagne a discretion, and any other light wine that may be preferred, and 2 bottles of brandy. Water can usually be obtained so it is useless to take it.

So many empties were tossed into the river there must have been a mosaic glass bottom from Maidenhead to Oxford. Along the banks, the picnickers also left rich pickings for today's treasure hunters armed with metal detectors. Giggling young ladies dropped earrings and coins fell from the pockets of young men as they lolled about full of potted beef and ginger beer. I have heard that to find anything you must search well back from the river because most Victorians were non-swimmers, and terrified of falling in. To be fair, they were not exactly encouraged to bathe in the Thames:

Bye-laws as to Sanitation, Bathing etc. – 1898

Bye-law 80 (sub-section 3) No person shall bathe or prepare to bathe between the hours of eight in the morning and nine in the evening during the months of June, July and August or during the remaining months in the year between the hours of eight in the morning and eight in the evening except at bathing places authorised by the Conservators and except in the river above Molesey Lock when wearing rowing costume.

I can't help wondering how strictly the authorities interpreted the words 'preparing to bathe', and whether a completely nude Victorian could have argued that they were merely preparing to lie in the sun.

Dorney Lake is the site of the rowing centre created for the schoolboys of Eton College. It also hosted the rowing events during the 2012 London Olympics. A detailed archaeological study was carried out during excavation work and thousands of worked flints were found. Among other artifacts recovered was a pot dating from between 3800 and 4200 BC.

A couple of bends further on is Boveney and the tiny Norman chapel of St Mary Magdalene. The riverside chapel, with its crooked clapboard belfry, was built to serve a now-vanished wharf, from which bargemen once ferried timber downstream from Windsor Forest. In recent years the oak stumps of a prehistoric footbridge were discovered on the riverbed here, along with wattle hurdles that once formed a trackway.

As the path approaches Eton, a tablet beside the river marks the site of the Eton College schoolboys' traditional bathing spot. The tablet quotes from the rules governing their behaviour:

Boys who are undressed must either get at once into the water or get behind screens when boats containing ladies come into sight.

Eton's annual prize-giving ceremony is held in June and at a picnic on the lawns a traditional dessert of strawberries and crushed meringues is served.

ETON MESS

500 g (1 lb) chopped strawberries
3 tablespoons kirsch
1 cup double cream
6 miniature meringues
Sprigs of fresh mint

Sprinkle the chopped strawberries with kirsch, cover and chill for 2–3 hours. Whip the cream and carefully fold into the strawberries. Gently fold in the roughly crushed meringues and serve decorated with sprigs of fresh mint.

During the long summer holidays there are regular tours of the college. Occasionally the school's private gardens open as well, to raise money for charity. Rob and I went on the garden tour one very wet weekend, decked out in raincoats and wellington boots. We began by visiting a rose-covered but muddy little island in the Thames before sploshing through the headmaster's garden then following another couple through an ancient door in a brick wall; rather like sheep. To our horror we found ourselves in the college museum, with staff staring pointedly at our muddy boots. Retreat was impossible, because someone had noticed the straying of the flock and locked the door in the wall behind us. We tried to blend in with the official college tour but I half expected to hear an announcement on the school's PA system: 'Those people wearing wellington boots report to the headmaster's office immediately.'

In 1919 an Australian army nurse visited the college after serving in France during the First World War. A letter home to her mother reveals a cultural divide as wide as the Gulf of Carpentaria. Completely unimpressed by the school's 500-year-old history, she scathingly described its 'tiny classrooms':

… old oak desks that are chipped and names that are cut everywhere by penknives. We would not own such schools in Australia. Nothing elegant about Eton. The floors are simply bare boards, not too clean and look worm eaten, the walls are quite bare, quite different to the Aussie schools with their nature studies and specimens in bottles, maps, and pictures.

The Swan Lifeline has its headquarters on Cuckoo Weir Island at Eton. At any one time there are around 100 sick and injured birds receiving specialist care at the centre. The swan population declined alarmingly when lead weights were used by anglers: the birds died from lead poisoning after swallowing the sinkers. One swan was found with twenty in its stomach, surely the swan equivalent of concrete boots. Lead weights are now illegal but most injuries are still caused by discarded fishing line. There is also a new threat to cygnets: mink, which have been liberated from fur farms by misguided animal rights activists.

Swans also need reed beds to breed in. According to the Queen's Swan Marker there is now far too much steel and concrete along the riverbanks. However, from a population of just 400 birds in the 1980s, numbers have now increased to well over 1,200.

WINDSOR TO WRAYSBURY

Approaching Windsor, the Thames Path becomes much busier, as Rob and I discovered after walking down from Dorney one Sunday morning. On several occasions we were overtaken by elderly gentlemen on bicycles who wobbled alarmingly as they politely tinkled their bells. Less considerate were the joggers who thundered past, flushed in the face and dripping with perspiration. We saw one group collide with an anxious old chap who had lost his small dog in a neighbouring field of barley. The man's cap was knocked off, and for a wonderful moment I thought he was going to shove a couple of runners into the river. It was a foretaste of things to come and I was reminded of Charles Dickens Jnr's comments about pedestrian hazards in London during the late Victorian era:

> *A butcher with his tray, a sweep with his brush, a carpenter with his saw protruding from his basket, and a scavenger loading mud into his cart, must be treated with the greatest of respect – they will treat you with none. Scarcely less dangerous are the ladies and gentlemen who persist in swinging umbrellas, parasols, and sticks about to the common danger…*

All such hazards remain, though some may some appear in a slightly different guise!

The fairytale sight of Windsor Castle looming above Brocas Meadow is a fitting finale to this section of the walk. The site for the castle was chosen by William I in around 1070 following the Norman Conquest. He enclosed 13 acres (5 hectares) above the Thames with a wooden stockade. Inside, a deep, dry moat was dug. Excavated chalk was used to form a 50-ft (15-m) mound on which the Normans built their keep. To obtain water a bore hole was sunk through the mound, then down to the level of the river, a total depth of 164 ft (50 m).

The Normans brought with them a recipe for *Pain Perdu,* or Lost Bread. The name refers to slices of bread which are covered in a sweet batter before being fried. The recipe was eventually renamed Poor Knights of Windsor. The 'Poor Knights' belonged to an order of military pensioners founded by Edward III in 1349. They lived at the castle in fairly impoverished circumstances, so no doubt found a recipe using stale bread very handy.

POOR KNIGHTS OF WINDSOR

6 slices of day-old bread
4 tablespoons single cream
2 eggs
1 tablespoon medium-dry sherry
butter for frying

Remove the crusts from the bread and cut into fingers. Beat together the eggs, cream and sherry until well blended. Dip the bread into the mixture and fry in hot butter until crisp on each side. Serve spread with warmed jam or sprinkled with caster sugar and cinnamon.

The castle has been rebuilt, enlarged and repaired by a succession of monarchs. William's great-grandson Henry II replaced the original wood with stone and built the walls and towers that enclose the north, south and east fronts of the castle. He also began the Round Tower. The most recent repair work was carried out by Queen Elizabeth II, after the devastating fire of 1992. However, if anything reduces the castle to rubble it will be the vibrations of planes that constantly roar over the parapets to Heathrow. Perhaps Her Majesty should have a word with the Prime Minister about the problem – it hardly seems worth being queen if you cannot order the flight path away from your home.

William the Conqueror actually rented the site of his fortress from the Lord of Clewer for twelve shillings per annum, a payment that continued until the sixteenth century. Rob and I took time out from exploring Windsor to visit Clewer village and its tiny Church of St Andrew, which is almost as old as the castle. The present building was begun in 1125 but there are traces of a Saxon church on the site. For many years a museum documenting the history of Clewer village was housed in the church's gatehouse. Unfortunately, when the gatehouse underwent restoration the collection was placed into storage, though some items are on display at Windsor's new museum.

Many of the artifacts were recovered in 1978 from a Victorian rubbish dump, excavated in the garden of St Andrew's vicarage. Rouge pots, cold cream jars and hat pins no doubt belonged to various vicars' wives trying to look their best. Domestic duties were represented by preserving jars and blacking pots, and garden work by plot markers and a mole trap. On a more sombre note, containers marked with an X were found. They originally held coal tar, used to treat smallpox sores, and were probably buried to avoid further infection. Clewer suffered a serious outbreak of smallpox in 1893, which raged throughout the summer. In the absence of an isolation hospital, patients were treated in marquees set up behind the church.

Clewer's mill was first mentioned in the Domesday Book and there were several buildings on the site prior to the existing seventeenth-century structure. Wheat was ground here until the 1950s. In 1815 there was a tragic accident when thirty-six-year-old John Brackenbury was crushed by a millstone. He died a few days later and was taken to a makeshift mortuary at the Swan Inn, located in Mill Lane. The Swan also served as the local coroner's court and it was here that an inquest into Brackenbury's death was held. His remains, described as presenting 'a most ghastly appearance', were buried to the left of the main path, facing the church. A tunnel once led from the back of the Swan Inn to St Andrew's Church and was only blocked up in 1989.

Visitors to the churchyard are often puzzled to find a number of graves inscribed with the name Magdalen. In the first half of the nineteenth century a lady called Mariquita Tennant, the Spanish widow of an English clergyman, began to take fallen women into her home called The Limes, in Mill Lane (the sixteenth-century building still stands). Mrs Tennant later founded the House of Mercy, where her 'saved' women could live permanently. As their gravestones indicate, they were required to take the name Magdalen, after Mary Magdalen.

Clewer's St John the Baptist Convent evolved from the House of Mercy and my first introduction to the village was through the following recipe attributed to the sisters.

CLEWER DATE TART

375 g (12 oz) self-raising flour
2 tablespoons golden syrup
1 egg
185 g (6 oz) butter
375 g (12 oz) stoneless dates
1–2 tablespoons water
150 g (5 oz) sugar
Milk

The filling – put dates, syrup and water in a saucepan and bring to the boil, stirring all the time. When soft and mushy, remove from the heat and cool. The pastry – Rub the flour and sugar into the butter. Whip the egg with a little water. Mix into a stiff dough. Grease a sandwich tin. Roll out the mixture and line the tin. Spread the date mixture on it and put another layer of pastry on the top. Pinch the two edges of pastry together. Brush the surface with a little milk and sugar. Bake in a moderate oven for about ¾ hour.

I fondly imagined the sisters rolling up the sleeves of their habits and producing the tarts in their rustic kitchen. However, my initial letter of enquiry to St John's produced a nostalgic note from Mother Jane which began: 'Oh Pauline, I well remember those date tarts ...' In a sad sign of the times she told me that the convent now employed a catering firm. Worse, she confessed that most of the sisters were on diets, battling middle-age spread. I had a horrible image of them microwaving batches of 'slimline' TV dinners after evensong.

The sisters have forsaken date tarts for reasons of health, unlike the young Clewer woman in the following limerick, whose motive for dieting was vanity:

A plump young woman from Clewer,
Was desperate for someone to woo her.
She sucked in her cheeks,
And fasted for weeks,
Until you could almost see through 'er.

Back on the High Street outside Windsor Castle, we paused to inspect Joseph Edgar Boehm's statue of Queen Victoria, which has a humorous connection with Australia. While Sydney's Queen Victoria Building was under renovation some years ago, a worldwide hunt began for a nineteenth-century statue of Victoria. Nothing suitable could be found, prompting an article in the *London Times*. Queen Elizabeth saw the piece and jokingly told her then private secretary, the Australian Sir William Heseltine, that her great-great-grandmother was in danger of being kidnapped by his countrymen. She suggested Heseltine put a guard around the statue but fortunately, before the burghers of Sydney were driven to such desperate measures, an alternative was found, abandoned by the Irish in a Dublin field.

Having spent much of my childhood arranging miniature furniture in an upturned apple box, the highlight of my visits to Windsor Castle is Queen Mary's dolls' house. When leading artists and writers of the day were invited to create works for the project, the acerbic Virginia Woolf refused. However, her friend Vita Sackville-West contributed, leading to the following exchange between the pair at a dinner party:

'Why don't you contribute to the Queen's dolls' house, Virginia?'

Virginia's response was a rather facetious suggestion as to what she might present:

'Is there a WC in it, Vita?'

As a matter of fact, Virginia, there are five. There is even a story that the original idea for the dolls' house came after the architect Sir Edwin Lutyens showed Queen Mary a tiny lavatory from the scale model of one of his buildings. I doubt if this is true, but apparently it *is* true that the Queen caught her earring in the beard of the dolls' house plumber. He was demonstrating to Her Majesty that the tiny cistern in the King's bathroom flushed half a champagne glass of water.

In 1861 the plumbing in the castle itself became a matter of concern when Prince Albert died from typhoid fever, reputedly caused by infection from the castle's medieval drains. (Queen Victoria never fully recovered from the death of her beloved consort, and when Benjamin Disraeli was on his deathbed twenty years later he refused a visit from the Queen, saying: 'She will only ask me to take a message to Albert!') Clearly, little had been done to improve matters at Windsor by the time Edward, Prince of Wales married Princess Alexandra in 1863. *Punch* magazine quipped that the royal marriage was to be held 'in an obscure Berkshire village, noted only for an old castle with bad drains'. However, Albert's death eventually led to a clean-up of the middle and upper Thames. The Thames Conservancy Board's jurisdiction was extended from Staines to Cricklade, and the discharge of raw sewage into the river from towns such as Windsor, Reading, Abingdon and Oxford was banned.

Before I leave the subject of sanitation, there are some superbly restored public toilets by the entrance to Windsor's River Street car park. They are immaculately maintained and feature wall tiles decorated with colourful scenes of the town during the Edwardian era, including ladies strolling along the banks of the Thames with their parasols.

The seventeenth-century Guildhall in Windsor was built by Christopher Wren. Its innovative design began to worry the town burghers, just as Brunel's bridge was to cause alarm at Maidenhead two centuries later. Unable to accept Wren's assurance that the building's raised floor was safe without supporting columns, they insisted he include some. Wren complied but secretly left them several inches short, just to prove his point.

In November 2003 the Guildhall was the location for an inquest into the drowning of a sixty-year-old Thames fisherman. The circumstances surrounding the man's death were very unusual. He was fishing at night near Windsor when a 3½ lb (1.5 kg) barbel pulled his rod from its tripod. The man grabbed the rod but lost his footing, and the powerful fish dragged him down a shingle bank and into the river. His efforts to save himself were hampered by the fact that he suffered from arthritis and had become entangled in the line of his second fishing rod. The hook from the second line was found imbedded in his clothing. In 2011 the Guildhall was converted into the Windsor and Royal Borough Museum.

At Windsor Bridge, riverboats offer scenic trips down to historic Runnymede, but since the Thames Path marches resolutely on, so did we. However, first there was a little hop across the river to Datchet via Victoria Bridge, a detour created to keep the public away from Windsor Castle's Home Park. Safely beyond the park, the path returns to the Berkshire bank via the Albert Bridge. Few people were upset that the original Datchet Bridge had to be demolished to protect Queen Victoria's privacy. It had a long, sad history of collapse and in the 1830s there was another Buckinghamshire versus Berkshire dispute over the cost of urgent repair work. The result was that Berkshire rebuilt in iron while Buckinghamshire merely patched their half with wood. As a loyal Bucks resident for many years, albeit part-time, I refute the suggestion that they used old beechwood chair legs but it was a bit of a disaster all the same. Where the two sections met in the middle, there was a 3-in (7.5-cm) difference in level.

It was to Datchet that the servants of a merry wife of Windsor carried Shakespeare's Falstaff. The 'gross watery pumpkin' was thrown into a muddy ditch from a clothes basket 'like a barrow of butcher's offal'.

Separated from Datchet by the Queen Mother Reservoir is Colnbrook, on the old London to Bath Road. It is the birthplace of one of the country's best-loved dessert apples. In 1825 retired brewer Richard Cox grew a seedling tree from a Ribston Pippin that produced fruit with a unique flavour, containing hints of pear, cherry and orange. It became known as the Cox's Orange Pippin.

But there is also a dark side to Colnbrook. Seventeenth-century travellers who chose to bypass the village by sailing up the Thames to Maidenhead may well have owed their lives to the decision. A story goes that waiting like spiders at Colnbrook's twelfth-century Ostrich Inn were its deadly landlords, the Jarmans. The couple were said to have perfected an ingenious method of murdering and robbing wealthy guests. They installed a trapdoor under an upstairs bed which was released in the dead of night. The occupant would be plunged into a cauldron of boiling fat in the kitchen below. The Jarmans dispatched at least sixty travellers before they were caught, and even then it was only because a victim's horse escaped and was found wandering nearby. I wonder if the name ostrich hints at locals who closed their ears to the travellers' bloodcurdling screams? There is a model of the trapdoor in the bar of the old coaching inn, now marooned within a maze of motorways almost directly under the Heathrow flight path. These days the ostrich on the pub sign must feel like burying its head against the scream of jets.

About 1½ miles (2.5 km) and a half to the south-east of Windsor is Old Windsor, occupied by the Saxons from around the seventh century. In a riverside meadow called Kinsgbury, near Old Windsor Church, excavations have revealed the ruins of a building thought to have been Edward the Confessor's eleventh-century palace. By Elizabethan times, nothing remained of the Kingsbury settlement except what was described as 'a ruinous cowshed'. Nearby is Tile Place Farm, a moated site within a clump of trees where two fourth-century Roman tombs were excavated in 1865. The tombs suggest there was once a Roman villa on the banks of the river.

In the Domesday Book, this area is called Windsores, thought to derive from the Anglo-Saxon *windels* meaning a windlass and the Latin *ora,* a riverbank. The suggestion is that a settlement sprang up at a point where goods were transferred from ship to shore – presumably to supply the royal residence.

There has been something of a role reversal in recent years as the royal estates now supply produce such as meat and fruit for the Old Windsor Farm Shop, located in a series of Victorian potting sheds in Datchet Road. There is also a cafe, where the ice cream comes from the Royal Dairy. I very much hope the scones served are made to a recipe the Queen sent to President Eisenhower in 1966, after he had enjoyed some during a visit to Buckingham Palace:

ROYAL DROP SCONES

4 cups plain flour
4 tablespoons caster sugar
2 cups milk
2 eggs
2 teaspoons bicarbonate of soda
3 teaspoons cream of tartar
2 tablespoons melted butter

Beat eggs, sugar and about half the milk together, add flour and mix, adding remainder of milk as required. Then add bicarbonate of soda and cream of tartar, and fold in the melted butter. Drop onto greased baking sheet by the teaspoonful. Bake at 200°C (400°F) for 15 minutes or until lightly browned. Makes about 16 scones.

I'm sure Her Majesty would agree with the person who declared that scones rhyming with Oxford dons are eaten with butter, but that scones rhyming with stones are eaten with margarine!

Perhaps the shop should be renamed in honour of George III, who took a personal interest in his farms at Windsor and Kew. The King wrote pamphlets on agriculture under the pseudonym Ralph Robinson and was given the nickname Farmer George for his love of the countryside. The following rhyme, written in 1796, refers to an apple pudding named for King George's wife, Charlotte:

The Charlotte brown, within whose crusty sides,
A belly soft the pulpy apple hides.

The sensuality of the lines may have been inspired by George's open affection for his wife, whose own 'soft belly' swelled with a total of fifteen children. Twelve years after their marriage the King welcomed Charlotte home after an absence by opening the carriage door himself and seizing her around the waist. George is remembered for his bouts of insanity and for losing the American colonies but I prefer to think of him proudly presenting Charlotte with a bucket of home-grown apples.

It seems George was rather preoccupied by apples. During his periods of insanity he would walk the corridors of Buckingham Palace wondering aloud how they managed to get into apple dumplings!

After a summer visit to the Old Windsor shop, Rob and I finished our evening meal with a bowl of 'royal' raspberries and a glass of Sandringham peach liqueur. I half expected to feel a bad-tempered Corgi nipping at my ankles under the dining-room table.

Approaching Runnymede is a riverside pub called The Bells of Ouzeley. The bells in the name refer to those from Oxford's Osney Abbey. In 1538 the abbey's bells were supposedly removed by the monks and taken downriver to escape the clutches of Henry VIII. The barge sank near Runnymede and the bells were buried in deep mud, never to be recovered.

And so to historic Runnymede, where on 15 June 1215, King John was forced to sign the Magna Carta by his rebellious barons. The site has a special romantic association for me. My first true love was a nine-year-old baron called Leigh Dunstan, who made my heart flutter in grade four when he brandished a blackboard pointer under the King's nose and shouted: 'Sign here if you please!' Of the Charter's sixty-three clauses, number thirty-nine is the most well known, spelling out the individual's right to justice and liberty:

> *No man shall be taken, imprisoned, outlawed, banished or in any way destroyed, nor will we proceed against or prosecute him except by the lawful judgment of his peers or by the law of the land.*

The right to Navigation on the Thames is recognized in clause twenty-three.

It seems hard to believe, but after the First World War the cash-strapped government of the day raised some money by selling the Runnymede site. It was purchased by Lady Fairhaven, who commissioned Sir Edwin Lutyens to design the two small lodges which now flank the western entrance to the meadows. Lutyens' lodges were viewed as a desecration of an almost sacred site, and an infringement of the rights won at Runnymede. On the eve of the official opening, objectors sprayed them with creosote. With no time to clean the buildings before the Prince of Wales arrived to perform the ceremony, officials could only try to disguise the mess with greenery. Could it have been this embarrassing incident that prompted Lady Fairhaven to donate the site to the National Trust in 1931?

The Trust run a teashop in one of the lodges, and over tea and scones I read Rob a humorous account of the signing, written by Marriott Edgar in 1937. The early verses have the barons, led by Fitzwalter, preparing the Charter. By the fourteenth verse they are about to confront King John, who was himself enjoying tea at 'Runningmead':

> *Next day, King John, all unsuspecting,*
> *And having the afternoon free,*
> *To Runningmead Island had taken a boat,*
> *And were having some shrimps for his tea.*
>
> *He had just pulled the 'ead off a big 'un,*
> *And were pinching its tail with his thumb,*
> *When up came a barge load of Barons, who said,*
> *'We thought you'd be here so we've come.'*
>
> *When they told him they'd brought Magna Charter,*
> *The king seemed to go kind of limp,*
> *But minding his manners he took off his hat*
> *And said 'Thanks very much, have a shrimp.'*

Perhaps the barons did accept a shrimp from the King. According to the thirteenth-century chronicler, Walter of Coventry:

> *At length, after much deliberation, they made friends, the King granting them* [the barons] *all that they asked and by his charter confirming this. The kiss of peace was exchanged, and homage and fidelity having been renewed, they ate and drank together.*

But subsequently it was all downhill for King John. Trying to deal with more disenchanted barons in the north, he lost the crown jewels when his baggage wagons sank in the quicksands of Norfolk's Wash. Arriving at Swineshead Abbey in a foul mood, he ate and drank too much and died ignominiously from an upset stomach.

At Wraysbury, directly across the river from Egham and the Runnymede meadows, is Ankerwycke, site of an eleventh-century Benedictine priory called St Mary's. There is also a wonderful old yew tree here known as the Ankerwycke Yew. It is believed to be well over 2,000 years old and has a girth exceeding 30 ft (10 m). The tree has become the object of worship by self-described 'new-age Druids' who have covered it in ribbons, coins and candles. Unfortunately burning candles present a great threat to the tree and such pilgrimages are actively discouraged.

We once joined a group of interested locals for a National Trust archeological walk around Ankerwycke. Our guide interpreted the ruins, pointed out the old stew ponds, and showed us a channel that brought barges of Chiltern chalk to the priory building site from the

Thames. He was just getting into his stride when a row erupted within the group over his passing reference to the Magna Carta. There was a sudden split between the Wraysbury (Middlesex) and Egham (Surrey) camps over exactly where the Magna Carta was signed: 'They always try to claim the credit over at Egham because they're a lot of bloody snobs,' a Wraysbury woman muttered to me. She and her supporters argued that the Ankerwycke monastery would have been a logical place for the signing, especially as scribes would have been available to help draft the documents.

I tried to ease the tension with a joke. 'A busload of retired Australians pulled up at Runnymede one day and their guide explained: 'Well, ladies and gentlemen, this is where the Magna Carta was signed.' 'So when did that happen then?' one old bloke called out from the back. '1215,' was the reply. 'Oh bugger,' said the fellow, looking at his watch. 'We only missed it by an hour!' I'd like to think it helped a bit.

© Rob Conolly

Did this ancient Ankerwyke yew watch over the signing of the Magna Carta?

© Rob Conolly

Did King John borrow a quill from the scribes at St Mary's Priory, Ankerwycke?

By the time things settled down we were at the old yew tree and I heard the guide's assistant ask quietly: 'Are you going to discuss the MC and the YT?' He turned pale, shook his head and talked about bluebells and snowdrops. I didn't blame him for avoiding more conflict, although there *is* a theory that the Magna Carta was signed under the yew and it was certainly ancient enough to be venerated by 1215. In 1977, the environmentalist David Bellamy and some like-minded supporters met under the tree to sign the Green Magna Carta.

M25 TO MOLESEY

If reaching the Oxford boundary marker was a milestone on our initial journey down the Thames, walking under the M25 and into Greater London was even more significant. The path runs under the motorway bridge and as we emerged our achievement was 'saluted' by a Concorde flying overhead. I feel rather sad that these glamorous bird-like jets have since been consigned to history.

Several urban myths have developed around the M25, which circles the capital. My favourite involves a Texan tourist who is said to have ventured onto the motorway at Heathrow, missed every exit, and arrived back at Terminal One several hours later. In Paris the following day he told the appreciative French that England was even smaller than he had imagined, and far less scenic!

There are other reminders for walkers that London is now very close. Beside the towpath is an iron 'coalpost'. It warned the nineteenth-century coal merchants plying the river that they would be charged a London levy. More importantly, there is a replica of the London Stone, official marker of the upstream limit of the City of London's control over the Thames from 1215 until 1857, when the Thames Conservancy was established. The original stone is housed in the library at the next Thames settlement: Staines.

While King John was riding out to Runnymede from Windsor Castle, his rebellious barons were approaching from Staines. This town has suffered a good deal of derision due to its M25 commuter-belt location and the fact that it was the birthplace of linoleum. When television's *Vicar of Dibley*'s village was in danger of being flooded, Revd Geraldine Granger feared she might be transferred to somewhere like Bolivia … or Staines and prayed: 'Please God, let it be Bolivia.' More recently the comedian Sacha Baron Cohen made Staines the home of his satirical character Ali G. It all became too much for the borough council and a decision was made to raise the town's image by highlighting its proximity to the river. On 20 May 2012 the town officially changed its name to Staines-upon-Thames, an action perceived by critics (including the local football team) as pretentious, and liable to simply extend the joke.

The ancient Britons certainly considered Staines a suitable enough place to settle, as did the Romans when they invaded in AD 43. The local museum in the Market Square displays artifacts from all eras: a Bronze Age axe, a Roman baby feeding bottle and samples of Staines linoleum!

While walking this section of the Thames Path we were caught in a sudden thunderstorm. On the river beside us a dozen swans shook hailstones from their wings and took off towards London like a formation of Second World War bombers. Their extended necks conveyed a sense of purpose almost equal to my own. For the first time I appreciated the immense effort required for swans to become airborne. From a distance they appear to rise effortlessly, but in reality they need a very long 'runway'. In 1995 the Staines Railway Bridge was painted with yellow stripes to stop the birds flying into it.

It is only a short walk from Staines to Penton Hook Lock. This 'hook' of land was formed by a tight loop of the river which at its narrowest point measured only 50 yards (46 m) across. Many victims of the 1665 Great Plague were buried here in a mass grave. Floodwaters often broke through the neck of the hook, allowing Thames barges through, and in 1815 a permanent short cut was created by the Penton Hook Lock Cut.

Beyond Penton Hook and tucked between the river and the immense Queen Mary Reservoir is Laleham. Several years after Rob and I first walked through here we drove back to the village for a closer look at All Saints' Church. It was locked, but a parishioner spotted us on her way to the shops and kindly popped home for a key. Despite the church's security measures, it is impossible to protect everything. Three days before our visit, two oak benches had been stolen from the open porch after standing there for over a hundred years. No doubt the benches ended up in an antique shop a safe distance from Laleham. I only hope the church never loses its charming hand-me-down chandelier from Westminster Abbey, presented after the abbey updated from brass to glass chandeliers in the 1960s.

Our lady with the key showed us the Lucan family chapel. Lord 'Lucky' Lucan created a media sensation when he disappeared in 1974, after allegedly murdering the family nanny in mistake for his estranged wife. Twenty-five years later, on 26 October 1999, a High Court ruling declared him legally dead. The judgment enabled Lucan's estate to be settled but oddly enough he remained patron of All Saints' Church until the next change of vicar. Reports of alleged sightings continue, and in February 2012 his brother claimed that the fugitive Lord Lucan was alive and living in South Africa.

Laleham's other claim to fame is that the poet Matthew Arnold, who wrote so nostalgically of the Thames in 'The Scholar-Gipsy', was born by the river here in Ferry Lane. His father ran a small private school in the village and later became headmaster of Rugby Public School. There are disadvantages in having a schoolmaster for a father; Matthew received his first 'report card' at the age of six months when he was described by his father as 'backward and rather bad-tempered'.

The ferry service at Laleham ceased about thirty years ago but it used to carry passengers across the river to Chertsey, and was operated by a Lucan family tenant. I like to imagine Edward Lear, author of *The Owl and the Pussycat*, amusing himself during the ferry ride by composing the following limerick:

> *There was an Old Lady of Chertsey,*
> *Who made a remarkable curtsey;*
> *She twirled round and round*
> *Till she sank underground,*
> *Which distressed all the people of Chertsey.*

The Thames continues to separate Middlesex and Surrey. In the nineteenth century Middlesex paid a higher fee than Surrey for the recovery of corpses from the river, leading to a distortion of death rates for the two counties. Bodies were regularly towed to the more lucrative bank under the cover of darkness. One night a man was caught trying to push a disintegrating body across the river near Chertsey Bridge with his fishing rod.

Chertsey Abbey was established in AD 666 and was twice raided by the Vikings. It was destroyed during the dissolution of the monasteries and Henry VIII used some of the stone to expand Hampton Court Palace. Only a fragment of masonry remains in Abbey Fields, along with depressions left by the old fish ponds that continue to refill after periods of heavy rain.

The abbey's curfew bell was cast around 1310. In 1471 it tolled the death of King Henry VI, whose corpse was carried by barge from London to Chertsey after he was murdered at the tower. Henry was buried in the abbey's Lady Chapel until Richard III moved the body to Windsor Castle to stop a constant flow of pilgrims.

On a more uplifting note, the curfew bell featured in a romantic act of courage at Chertsey in the fifteenth century. During the War of the Roses, the sweetheart of a local girl called Blanche Heriot was captured by the Yorkists. His name was Herrick Evenden and his execution was to be signalled by the tolling of the curfew at Chertsey Abbey. A messenger rode off to London to obtain a pardon from King Edward IV but was delayed at Laleham Ferry. As the curfew hour approached and the bell ringer took up his rope, a desperate Blanche climbed the tower and swung from the clapper of the great bell like a human pendulum. She muffled the tolls with her body until the messenger returned from London and her lover was reprieved. The story inspired American poet Rose Hartwick Thorpe's ballad 'Curfew Must Not Ring Tonight':

> *As you swing to the left,*
> *And you swing to the right,*
> *Remember the Curfew*
> *Must never ring tonight.*

A life-size statue of Blanche swinging on the clapper has been erected beside Chertsey Bridge. The abbey bell is now number five in a peal of eight bells at Chertsey's St Peter's Church. Curfew is still rung at the church, from Michaelmas (29 September) until Lady Day (25 March) at 8 p.m.

Of the ten commandments Chertsey's bell ringers were required to keep, I was intrigued by the lofty sentiment expressed in No. 2:

Thou shalt not follow one rope too long, for the eyes are the windows of the mind and if they be glued to one rope how shall the mind be lighted?

© Rob Conolly

Brave Blanche Heriot became a human pendulum, silencing Chertsey's curfew bell to save her sweetheart

No. 5 was far more prosaic:

Thou shalt not bump the stay of the bell lest it break and thou be carried up to heaven.

Back at the river another bell caught our attention. It was a landing bell, rung to summon a boat from a house on the opposite bank. I was tempted to give the rope a little tug as I passed, and bolder types probably do. I wonder whether New Year's Eve revellers force the occupants of Willowdean to follow Blanche Heriot's example and muffle the bell's clapper?

The busy M3 crosses the river and towpath at Laleham on its way to Winchester and beyond, but as the traffic noise recedes there is an enjoyable walk towards Shepperton through water meadows. Only one thing disturbed my peace of mind: the sight of a lone fisherman sitting on the riverbank with a bulging Royal Mail bag beside him. I have the highest regard for Royal Mail and could only hope the bag contained fish, or a large packed lunch; anything but undelivered letters from Australia.

Shepperton Lock is one place where Thames Path walkers can opt for a ferry ride without 'missing a stich' on the walk. Barge teams crossed the Thames and picked up the towpath again on the south bank, at Weybridge. Walkers can follow suit, as a ferry service still operates. However, there is an alternative route via riverside Shepperton and delightful Church Square. Several old pubs surround the church, including The Anchor, where highwayman Dick Turpin was a regular visitor. According to legend, Turpin's pistol was found at The Anchor years later, inscribed 'DICK'S FRIEND'.

The present church was built in 1613 to replace a building destroyed by flooding in the winter of 1605. Thomas Love Peacock (1785–1866), the Victorian novelist and poet, wrote a memorial for his three-year-old daughter Margaret, who is buried in the churchyard. The lines were inscribed on the gravestone despite opposition from the vicar of Chertsey, who complained that it did not include the word God. I read the first lines and decided the vicar must have had a heart of granite:

Long night succeeds thy little day;
Oh blighted blossom! Can it be,
That this grey stone, and grassy clay,
Have clos'd our anxious care of thee?

Peacock also wrote a poem which an English friend of ours wryly calls 'The Aspiring Emigrants' Anthem'. It begins:

Henry VIII; an imposing figure, but obesity hastened his death

Instead of sitting wrapped up in flannel
With rheumatism in every joint,
I wish I was in the English Channel,
Just going 'round the Lizard Point.

The Shepperton 'detour' returns to the Thames Path via Walton Bridge, but meanwhile the ferry discharges its passengers at Weybridge. In 1538 Henry VIII stripped more stone from Chertsey Abbey's steeple and library and sent it downstream to Weybridge to build Oatlands Palace for his new queen, Anne of Cleves. Having a royal palace in the neighbourhood created something of an embarrassment for the locals, who asked to be excused from carrying the King's baggage because they only had one cart. Trying to cross busy Church Street, Rob and I wished transport was still that scarce!

Henry VIII rarely visited Oatlands Palace, although it is said he secretly married Catherine Howard in the chapel. It was demolished in 1650 following the execution of Charles I. At Weybridge's Elmbridge Museum there are decorative floor tiles and Cotswold limestone columns from Chertsey Abbey, as well as one of its grinning gargoyles.

On the way downriver to Walton-on-Thames there is a choice for walkers: either following the straight line of the 1935 Desborough Cut or wandering up and down the loops it bypassed. The cut was named in honour of Lord Desborough. The name Walton derives from the Old English *Wealh* and *Tun* meaning 'farm of the Britons'. The area was inhabited from Stone Age times, perhaps because the river could be forded here.

In Walton's St Mary's churchyard is the grave of demon bowler Edward 'Lumpy' Stevens, who died in 1810. Stevens was responsible for a major development in the game of cricket. His accuracy was such that on three occasions in one innings, he bowled a ball straight through the then 'two stump' wicket of star batsman John Small without dislodging the bail. In 1774, largely as a result of this match, a third stump was introduced. There is something very satisfying about watching a batsman's middle stump fly, and as lifelong cricket fans Rob and I wanted to pay our respects to Lumpy. We found his weathered gravestone by the south door of the church.

Two centuries later the skill of a batsman would cause officials to examine the rules of cricket again, and oddly enough there was another Walton-on-Thames connection. The English cricket captain Douglas Jardine lived in Ashley Road, Walton, and at his home, Woodside (since demolished), he came up with a strategy to counter the amazing batting ability of Australia's Don Bradman. Unfortunately, batsmen rather than stumps became the target in Jardine's 'bodyline' bowling and during the 1932/33 test series in Australia, relations between Australia and England sank to an all-time low. We wondered how the stress of the whole affair affected Jardine's mother Alison, who died only three years later in 1936. She is remembered by a brass plaque set into the south wall of St Mary's All Saints' chapel.

Jerome K. Jerome and his friends called at St Mary's to see a torturous contraption known as a scold's bridle, and I must say Rob showed a disturbing interest in it as well. It was presented to the community by the city of Chester in 1723, inscribed with the date 1633 and the verse:

Chester presents Walton with a bridle
To curb women's tongues which talk too idle.

It is a replica of the original, which disappeared in the 1960s. I hope it is not being used by someone determined to watch test cricket in peace. While Rob was smirking over the bridle, I was in the chancel looking for a marble slab covering the grave of William Lilly. Lilly was a noted astrologer in the seventeenth century who played a dangerous game by advising both Roundheads and Cavaliers during the Civil War. He managed to get himself arrested by both sides. There was more trouble after he successfully predicted the Great Fire of London, because some people thought he had tried to enhance his reputation by starting it. However, Lilly was a model citizen at Walton. He was appointed church warden in 1663 and not only settled post-war parish debts from his own pocket but became a generous benefactor to the town's poor.

Visitors to the Cob and Pen bar at Walton's Swan Inn in Manor Road may notice a copy of a marriage certificate on display. The marriage, on 25 October 1910, was between the landlord's daughter Eva Leale and composer Jerome Kern. Kern had wandered into the hotel with friends and captivated the lovely Eva with his piano playing. He is remembered for classics such as 'Old Man River', 'Smoke Gets In Your Eyes', 'The Last Time I Saw Paris' and 'Look For The Silver Lining'. A concert was held at St Mary's to mark the centenary of his death on 27 January 1985. Across the Atlantic, President Reagan pronounced 'Jerome Kern Day', and there were celebrations throughout the United States.

Downriver from Walton on the northern bank is Sunbury. In Oliver Twist, Bill Sikes passed through here on the way to Chertsey, with Oliver in tow. Sikes was planning to burgle Rose Maylie's house:

As they passed Sunbury Church, the clock struck seven. There was a light in the ferry-house window opposite; which streamed across the road and threw into more sombre shadow a dark yew tree with graves beneath it. There was a dull sound of the old tree stirred gently in night wind. It seemed like quiet music for the repose of the dead.

As it turned out, young Oliver very nearly ended up dead; he was shot in the arm during the bungled robbery.

To celebrate the new millennium, a remarkable embroidery was created at Sunbury. The main panel, which measures 9x3 ft (3x1 m), is a detailed view of the village centre. Dozens of buildings can be identified, with the Thames flowing in the foreground. When one man commented on the absence of a snake among the local flora and fauna he was jokingly challenged to embroider one himself, which he did. He was among 140 people involved in the project, many with no previous needlework experience. In June 2001, the Queen went to see the embroidery and took tea with the workers. To everyone's amusement she had heard about the snake and singled out the man involved.

The embroidery was originally displayed where it was created, at Riverbank Cottage in Thames Street. However, funds were raised for a purpose-built home which opened in 2006 beside Sunbury's historic walled garden, still only a short walk from the river. This garden once produced fruit and vegetables for the local manor house but today its parterres and knot gardens are open to everyone. A flowerbed has been planted in memory of Diana, Princess of Wales. Gardeners will also be interested in Sunbury's century-old standard wisteria, growing down by the river. Its future was in doubt following the floods of 2003 and staff from Kew Gardens had to be called in to give it some TLC.

Back on the south bank by Sunbury Lock we noticed an exuberant little house where Noddy peeped over the front fence, Sylvester the cat grinned from the shrubbery and a rocking horse galloped along the roof of a garden shed. Perhaps the owner's kindly intention was to raise the spirits of riverside walkers in the knowledge that the Thames Path soon passes through the gloomy walls and banks of the Molesey reservoirs and the concrete remains of Second World War anti-tank defences.

One of the earliest references to Molesey was in the seventh century, when as *Muleseg* it belonged to Chertsey Abbey. A quaint sixteenth-century pub in East Molesey, The Bell, claims to have been a favourite drinking spot of the debonair highwayman Claude Duval. Duval once held up a coach, relieved the traveller of his gold, then cheekily waltzed his victim's wife along the roadside. Incidents such as this prompted the following epitaph on the highwayman's now vanished tombstone:

Here lies Du Vall: Reader, if Man thou art,
Look to thy purse; if Female to thy heart!

Beyond Molesey is Garrick's Ait (or island) with its domed temple built by the eighteenth-century actor and theatre manager David Garrick, to house his statue of William Shakespeare. Garrick owned a riverside estate opposite the island. He ran London's Drury Lane theatre and is famous for the patriotic lines:

Heart of oak are our ships,
Heart of oak are our men.

Houseboats on the river near Molesey; a delightful display of English eccentricity

Moored beside a longer river island is a row of diverse houseboats. Some have lost all resemblance to boats except for the fact that they are floating. Rob photographed a bright yellow 'bungalow' with a tiled roof and a double-storey purple mansion with a huge upper terrace. A retired tugboat looked completely out of place wedged between them.

Ahead is Molesey Lock, where fishermen must feel a shiver of anticipation as they throw in a line. It was here that the biggest trout ever taken from the Thames was hooked, on 20 May 1883. It weighed in at 14 lb 10 oz (7 kg). The trout was stuffed and is on display at Henley's River and Rowing Museum. Trout numbers in the river are increasing so there is always hope that an even bigger fish will be landed one day. In recent years one weighing 4 lb (1.8 kg) was taken at Penton Hook.

The Thames Path (still the original towpath) now crosses to the north bank via Hampton Court Bridge where it becomes Barge Walk. The name not only commemorates the commercial craft that ferried material and men to the palace during Henry VIII's extensive building programme, but the royal barges that conveyed Henry and succeeding monarchs upriver from London.

HAMPTON COURT TO TWICKENHAM

Appropriately, one of the first views of Hampton Court is the original Tudor palace built by Cardinal Wolsey. Wolsey failed to obtain papal consent for the annulment of Henry VIII's marriage to Catherine of Aragon, and tried to save his neck by giving the house to the King. He ended up being arrested for high treason anyway, only escaping the axe by dying prior to his trial. We were walking between the palace and the river recently when who should come strolling towards us but Anne Boleyn, the woman behind Henry's desire to be free. Thankfully Miss Boleyn did not have 'her head tucked underneath her arm' as the old song goes. Her hair was in a coiled plait and she was wearing a silky back gown under a full-length cerise cape. I thought I caught a whiff of freshly baked almond tarts from the wicker basket over her arm, but she smilingly informed us that she was an actor employed at the palace. Disappointingly, the basket contained only her Anne Boleyn buckled slippers and her mobile phone.

Hampton Court was a place of romantic dalliance long after Henry courted Anne, though sometimes the bounds of propriety were overstepped. Alexander Pope's eighteenth-century satirical poem 'The Rape Of The Lock' was inspired by an incident at the palace involving a young lady called Arabella Fermor. A cheeky Lord Petre had snipped off a lock of Arabella's hair and she was not amused:

> *For ever cursed be this detested day,*
> *Which snatch my best, my favourite curl away!*
> *Happy! ah ten times happy had I been*
> *If Hampton Court these eyes had never seen!*

George III's memories of Hampton Court were unhappy too, because it was here his bad-tempered father once boxed his ears. After becoming king in 1760, George preferred to live at Windsor Castle. His son the Prince Regent was more interested in building onion-domed Brighton Pavilion, and Hampton Court became rather run down. Visitors were shown around the shabby buildings for a shilling a head until a century later

William IV thought they deserved more for their money and carried out some much-needed repairs.

It costs visitors a good deal more than a shilling to look around the palace today, but it has been restored to its full glory and maintaining an historic building of this size is an expensive business. There are all sorts of problems to contend with. Windows are loosened by vibrations from jets roaring overhead to Heathrow and caustic poo from roosting pigeons dissolves the ancient brickwork. One of the most bizarre forms of damage affects statues in the palace gardens; the problem is caused by Hampton Court's proximity to the river, as water rats sneak up during the night to sharpen their teeth on the toes of the stone figures. Some ancient but innovative building techniques have been discovered during repair work inside the palace. For example, to soften the overhead footsteps of courtiers, ceilings had been filled with crushed shells, which acted as an effective sound-proofing material.

I was anxious to see the Chapel Royal roof, carved at Sonning for Henry VIII and sent downriver by barge in prefabricated sections (see page 99). One hundred woodcarvers and labourers worked on the roof for nine months. It has delightful pendants, decorated with gilded cherubs playing musical instruments. The vaulted ceiling is decorated with the King's motto, *Dieu et mon droit* (God and my right), spelled out in gold all over the roof. Most of the Ns are the wrong way round but this was the fault of the royal painters, not our wonderful middle Thames craftsmen.

Barge Walk also passes the Banqueting House, built in the reign of William III. In 1702 King William was riding at Hampton Court Park when his horse tripped over a molehill. The King escaped the fall with a broken collarbone but complications set in and he died the following month from pleuro-pneumonia. His enemies, the Jacobites, allegedly made congratulatory toasts to the mole for having brought the King down, referring to the animal as 'the little gentleman in black velvet'.

William was followed at Hampton Court by his sister-in-law Queen Anne, who pulled out all her predecessor's box hedging because she hated the smell of it ... and hadn't much liked William either. It was during Anne's reign that the famous yew maze was planted in the seventeenth century, although it is doubtful whether the Queen ever walked the half mile to its centre. She suffered ill health all her life, including rheumatism and dropsy, which caused her body to swell alarmingly. When she died in 1714 it was noted that her coffin had to be made square. Anne loved chocolate and brandy, which probably did not help her various medical conditions. However, the chicken soup she regularly took at breakfast is virtually calorie free.

QUEEN ANNE'S BROTH

1.2 litres (2 pints) chicken stock
1 onion, chopped
1 clove garlic
2 sprigs parsley
2 sprigs thyme
2 sprigs mint
2 sprigs lemon balm
12 coriander seeds
large pinch saffron
4 cloves
salt and pepper

Place all ingredients in a pan and bring to the boil. Simmer for 30 minutes. Cover and allow the herbs to infuse. Serve with fingers of toast.

A slightly older horticultural wonder than the maze is a 230-year-old grapevine, the world's oldest and largest. It was planted by Capability Brown circa 1768 and still produces 500–700

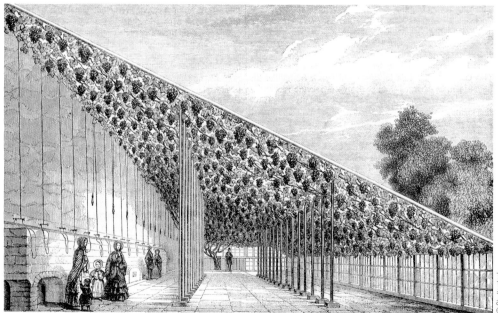

The vast grapevine at Hampton Court attracted visitors in Victorian times, as it does to this day

bunches of black table grapes annually. The fruit is harvested in September and sold to visitors in Hampton Court's shops. Capability Brown was the royal gardener at Hampton Court between 1764 and his death in 1783. We should be grateful that he had a sense of history and refused to alter the layout of the palace grounds 'out of respect for my profession'.

Downriver at Kingston upon Thames is Coombe Conduit, built by Cardinal Wolsey to carry fresh water a distance of 3 miles (5 km) to Hampton Court. The Thames was still reasonably clean in those days but Wolsey was probably dwelling on the foul contents of the sewer pipes (3x5 ft, 1x1.5 m), which he installed to run from Hampton Court to the river. The conduit consists of two small buildings, one now in ruins, connected by an underground passage.

Seven Anglo-Saxon kings were crowned at Kingston, on the stone from which the town takes its name. It sits outside the Guildhall and set into its plinth is a coin from the reign of each sovereign. As Rob photographed the coronation stone one morning, a small crowd gathered. We were bemused to discover that they were mostly locals, more used to hurrying past the monument on their way to work without giving it a second glance. Throughout our journey down the river we were struck by how appreciative people were of our interest in English history, and how their own interest rose in response.

The names of the Saxon kings read like an incantation, and if repeated at midnight might summon the spirits of at least six: *Eadweard, Adelsten, Eadmund, Eadred, Eadward and*

© Rob Conolly

Once interested onlookers dispersed I posed beside the Coronation Stone at Kingston

Edelred. The seventh, *Eadwig* (a name it is difficult not to smile over), may prefer not to revisit Kingston. Having sneaked away from his coronation feast to canoodle with a young woman, the fifteen-year-old was discovered by outraged clergymen. His discarded crown was jammed back on his head before he was ignominiously marched back to the dining hall. The girl in question was castigated as a 'strumpet' but she was actually the daughter of a noble-woman and in Eadwig's defence, reader, he married her!

Apparently Eadweard, known as Edward the Elder, chose to be crowned at Kingston rather than the Saxon capital of Winchester for diplomatic reasons. He wanted to unite the Angles, who lived north of the Thames, with the southern Saxons, in his struggle against the invading Danes.

Visitors who happen to be in Kingston around lunchtime on Mondays can call at the parish church for soup, coffee and a free concert. On the first Sunday of the month the concerts give way to bell ringing. The church has a full peal of twelve bells. On 28 May 1984 an all-female group spent a marathon seven hours ringing 10,560 changes, in which the bells are struck in a different order for each ring or 'change'. Theoretically the changes possible on twelve bells could keep ringers busy for nearly thirty-eight years. In the time of Elizabeth I there were only six bells at Kingston, one carrying the lovely inscription: 'Untouched I am a silent thing, but strike me and I sweetly sing.' The bells sometimes sang for the Queen herself, such as in 1571 when ringers were paid eleven pence for marking the occasion of Her Majesty 'goyeng to Ottland' – 'Ottland' referring to the royal palace at Weybridge

In 1745 a woman innkeeper from Kingston was ducked in the river by the old bridge as punishment for being a scold. The authorities could have shut her up by borrowing Walton's scold's bridle but of course a ducking was far more dramatic; witness the fact that more than 2,000 spectators turned up. The town's existing bridge was built in 1825.

As we drew closer to London I felt a rising sense of urgency. I had not actually become a bolter, but when dawdlers obstructed the path and slowed me down I was tempted to poke them in the bottom with a little stick. We left Kingston via Canbury Gardens and having noticed the feverish glint in my eyes, Rob suggested we stop for morning tea along the gardens' avenue of plane trees. To my amusement a squirrel hopped onto the back of our seat and tapped Rob on the shoulder for a handout. However, he was in even more of a hurry than me and when we gave him some walnut bread he quickly picked out the nuts and took off towards Teddington Lock, leaving the rest for the ducks.

Teddington Lock has the longest weir and largest locking system on the river. There are actually three locks. The largest, Barge Lock, is capable of holding six barges plus a tug. Launch Lock, built in 1815, is much smaller, and Skiff Lock is so tiny it has been dubbed Coffin Lock. From this point on, the river is tidal. As the seventeenth-century poet Sir John Denham wrote:

Thames, the most loved of all the ocean's sons,
By his old sire, to his embraces runs,
Hasting to pay tribute to the sea,
Like mortal life to meet eternity.

Perhaps my urgency was due to that same pull of the sea.

The Thames Path now effectively 'splits' and follows both north and south banks to the Flood Barrier. Those pressed for time face a difficult choice, but most people swap from side to side as the fancy takes them. Over the years Rob and I have walked both banks.

At Teddington, on the north bank, work on cathedral-like St Alban's Church began in the 1880s when the existing parish church became too small to cope with its congregation of God-fearing Victorians. But even before it was finished, society had become more secular and the pews were beginning to empty. The church was deconsecrated in 1977 and has since been converted into an arts centre. St Alban's did have one claim to fame: a local boy called Noël Coward used to sing in the choir.

The south bank route crosses Ham Lands, which were heavily quarried for gravel early last century. In the 1960s the deep pits were filled with rubble from all over London, including Second World War bomb sites. The soil held an enormous variety of plant seeds (around 230 species) and has resulted in a nature reserve that attracts all kinds of birds and butterflies. It is moving to think there are flowers blooming in this idyllic spot that are 'descendants' of those blown to pieces in London gardens.

Further on is the National Trust property, Ham House. Built in 1610, it was expanded and lavishly decorated in the 1670s by Elizabeth Dysart and the Duke of Lauderdale, her second husband. During this period the house became the centre of fashionable society and court life. It is unique in that its interior style and décor has scarcely changed in 300 years. A painting in the house by Henry Danckerts shows Dorney Court's head gardener John Rose presenting his pineapple to Charles II in 1661. Unfortunately, by the time Elizabeth died she had suffered a dramatic reversal of fortune. Her spending on the property had left her deeply in debt, and perhaps with an unquiet spirit. It is said that her ghost still walks the house.

Fortunately the grounds of Ham House survived the often heavy-handed eighteenth-century English Landscape movement and in recent years the National Trust have recreated the walled kitchen gardens to more accurately reflect Elizabeth's era. The organically grown herbs and vegetables produced are used in seventeenth-century dishes served in the Orangery restaurant. We visited Ham House early in the season, when there was scarcely another visitor in sight. It would have been easy to believe we had been transported to the seventeenth century, except for the incongruous sight of new-age travellers encamped at the end of the drive.

The Duke of Lauderdale's herd of highland cattle grazed the water meadows beside the Thames, and the National Trust have added a great deal of interest for visitors by restoring the property's original dairy. A butter churn and a selection of milk jugs and bowls stand on original marble-topped benches, backed by hand-painted Wedgwood tiles. The benches are supported by unique, cast-iron 'cows' legs'. The dairy's open milk bowls made me think of the butterflies at Ham Lands, and of folklore surrounding the name butterfly. It was believed fairies stole milk and butter by transforming themselves into gossamer-winged insects, hence 'butter fly'. Ham House has also retained its ice house, which allowed the creation of desserts already popular in Europe such as sorbets, blancmanges and early versions of ice cream.

We approached Petersham through a sun shower and watched a double rainbow arch across Richmond Hill on the far side of Petersham Meadows. These water meadows are still

© Rob Conolly

Someone with a sense of humour designed the benches in eighteenth-century Ham House dairy allowed to flood in the traditional way but the Thames no longer freezes solid, as it did in 1788 when loaded carts could be driven across the river. During the thaw, lumps of ice weighing 1 tonne were thrown 100 ft (30 m) onto nearby properties. In October 2001 the meadows were leased for 125 years to the Petersham Trust. Annual rent was settled at a bunch of wild flowers, not bad for a site valued at around £70 million. The trust was set up to preserve the meadow from the clutches of developers.

It was in Petersham water meadows that we encountered the final herd of dairy cows on our journey down the Thames. I brushed against their flanks without a qualm, as cattle have grazed here for hundreds of years and are far too civilized to crush the ribs of walkers. Perhaps their ancestors were those milked by dairymaids for a drink called syllabub, popular among the area's gentlefolk. To make an authentic syllabub, milk was squirted directly into a bowl of sweetened wine.

Just across the river in Twickenham, the eighteenth-century wit Horace Walpole treated some French house guests to a syllabub made from his own dairy herd at Strawberry Hill, a property he eloquently described as being 'set in enameled meadows, with filigree hedges'. I doubt if the urbane Walpole did the milking himself because experience and strong wrists are required for making syllabub 'under the cow'. The idea is to achieve a natural froth, which forms only in a strong stream. Nevertheless, the image of Horace nestled into the flank of a cow while dressed in one of his favoured lavender suits is very appealing.

In her eighteenth-century classic, *The Art of Cookery Made Plain and Easy,* Hannah Glasse gave instructions for making the drink 'from the cow': 'Make your Syllabub of either Cyder or Wine, sweeten it pretty sweet, and grate nutmeg in, then Milk the milk into the Liquor.' She pointed out that if the syllabub was being made at home the milk should be the same temperature as from the cow and that a froth could be achieved by pouring it from a teapot, 'holding your Hand very high'. In the following, more modern recipe, the froth is achieved with a whisk:

WHYPT SYLLABUB

juice and rind of 2 lemons
300 ml (½ pint) sweet white wine such as sherry or Madeira
1 tablespoon sugar
300 ml (½ pint) whipping cream
freshly ground nutmeg

Infuse the wine with the whole lemon rind for several hours then remove. Put the rest of the ingredients into a bowl and whisk until well frothed. Pour into glasses and leave until the wine and the cream separate.

The Druid's Head Tavern back in Kingston claims to have been one of the first places to sell syllabub, in the seventeenth century. I was disappointed to find that it no longer appears on their menu, which seems rather short-sighted. I will judge this book an unqualified success if it suddenly reappears!

Satirist and poet Alexander Pope was another celebrated resident of Twickenham. He was born in 1688 and grew up in the village of Binfield, south of Windsor, where oddly enough he was attacked by a cow while playing in neighbouring fields as a toddler. The animal tore off his feathered bonnet with its horns and wounded him in the throat. He made a full recovery but with great bad luck he subsequently contracted Pott's disease, a tubercular infection contracted through cows' milk. The infection weakened and twisted his spine, leaving him hunch-backed and only 4 ft 6 in (1.3 m) tall. Pope suffered from severe headaches and physical discomfort for the rest of his life, which may have sharpened his acerbic wit. Someone once compared his glittering couplets to crystal drops of water as opposed to Shakespeare's raging torrents. A contemporary, Lady Mary Montague, dubbed him 'The wicked asp of Twickenham', although it seems there were occasions when, like the rest of us, he struggled for inspiration:

You beat your pate and fancy wit will come,
Knock as you please, there's nobody at home.

His wry comment on gossip still resonates 300 years on:

And all who told it added something new,
And all who heard it, made enlargements too.

Pope's Thames-side villa was sometimes marooned by floodwaters, with small fish conveniently delivering themselves to the kitchen via the drains. During a spell of particularly wet weather in 1720, he cheerfully compared his home to Noah's Ark. The poet is credited with growing England's first weeping willow in his garden at Twickenham. Willows are native to China but spread westward with the trade caravans to the Middle East, then finally on to Europe. Around 1730 Pope planted a willow twig broken from a woven basket of figs received from Turkey by his friend and neighbour the Countess of Suffolk. The twig took root and its descendants eventually spread along the riverbanks. Thames Path walkers should be grateful they did so because there is no more beautiful scene than willows dipping into a quiet curve of the river.

The *pièce de résistance* of Pope's garden was its famous grotto, built as a tunnel under Cross Deep Road, which dissected his property. It was decorated with Cornish diamonds, gold ore, amethysts, sea-shells, corals and multi-coloured crystals. Pope described it as follows:

From the river Thames you can see through an ivy arch, up a walk of the wilderness, to a kind of Temple wholly composed of shells in the rustic manner; and from the distance, under the temple, you look down through a sloping arcade of trees and see the sails on the river passing suddenly and vanishing, as through a perspective glass. When you shut the door of this grotto, it becomes in the instant, from a luminous room, a camera obscura, on the walls of which all the objects of the river, hills, woods and boats, are forming a moving picture in their visible radiations.

The grotto, sadly stripped of its splendour, now lies under St James Independent School for Boys. It can be visited by appointment on Saturday mornings. Pope's grave in Twickenham Church is simply marked with the letter P, but he did compose epitaphs for himself, including the following:

Under this Marble, or under this Sill,
Or under this Turf, or e'en what they will;
Whatever an heir, or a friend in his stead,
Or any good creature shall lay o'er my head;
Lies He who ne'er car'd, and still cares not a Pin,
What they said, or may say of the Mortal within.
But who living and dying, serene still and free,
Trusts in God, that as well as he was, he shall be.

Despite the sentiments expressed in the lines, Pope really did care where he was buried. He wanted to lie in Westminster Abbey but since he was a Roman Catholic it was impossible. Perhaps he should have claimed a connection to the 'Pope' family of Vatican City, with a view to burial in the equally impressive St Peter's Basilica.

By the footbridge to Twickenham's Eel Pie Island is a pub called the Barmy Arms, no doubt a mecca for the self-styled Barmy Army, which supports England's test cricket team so

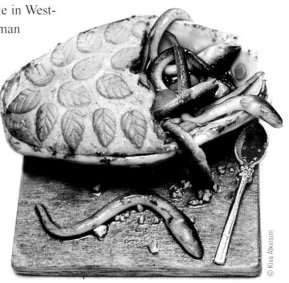

© Kva Atkinson

Not for the faint-hearted! A wacky eel pie in miniature

enthusiastically, especially when playing for the Ashes against Australia. Eel Pie Island is where Mistress Mayo sold her famous pies to Henry VIII. The island later became a favourite destination for Victorian day-trippers with a taste for eels and ale. The Eel Pie pub in Church Road sells pies and in the interest of research I felt obliged to try one. To my relief I discovered they now contain meat, eels being rather scarce.

The house in the bend of river beyond Eel Pie Island is Marble Hill House. It was built in 1723 for Henrietta Howard, mistress of the Prince of Wales (the future George II), who picked up the construction bill of £12,000. Henrietta had a bad start in life. Her father was killed in a duel when she was a child and she was only thirteen when her mother died. She became lady of the bedchamber to Caroline, the Princess of Wales, but began to spend far more time in the Prince's bedchamber. Eventually George grew tired of his mistress and allowed Caroline to dismiss her, but at least Henrietta ended up in a beautiful house, with an enviable view across the river to Richmond Hill.

RICHMOND TO PUTNEY

Richmond Bridge is now London's oldest. It was built between 1774 and 1777 to replace a horse ferry, which ran between Ferry Hill and Twickenham for 300 years. Its construction was funded by Tontine Shares. Shareholders received a percentage of the bridge tolls (initially a halfpenny for a pedestrian, a penny for a wheelbarrow!) until he or she died. Their shares were then distributed among the living until only one person remained; presumably very old and very rich.

Just below the newly built bridge was a mansion called Heron Court, owned by the Duke of Queensberry. In 1808 the Duke loaned this house to Emma Hamilton, who was in dire financial straits following the death of her lover Horatio Nelson three years earlier. Emma lived at Heron Court with Horatia, her illegitimate daughter by Lord Nelson, until creditors forced her into a debtor's prison in London. Young Horatia probably enjoyed feeding the swans in the river but the world-weary Duke of Queensberry considered the Thames rather tedious, famously complaining: 'There it goes – flow, flow, flow, always the same.' It was rumoured that 'Old Q' enlivened his summer at Richmond by arranging rather spicy entertainment involving young ladies.

Richmond Bridge has a romantic association with Vincent van Gogh. When the artist first visited England in 1873, he boarded with a Mrs Loyer of Lambeth, and fell in love with her daughter Eugenie. Unfortunately Vincent was so shy that the girl hadn't the faintest idea of his feelings. Heartbroken when she became engaged to another lodger, he took to wearing one of her earrings as a badge of lost love. Three years later van Gogh returned to England and lived at Holme Court in Twickenham Road. Eventually he threw the earring into the Thames from the bridge. I once poked around with a stick trying to find it, but the only fission of excitement came when I fished out the ring pull from a soft-drink can.

Something far more grisly was hurled from the bridge six years later. Following an argument on 2 March 1879 in her home at 2 Mayfield Cottages, a fifty-five-year-old local widow, Mrs Julia Martha Thomas, was pushed downstairs by her servant Catherine (Kate) Webster. Irish-born Webster then panicked and strangled her mistress. In an effort to hamper identification she boiled the body in a copper and dismembered it with a razor and saw. She then dumped a box of remains in the Thames but unluckily for her it was retrieved by a passer-by the following day, a mile downstream at Barnes. The head was missing but police found other proof of identity and Webster was convicted of murder at the Old Bailey:

The terrible crime at Richmond at last,
On Catherine Webster now has been cast.
Tried and found guilty she is sentenced to die,
From the strong hand of justice she cannot fly.

Webster, who had previously served time for theft, was hanged at Wandsworth prison on 29 July 1879.

In October 2010 the skull of a middle-aged woman was unearthed during construction of an extension to the home of Sir David Attenborough, next door to Mayfield Cottages. It was found while workmen were excavating the site of a pub frequented by Webster known as The Hole in the Wall. Exhaustive tests were carried out, revealing fractures consistent with a fall downstairs. More significantly, there was a low collagen level: a grisly indication that the skull had been boiled! In July 2011 the coroner declared: 'Putting all the circumstantial evidence together there is clear, convincing and compelling evidence that this is Julia Martha Thomas.'

Sir David Attenborough travels the world, but a skull unearthed in his own backyard solved a 130-year-old murder!

In Paradise Road at Richmond, a blue plaque marks Hogarth House, where Leonard and Virginia Woolf lived for nine years. The couple chose Paradise Road because it was close enough to the railway station for easy retreats to Bloomsbury. They set up the Hogarth Press here in April 1917. It was a very successful venture, though not without teething troubles. Virginia wrote to her sister Vanessa Bell: 'Our press arrived on Tuesday. We unpacked it with enormous excitement, finally with Nelly's help, carried it into the drawing room, set it on its stand and discovered it was smashed in half!' Among the first books to roll off the Hogarth Press was Virginia Woolf's own *Kew Gardens*.

During peace celebrations at the end of the First World War, Virginia walked up Richmond Hill to watch the fireworks. In her diary she wrote:

Rising over the Thames, among trees, these rockets were beautiful; the lights on the faces of the crowd was strange; yet of course there was a grey mist muffling everything and taking the blaze off the fire.

It was at this point on our original walk that we were joined by Harleyford neighbour Bill Wilson, who had dropped us off at Cricklade in readiness for our long walk down to Oxford. Since then we had talked so incessantly about the Thames Path that Bill realized the only way to shut us up was to join in. He would eventually accompany us on the final stretch from Westminster to the Flood Barrier, but we suggested a wander through Richmond and Kew as an introduction. Anxious that he should enjoy the experience, we began by following in Virginia Woolf's footsteps and climbing Richmond Hill for a glorious view over Petersham Meadows to the river. Afterwards we visited the remains of Richmond Palace.

The palace was built in 1498 by Henry VII, on the site of an earlier royal residence. Henry died at Richmond Palace in 1509 and in 1603 Queen Elizabeth I also died there, apparently from septic tonsils. There is a story that at the moment of the Queen's death, a sapphire ring was removed from her finger and thrown down to a horseman who rode flat out to Edinburgh to deliver it to James IV of Scotland as a signal that he was now James I, King of England. The journey took sixty-two hours, with the rider, Robert Carey, greeting the King in a bloodied state after a bad fall and a kick in the head from his horse. The accident had occurred 97 miles (156 km) south of Edinburgh.

While we were at the ruins, a resident came out of a nearby house to chat. She told us that Elizabeth died on a pile of cushions in a room above the palace gateway, after refusing to take to her bed. The story may be true, although it is suspiciously convenient for tourism that the red brick gateway is all that remains!

The old Queen's final journey down the Thames from Richmond moved a contemporary poet to write:

The Queen was brought by water to Whitehall
At every stroke the oars did tears let fall:
More clung about the barge, fish under water
Wept out their eyes of pearl and swum blind after.

The moment of Elizabeth I's mother's death is remembered in Richmond Park. By Richmond Gate is a mound on which Henry VIII is said to have stood on the morning of 19 May 1536, waiting for smoke to rise from the Tower of London as a sign the executioner's axe had fallen on Anne Boleyn. At noon, the signal came. Satisfied that 'adulteress' Anne was safely dispatched, the King also rode hard, not to Scotland but to Wiltshire, where with unseemly haste he married his lady-in-waiting, Jane Seymour. Soon after the couple's marriage, the fiery four-year-old Elizabeth, conscious of a loss of status, snapped: 'How hap it was yesterday Lady Princess and today but Lady Elizabeth?' When one considers her father's unfortunate marital record, it is little wonder she chose to remain single.

Incidentally, Richmond's connection with royalty and with Henry VIII in particular caused great distress for an ex-colleague of mine. Madeleine grew up in the borough just after the Second World War and as a plump schoolgirl in a box-pleated tunic she was dubbed Henry VIII by her brother. His cruel taunts prompted Madeleine to trade her uniform for a goldfish, courtesy of the local rag-and-bone man. The uniform was retrieved next day by her furious mother and the goldfish died almost as promptly. Fortunately Madeleine has other, happier memories of her childhood in Richmond. She spent hours paddling in the river and loved visiting her artist uncle, who worked in a studio above an old boatyard.

Richmond Palace's Tudor gateway opens onto Richmond Green, now a very exclusive residential area. Its row of perfectly preserved Georgian terraces is known as Maids of Honour Row. The terraces were built for the ladies who attended Queen Caroline, wife of George II. If Henrietta Howard had not caught the eye of King George, she may well have ended up here, overlooking the green, instead of at Marble Hill House overlooking the Thames. The green began as a sheep field but with the arrival of royalty it became a medieval jousting ground. The lance-thrusting jousters may have long gone but on lazy summer Sundays there is entertainment from bat-wielding village cricketers. Nearby, Richmond's ancient monastic communities are remembered in Retreat Road and Friars Lane.

Richmond Park was first enclosed by Charles I in 1637 to indulge his passion for deer and game hunting. Around 1751, George II appointed his youngest daughter Princess Amelia as park ranger and she immediately alienated the local people by denying access to the park to all but her friends. A local brewer called John Lewis managed to obtain a court order against the Princess, forcing her to place public ladder stiles on boundary walls. You have to admire the wretched woman's cleverness because she deliberately had the rungs spaced so far apart that only a long-legged few were able to climb them. After further legal action she was forced to have the ladders amended so that even old women and children could enter the park.

Before venturing too much further, we should return to the northern or Middlesex bank, where the Thames Path has continued past Marble Hill Park to Isleworth. A ferry still takes passengers across to Richmond on weekends between May and September. The church at Isleworth was almost completely rebuilt after being destroyed by fire in 1943, not by a Second World War bomb but by two schoolboys armed with a box of matches. The fourteenth-century tower is all that remains of the original building.

The existing house at nearby Syon Park was built for the Northumberland family on the site of a nunnery dissolved by Henry VIII. The foundations of the nunnery were discovered by television's archeological show, *Time Team*. When King Henry died his coffin was rested at Syon Park on its way to burial at Windsor Castle. Allegedly, the coffin burst open during the night and next morning dogs were found licking at his bloated remains. There were mutterings that the desecration was an appropriate retribution for the dissolution of the abbey. The relatives of Henry's fifth wife might have felt a sense of satisfaction too, because the King had Catherine Howard imprisoned at Syon Park before she was beheaded. The house has some wonderful rooms created by the eighteenth-century architect and designer Robert Adam. It was used as a setting for the film, *The Madness of King George.*

Across the Thames is Kew, and its 121-hectare (300-acre) gardens, containing more than 40,000 plant species from around the world. As the eighteenth-century poet Erasmus Darwin wrote:

> *So sits enthroned in vegetable pride*
> *Imperial Kew by Thames's glittering side;*
> *Obedient sails from realms unfurrowed bring*
> *For her the unnamed progeny of spring;*

The gardens became famous during the reign of George III, when the botanist Sir Joseph Banks was acting as unofficial director. (Banks had been with Captain James Cook when he sailed into Botany Bay, New South Wales, in 1770.) Kew Gardens is worth visiting all year round and requires a full day to do it justice. In winter there are usually a few Australian tourists standing like potted plants in the Palm House, eyes glazing in pleasure as their blood thaws. The Refreshment Pavilion is a pleasant place to linger too, although it became a little too hot in February 1913, when angry Suffragettes burned it to the ground. Two natural disasters have also created havoc at the gardens. In 1879 a severe hailstorm broke 40,000 panes of greenhouse glass and in the great storm of 1987 hundreds of historic trees were destroyed. By the way, children will enjoy some of the bizarre exhibits in the gardens' museum. Illustrating the versatility of plant material are a set of rubber false teeth, a cork hat, and a shirt made from pineapple fibre.

The English naturalist Edith Holden, who wrote and so beautifully illustrated *The Country Diary of an Edwardian Lady,* drowned in the Thames at Kew at the age of forty-nine. On 16 March 1920 she fell into the river near Kew Gardens Walk while trying to hook buds from a chestnut tree with the handle of her umbrella. In 1977, after lying undiscovered for many years, the 1906 diary was published in facsimile.

Located close to the gardens on Kew Road is the Maids of Honour Teashop. According to legend, Maids of Honour tarts were so named because Henry VIII came upon Anne Boleyn and her ladies enjoying them at Richmond, courtesy of Anne's predecessor

Catherine of Aragon's pastry cook. The tarts were first made commercially in 1750 by Thomas Burdekin, at his premises on Richmond's Hill Street. Alfred Newans is said to have paid £1,000 for the recipe in 1887 and the tearooms at Kew are still run by his descendants. You can try the tarts on the premises with a pot of tea or take some away for a picnic in the gardens. The original recipe remains a closely guarded secret but there have been many attempts to replicate it.

We took a break for morning tea at the Maids of Honour Teashop but Manchester-born Bill rejected the tarts out of hand. As a northerner he has a prejudice against flaky pastry as opposed to no-nonsense suet crust. However, I love the tarts' delicate almond flavour and hint of nutmeg. Having made them myself, I lean towards an alternative theory about the name; that it was inspired by the soft fillings that 'bob' in a curtsey as they are taken from the oven.

MAIDS OF HONOUR TARTS

250 g (8 oz) puff pastry
250 g (8 oz) ground almonds
125 g (4 oz) caster sugar
2 beaten eggs
30 g (1 oz) flour
4 tablespoons double cream
good pinch ground nutmeg
2 teaspoons lemon juice
sifted icing sugar to decorate

Preheat oven to 200°C (400°F). Grease and flour 20 patty tins. Roll out pastry on lightly floured board and line the tins, trimming the edges. Mix together the ground almonds and sugar, stir in beaten eggs, flour, cream, nutmeg and lemon juice. Divide between the pastry cases and bake for about 15 minutes. Turn onto a wire rack and let cool a little before serving, dredged with icing sugar.

Kew's St Anne's Church was built on a disused gravel pit after permission was granted by Queen Anne in 1714. It was extended in 1770 and a few more times after that as the population of the parish grew. Inside the church is a monument to the eighteenth-century painter Thomas Gainsborough, whose grave is located on the south side of the churchyard. The pall-bearers at his funeral were six fellow artists, including Joshua Reynolds. Gainsborough did not actually live in Kew but spent a lot of time there, staying with his daughter or with his friend and fellow painter, Joshua Kirby.

GAINSBOROUGH TART

175 g (6 oz) shortcrust pastry
2 tablespoons raspberry jam
25 g (1 oz) butter
1 egg
50 g (2 oz) caster sugar
100 g (4 oz) desiccated coconut
¼ teaspoon baking powder

Line a 20 cm (8 in) sandwich tin with the pastry and spread with the jam.
Melt the butter, stir in the beaten egg, sugar, coconut and baking powder
and pour into the pastry case. Bake at 180°C (350°F) for about 30 minutes.

Running off Kew Green is Ferry Lane, named for a long-vanished ferry which once crossed the river to Brentford. The lane now ends at a car park, but there is more to this seemingly unromantic spot than meets the eye. Under the tarmac lies the lawn on which Queen Elizabeth I is said to have had secret assignations with her lover, Lord Leicester.

Today, Kew Bridge links the Surrey bank with Brentford, where the Grand Union Canal enters the Thames. For a brief while the Thames path actually takes advantage of the canal towpath. A Civil War memorial at Brentford commemorates the Battle of Brentford, which took place on 11 November 1642, when Royalist forces were advancing on the capital. The King's men were victorious, but it was the closest to London they ever got. A Royalist soldier left a colourful account of a counter attack by the Parliamentarians the following day, when the enemy approached Brentford via the Thames:

That night most lay in the cold fields. Next morning we were startled afresh by the loud music of some canon … We sank four of five of their vessels with the canon in them, took the rest and eight pieces in them, for our breakfast.

However, with winter closing in and London heavily defended, the Royalists were soon forced to withdraw and King Charles subsequently established his headquarters at Oxford. I love the soldier's quip about eating enemy ships for breakfast but in reality Civil War troops were likely to begin the day with a piece of hard cheese, a rasher of bacon and some unleavened bread.

Nearby is Strand-on-the-Green, one of the best-preserved riverside communities on the river, with its row of early-eighteenth-century almshouses. There are some great pubs here as well, including The Bull's Head and The City Barge.

Downstream by Chiswick Bridge there is a view across the Thames to the old Mortlake Brewery. When we drove down from Harleyford to walk the south bank between Mortlake and Putney, Rob parked in the lane between the brewery and the Ship Inn. As we walked under the arches of Chiswick Bridge a flock of low-flying Canada geese skimmed the river, passing under the central arch in full voice and in perfect formation.

The Ship Inn is a popular spot for watching the finish of the annual Oxford and Cambridge boat race, which begins at Putney, 4 miles (6.4 km) downstream. In 2003 Oxford beat Cambridge by 1 ft (30 cm), the closest margin in the history of the race apart from a controversial 'dead heat' in 1877. The judge that year was John Phelps, who was allegedly asleep as the boats crossed the line. He woke in a befuddled state to declare the race 'a dead heat to Oxford by four feet'. There are not always two boats at the finish. In 1984 Cambridge struck a barge and sank before the race was underway and in a strange coincidence, both crews sank during a gale in 1912, the year the *Titanic* went down.

In 2012, for the first time in the race's 158-year history, proceedings were disrupted by a rogue swimmer. Claiming he was protesting against 'elitism', the Australian (yes, I'm afraid so) swam directly into the path of the boats, which were heading for a climactic finish, although Oxford had a slight edge. Olympic rower Sir Matthew Pinsent was helping officiate and spotted the interloper, who had to be dragged out. The race was halted for half an hour. After it restarted Oxford veered into the Cambridge crew and snapped an oar. Cambridge then cruised to an easy victory but celebrations were muted as Oxford's bowman had pushed himself too hard trying to compensate for the loss of an oarsman. He collapsed unconscious and was rushed to hospital. It was a race to be remembered for all the wrong reasons.

The towpath continues under Barnes railway bridge to Barnes Terrace. In a book called *Down the Thames* published in 1949, Martin Briggs wrote about the area and noted sadly: 'Barnes Terrace, the only distinctive feature close to the Thames, is now so shabby and so much damaged by bombing that its half-dozen old houses still standing are unlikely to survive much longer.' Happily they did survive, complete with their charming bow windows and balconies.

In 1812 one of the houses here, D'Antraigues, was the scene of a dramatic double murder and suicide. A French count and his wife had been living at the house but decided to leave Barnes without taking the count's Italian valet with them. In a tragic overreaction, the valet stepped into the departing coach, shot the count, stabbed the countess, then killed himself as well.

One of Barnes' most well-known residents is Tim Henman, that ever-so-nice English tennis player who so valiantly tried to win Wimbledon for many years while carrying the weight of a nation on his shoulders. Tim's local pub, the Sun Inn, was regularly dubbed the Henman Arms for the duration of the tournament. In 2003 the BBC visited the pub and attached a heart-rate monitor to a fan watching Tim play in the quarter-finals. The man's stress level rose alarmingly before his hero bowed out and there is no doubt that if and when the next Englishman wins Wimbledon, the entire country will be in need of resuscitation.

The river loops around to Barnes Elms and just a short stroll from the towpath is a 100-acre (40-hectare) wetland centre. Thirty different habitats have been established around a number of redundant reservoirs, supporting 130 species of bird and a wide range of butterflies and amphibians. An observatory overlooks the main lake and there are six hides for serious birdwatchers. It is a very special place, particularly as it is so accessible to Londoners.

When we walked from Mortlake to Putney, the Thames was exceptionally high. I thought we might have to roll up our jeans and wade through at one stage. On the opposite bank at Chiswick, weeping willows were looking less than their elegant best. Their long skirts were floating around their knees in soggy bunches and becoming entangled with plastic bags and lunch wrappers.

Chiswick's Church Street is one of London's most charming. At the river end is the Old Burlington, a fifteenth-century pub now retired from duty. The parish church is dedicated to the patron saint of fishermen, St Nicholas. It was heavily restored in Victorian times but its fifteenth-century tower remains intact. The holy water stoup was dredged from the Thames and is thought to have been a Roman grinding stone. Regrettably, other treasures became

© Shutterstock

Oliver Cromwell. Does his headless body lie in Chiswick's St Nicholas church?

early victims of theft. In 1552, a valuable plate was 'stowlin out of the church' leaving only '2 brass potts and 4 pewter dyshes'.

In the Fauconberg vault buried beneath the chancel of St Nicholas lies Lady Fauconberg, third daughter of Oliver Cromwell. An unidentified, shorter tomb may hold the headless body of her father. Cromwell died from natural causes and was originally buried in West-minster Abbey. However, old enemies exhumed the corpse and carried out a belated 'execution' at Tyburn Gallows. His head was retrieved and treated with extreme disrespect; it was eventually buried in a secret location at Cambridge University. There is a possibility that family members were able to save the rest of the body for burial. No doubt there will be a push to exhume poor old Oliver again soon, with the aim of matching head and body through DNA samples. The records at St Nicholas date back to 1622 and ironically it was Cromwell's soldiers who are said to have burned the earlier ones to keep themselves warm while occupying the church. In 1656 an entry reads:

Pay'd Goody Blake 1/6 pence for cleaninge ye church after ye soldiers.

The old churchyard wall also survives at Chiswick along with a small plaque noting that it was built in 1623 to keep pigs out. The wall encloses the tomb of eighteenth-century engraver and artist William Hogarth who spent his summers at Chiswick. Hogarth satirized the vices and manners of his age in works such as 'A Rake's Progress' and 'Marriage à-la-Mode'.

There are some elegant residences at Chiswick although William III managed to damn one with faint praise. While visiting Sir Stephen Fox at Manor Farm House he commented: 'This place is perfectly fine. I could live here five days!' Of course His Majesty did have Hampton Court and Windsor Castle to go home to. Walpole House in Chiswick Mall was built on the site of the home of the Duchess of Cleveland (1641–1709), mistress of Charles II and mother of several of his children. Her colourful love life is said to have included an affair with a rope dancer, which conjures some interesting images. The Duchess may have shocked people during her lifetime but nevertheless her coffin was carried to the church by two dukes, with four peers of the realm acting as pall-bearers. Walpole House later became a school, attended by the writer William Thackeray. In his novel *Vanity Fair*, Thackeray used the school as the model for Miss Pinkerton's Academy for Young Ladies. It was here the capricious Becky Sharp famously threw Miss Pinkerton's parting gift, a copy of *Dr Johnson's Dictionary*, into the garden as she drove off in a carriage. I have never quite forgiven her for this act of sacrilege.

Beyond Chiswick Mall a boundary stone marks the entrance to Hammersmith, where William Morris lived and worked at Kelmscott House, named after his much-loved manor on the upper reaches of the Thames. Hammersmith suspension bridge is an ornate Victorian confection in green and gold. It was built by Sir Joseph Bazalgette in 1887 and in a former

© Rob Conolly

Beautiful Hammersmith Bridge, still straddling the Thames despite numerous terrorist attacks

life it was painted brown and cream, prompting locals to dub it 'the coffee cake'. For some reason terrorists have targeted Hammersmith Bridge. The IRA tried to blow it up in 1939, but were foiled by a passer-by. Chiswick resident Maurice Childs was walking across the bridge late one night when he saw smoke and sparks coming from a suitcase. I am not sure whether to label Maurice brave or foolish, but he opened the case and discovered a bomb, which he sensibly hurled into the water. The bomb exploded harmlessly, sending up a spectacular column of water. A second, undiscovered bomb went off a few minutes later, badly damaging some girders.

On 26 April 1996, terrorists planted 40 lb (18 kg) of explosive on the south side of the bridge. On this occasion only the detonators went off but the attempt sent chills through Londoners because a full blast would have caused enormous damage to nearby flats, as well as destroying the bridge. In 2000 it came under attack yet again. At 4.30 a.m. on 31 May, a bomb attached to a girder on the Barnes side exploded. Thankfully it was much smaller, causing only 'severe local damage'. Surveillance cameras have since been installed, providing some comfort to locals and also to walkers following the Thames Path under the bridge.

Downstream, Putney Bridge was also built by Bazalgette. As at many crossing points on the river, there was once a ferry here, followed by a wooden toll bridge. In November 1796 while distressed over her lover Gilbert Imlay's affair with an actress, the writer and early feminist Mary Wollstonecraft tried to commit suicide by jumping off the bridge. The attempt appears to have been a serious one because she stood in torrential rain until her heavy clothing was soaked, so that she would sink more easily. In a note left for Imlay she wrote: 'When you receive this, my burning head will be cold … I shall plunge into the Thames where there is least chance of my being snatched from the death I seek.' But Mary was rescued by a sharp-eyed passer-by. Bram Stoker, author of the horror story *Dracula,* also dragged a drowning person from the river. Apparently the man was still breathing when he was laid out on Stoker's kitchen table at Chelsea but died before medical help arrived. Unfortunately Mrs Stoker, who was unaware of the incident, walked in to be confronted with a dead body. In this case the horror was all too real and the Stokers quickly moved out. About seventy bodies are recovered from the Thames every year, most being the result of suicide.

Another major milestone on the Thames Path is reached at Putney. The towpath, which began back at Lechlade in Gloucestershire, finally comes to an end. A loading slipway remains as a reminder of all the cargo hauled upriver by the barge teams.

There was a touch of the surreal about the outdoor cafe we visited in Putney High Street at the end of our day's walk. We were drinking cappuccinos in cups the size of soup tureens when I glanced at the seat beside me and saw an inch-high gnome standing on a mound of gold coins. I hope no one turned up to claim him because I put him in my pocket and took him back to Australia, where he lives under a tree fern in our garden. The gold coins did not make it that far. They were full of chocolate and we ate them on the way home while planning our next walk, through Wandsworth and Battersea to Lambeth.

WANDSWORTH TO BATTERSEA

The Thames Path negotiates the mouth of the River Wandle then passes a recycling centre and huge waste-transfer station. Barges still ply the river here, loaded with refuse bound for landfill sites in Essex. Ahead is Wandsworth Bridge. Early last century a very rare 'Thames Treasure' turned up in mud by the bridge. It was a completely intact Iron Age dagger, though sadly not intact for very long. The man who found it was forcing the dagger from its sheath when the hilt came off in his hand. Worse still, he threw the hilt back into the river! The remainder eventually found its way to the British Museum but I doubt if experts were consoled until a wonderful example with bronze hilt and sheath was taken from the Thames at Cookham.

Approaching Battersea, the spire of eighteenth-century St Mary's Church appears. Tap the right flagstone in the crypt and you will hear a hollow sound, as a tunnel runs from St Mary's to Chelsea, across the river. It was funded by members of St Mary's congregation who lived at Chelsea and were tired of the outrageous fees charged by ferrymen. The tunnel was sealed during the Second World War for security reasons. There is a monument in the church to Sir Edward Wynter, soldier and adventurer. Sir Edward died in 1685 and his epitaph records deeds of heroic proportions:

Alone, unarm'd, a tyger he opressed,
And crushed to death the monster of a beast;
Twice twenty Moors he also overthrew,
Single on foot; some wounded; some he slew
Dispersed the rest. What more could Sampson do?

Not much really.

The poet William Blake came to St Mary's in 1782 to marry Catherine, daughter of a local market gardener. The couple's wedding certificate is held at the church, signed by William but with a cross from Catherine, who was illiterate. Later the painter Turner would visit, to sit in the bay window of the vestry and paint his studies of clouds and sunsets over the river.

St Mary's tunnel emerged on the north bank at Chelsea's Cremorne Pier, where pleasure-seeking Londoners once disembarked to visit Cremorne Gardens. Spectacular events were organized for their entertainment, such as a young woman crossing the Thames on a tightrope. In 1852 the owner, Monsieur Poitevon, went that little bit too far. He harnessed a blindfolded bull to a hot-air balloon and had his wife ride the bucking beast side-saddle as it sailed across town to Ilford. The bull landed safely with Madame Poitevon and was led away by its gilded horns to recover in a stable. However, Poitevon was summonsed by the RSPCA. The public often went too far as well, consuming huge quantities of alcohol and indulging in illicit sex. Cremorne Gardens closed in 1877 because of its unsavoury reputation. Perhaps in gratitude for the profits they had made, a local brewery salvaged the magnificent entrance gates. They have now been restored and reinstated at what remains of the pleasure grounds: a tiny patch of green.

Before venturing deeper into Chelsea we visited neighbouring Fulham. A triangle formed by Fulham High Street, New King's Road and Burlington Road was the location for the Fulham Pottery, which operated for over 300 years. It was established by John Dwight in 1671 after he was granted a patent by Charles II for 'the mistery and invencion of making transparent earthenware …' No doubt the King was anxious to encourage such enterprise as London was still recovering from the Great Fire of 1666 in which some 13,000 houses had been destroyed, along with their contents. A site so close to the Thames was ideal for transporting Dwight's household goods to the city.

The country's social history can be traced in the Pottery's output; from seventeenth-century hunting mugs to Victorian blacking bottles and stoneware hot-water bottles. During the First World War, the company produced containers for the rum issued to soldiers fighting in the trenches of France. The Pottery closed in 1986, but examples of its work can be seen at Fulham's Archives and Local History Centre.

Back at Cremorne Gardens a right-hand turn takes the Thames Path into Chelsea's Cheyne Walk, where blue plaques mark the homes of many famous writers and artists. Before the writer Thomas Carlyle moved to No. 5 (now No. 24) Cheyne Row in 1834, he described Chelsea to his wife Jane as 'a singular, heterogeneous kind of spot, very dirty and confused in some places, quite beautiful in others, abounding with antiquities and the traces of great men'. Jane responded with a word of caution about the proximity of their prospective home to the Thames: 'But is it not too near the river? I should fear it would be a very foggy situation in the winter, and always damp and unwholesome.' However she was very taken by the fact that it had a small room shelved ready for china. It was in this china closet that a servant girl gave birth while an oblivious Carlyle took tea in the adjoining room. The baby was smuggled out of the house at night.

J. M. W. Turner was another famous resident of Chelsea. Never particularly sociable, he became even more reclusive in old age and took to calling himself Admiral Booth. Appropriately enough for a self-styled 'naval man', he lived almost exclusively on a mixture of rum and milk, probably because he had lost most of his teeth. Turner died in 1851, overlooking the Thames. According to the doctor who attended him on his last morning, the sun suddenly broke through clouds and flooded the room. It was the perfect farewell for an artist who had spent his life capturing light in all its moods.

Writer George Eliot's stay at 4 Cheyne Walk was tragically brief. In 1880, two years after her lover George Lewes died, Eliot married John Cross. The couple moved to Chelsea, believing the riverside village would benefit her failing health, but nineteen days later she caught a chill and died. Virginia Woolf attributed Eliot's death to her brave and unceasing struggle for knowledge and freedom: 'the body, weighed with its double burden sank worn out.' John Cross was left to grieve in the house which, as he put it, 'we had meant to be so happy in'.

No. 16 Cheyne Walk became the home of another widower, Dante Gabriel Rossetti, after his wife, Elizabeth (Lizzie) Siddal died. In 1852 Lizzie had become Rossetti's pupil, lover and model. Her background was humble and it was said she was introduced to literature by reading lines by Tennyson on the wrapping paper from a pound of butter. The couple did not marry until 1860 and within two years Lizzie was dead. Always delicate, she had become addicted to laudanum and died from the drug aged thirty-two, when she and Rossetti were living by the Thames near Blackfriars Bridge. Rossetti placed all the love poems he had written to his wife in her coffin; a grand gesture, though diminished by the fact that seven years later he thought better of it and had them dug up and published.

When Rossetti moved to Cheyne Walk he lavished attention on his house and held parties in a garden full of unusual pets. The actress Ellen Terry wrote of seeing a white bull tethered on the lawn, and there was a flock of shrieking peacocks which terrorized the neighbours. The interior of the house must have resembled a scene from *Alice in Wonderland*, with dormice perched on tiny bamboo chairs and Rossetti's pet wombat being allowed to sit at the dining-room table. Sadly, the wombat squandered any chance of improving the image of the uncouth Australian when it ate a guest's hat.

In 1717 the equally eccentric Don Saltero moved his well-known coffee house to 18 Cheyne Walk. Saltero operated one of London's first private museums. A catalogue printed in 1709 included the following curiosities: Mary Queen of Scot's pin cushion, Queen Elizabeth's strawberry dish, a pair of nun's stockings, a starved cat found between the walls of Westminster Abbey, and a necklace made of Job's tears. Displaying a healthy scepticism, Richard Steele wrote of Don in *Tatler*: 'He shows you a straw hat, which I know to be made by Madge Peskad within 3 miles of Bedford; and tells you, "It is Pontius Pilate's wife's chambermaid's sister's hat."' In his defence, Saltero did not claim to be a serious antiquarian.

He called himself a 'gimcrack whim collector', which was probably a fair description, despite the fact that some of his treasures are said to have ended up in the British Museum. One day I am going to visit the museum and ask if it is possible to see Mr Saltero's elf's arrow.

In front of Chelsea Old Church sits the larger-than-life figure of Sir Thomas More, English statesman, humanitarian and Roman Catholic saint. More was beheaded in 1535 for treason, after refusing to support the annulment of Henry VIII's marriage and rejecting the King's religious reforms. Sir Thomas looks formidable in his black robes but I remembered his opposition to the Enclosures that made peasant farmers homeless, and paid my respects on their behalf. Sir Thomas had a lovely home and garden at Chelsea, and while he was languishing in the tower awaiting execution, his politically naïve wife wrote asking why he didn't come home and enjoy it all.

Chelsea has always been my favourite London suburb. I follow Chelsea Football Club and dream of owning a quaint mews house where I could invite the entire team home for tea and Chelsea buns. The buns became famous in the mid eighteenth century. They were made at a bakery in Pimlico Road by Richard Hand, an eccentric character who went about in a dressing gown and a fez. London's fashionable society flocked to Hand's Chelsea Bun House, and among his loyal customers were King George II and Queen Caroline.

CHELSEA BUNS

300 g (10 oz) plain flour
100 g (3 oz) butter
100 g (3 oz) caster sugar
15 g (½ oz) fresh yeast
300 ml (10 fl oz) milk (preferably sour)
2 large eggs
60 g (2 oz) currants
large pinch mixed spice

Warm the flour and sift into a warm basin. Rub in half the butter and add half the sugar. Cream the yeast with 1 teaspoon of sugar. Warm the milk to blood temperature and pour it onto the beaten eggs. Add the yeast. Pour the liquid into the centre of the flour then beat well and allow it to rise for 1½ hours, until double in bulk. Turn onto a floured board. Knead lightly to shape and roll out to a square. Spread with remainder of butter and sprinkle with some of the sugar then fold up. Roll out again and sprinkle with the rest of the sugar, the currants and the spice. Roll up and cut into slices about 4 cm (1.5 in) thick. Stand close together on well-greased, warmed baking tray, cut side down. Prove for 15–20 minutes. Sprinkle with sugar and bake at 230°C (450°F) for about 20 minutes.

The Chelsea Physic Garden was founded in 1673, by the Worshipful Society of Apothecaries. Since then dedicated botanists have gone to great lengths to expand the garden's collection of plants. In 1848, Robert Fortune used miniature greenhouses to transport camellias from China, but my favourite story involves the French botanist Dr Jussieu. Jussieu travelled to Syria and brought back a seedling Cedar of Lebanon, potted up in his hat and kept alive with water from his meagre ship's ration. The traffic in plant material was not all one way, as the first cotton seeds planted in the American south came from the Physic Garden's laboratory. After the gardens closed one afternoon, we watched a little boy with a shrimping net beg to be allowed in to catch some minnows for a school project. We were as pleased as he was when the gate-keeper relented and he was allowed to slip inside.

Ahead is Wren's Royal Hospital, founded as a home for old soldiers in 1682. The hospital's Chelsea Pensioners still wear distinctive eighteenth-century-style uniforms, scarlet in summer, blue in winter. The annual Chelsea Flower Show is held in the grounds of the hospital, and in 1996 Rob and I covered the event for an Australian magazine. The Thames must have been creeping into our consciousness even then because our article featured a prize-winning garden inspired by *Wind in the Willows*. Ratty's cosy riverbank home had been recreated, surrounded by a wild-flower meadow studded with English daisies, cowslips and buttercups. A rowing boat complete with wicker picnic basket bobbed in a miniature Thames. By the way, Mrs Beeton would have approved of Ratty's generous picnic fare (see page 141), although as he explained to a wide-eyed Mole: 'It's only what I always take on these little excursions; and the other animals are always telling me that I'm a mean beast and cut it VERY fine!'

Two bridges link Chelsea with Battersea: Battersea Bridge and Albert Bridge. The latter is pretty enough to have been piped in royal icing by a member of the Women's Institute. It has fine white suspension stays, and panels decorated in pink, pale green and gold. There is no suggestion that the bridge is unsafe, but it is sometimes dubbed 'The Trembling Lady' due to the movement created by soldiers from the Chelsea Barracks as they march across. A sign actually warns approaching troops to break step.

Battersea Park was originally marshland but in 1854 the industrious Victorians built it up with earth excavated during the construction of new docks, further downstream. It was also the Victorians who established Battersea Dogs Home, strongly supported by Charles Dickens. The home makes the justly proud claim that no dog suitable for rehousing is ever put down, regardless of the time required to find a suitable placement. Upriver at Old Windsor there is a country estate which accommodates large breeds, and incorporates a canine maternity home. The British owe a great debt to the Battersea Dogs Home. During the Second World War, some of its inmates were trained to lay cross-country cables under enemy fire, to carry ammunition and to be parachuted into minefields.

Chelsea Bridge lies ahead, convenient for those wishing to pop across the river to see the statue of William Huskisson in Pimlico Gardens. Huskisson was a politician, but is best remembered as the world's first victim of a train accident. The tragedy occurred in 1830 during the official opening of the Liverpool to Manchester rail line. Huskisson was run over by Stephenson's Rocket after leaving his coach, allegedly to make peace with the Duke of Wellington after the pair had fallen out. The Duke was prime minister at the time.

The Thames Path is forced to detour around the still-empty shell of Battersea Power Station. There are now grand plans to transform this building, one of Europe's largest brick structures, into a leisure and residential complex. The power station was designed by Sir Giles Gilbert Scott, who was also responsible for a much smaller but no less famous London structure: the red telephone box.

Downstream, the futuristic headquarters of the overseas intelligence organization, MI6, accommodates the Thames Path with a leafy river terrace. All London's new riverfront properties must provide access for walkers, a heartening positive among the many negatives of the city's constant redevelopment. The terrace continues past a few more office blocks then gives way to the Albert Embankment. Anticipating the next Thames 'village', I embarrassed Rob by launching into my own 'all singing all dancing' version of 'Doing The Lambeth Walk'.

MILLBANK TO EMBANKMENT

Lambeth Bridge replaced an earlier bridge which in turn took over from a horse ferry, remembered by Horseferry Road, across the river in Millbank. Although the ferry was large enough to take a coach and six horses, it could not always cope with the demands placed upon it by Archbishop Laud (1573–1645). On several occasions the ferry sank under the weight of his possessions, which were being transported to Lambeth Palace, home of the Archbishops of Canterbury for more than a thousand years. Laud's High Church policies were a major cause of the Civil War and he was executed in 1645 for his persecution of Puritans. Ironically, the ferry sank again in 1656 with Oliver Cromwell's coach on board.

MI5 have their headquarters at Millbank and I was amused to hear a radio station giving advice on the art of spy spotting. Apparently MI5's top echelon socialize at London's exclusive Travellers Club but the *real* spies pop around the corner to Starbucks, in Horseferry Road. The programme assured listeners that most spies are now female so the idea is to linger over a cup of coffee while keeping your eyes peeled for a young woman muttering into her stiletto.

Millbank Prison was located on the banks of the Thames, constructed in 1816 to house both male and female convicts. A colourful description in *The Criminal Prisons of London* by Mayhew and Binny reads:

> *This immense yellow-brown mass of brickwork is surrounded by a low wall of the same material, above which is seen a multitude of small squarish windows, and a series of diminutive roofs of slate, low like retreating foreheads. There is a systematic irregularity about the in-and-out aspect of the building, which gives it the appearance of a gigantic puzzle; and altogether the Millbank prison may be said to be one of the most successful realizations on a large scale, of the ugly in architecture, being an ungainly combination of the madhouse with the fortress style of building …*

In 1843 Millbank became a holding depot for convicts awaiting transportation. A stone bollard marks the head of steps leading down to the Thames, from where prisoners began their long journey into exile. The prison's surroundings were almost as depressing as the cells, as Charles Dickens noted in *David Copperfield*, published in 1849:

> *The neighbourhood was a dreary one at that time; as oppressive, sad, and solitary by night, as any about London. There were neither wharves nor houses on the melancholy waste of road near the great blank Prison. A sluggish ditch deposited its mud at the prison walls. Coarse glass and rank weeds straggled over all the marshy land in the vicinity.*

My interest in the prison is very personal. Four of my ancestors were held here in 1845 before being sent to the hellish penal colony of Norfolk Island and hence to a probation station in Van Diemen's Land. They were my three times great-grandfather Solomon Shadbolt, my great-great-grandfather George Shadbolt and his Shadbolt cousins Jonathan and Ben, all from Datchworth in Hertfordshire. I cannot pretend they merely stole the proverbial loaf of bread. They were convicted of robbing a widow's drapery shop and the sentencing judge described them as a family of notorious thieves who had baffled the efforts of police for years! Poor old Solomon died just prior to his release. Jonathan disappeared to the goldfields and was never heard of again. My great-great-grandfather George became a successful and highly respected farmer and blacksmith, serving as first superintendent of his local Sunday school. Ben went to New Zealand where he became an extremely rich 'gentleman', though perhaps his wealth was acquired through more nefarious means than the God-fearing George.

In the 1890s Millbank became the home of the Tate Gallery, built on the site of the penitentiary. Following a £30 million redevelopment, it is now known as Tate Britain, displaying British art from the 1500s to the present and continuing to host the annual and often controversial Turner Prize. In 2003 the winner of the competition was Grayson Perry, a happily married transvestite potter who made his acceptance speech wearing a knee-length purple party dress decorated with bows and patterned with rabbits and hearts.

Two minutes' walk from the Gallery, The Morpeth Arms pub was built to slake the thirst of warders from the old gaol. The cellars are believed to be connected to a tunnel from Millbank, dug by convicts desperate to escape. The pub was constructed during 1845, the very year my ancestors were incarcerated. The Shadbolts therefore missed any opportunity of making a break but perhaps this actually saved their lives. A blue plaque notes that The Morpeth Arms is haunted by men who, already weakened by cholera and the other infectious diseases rife among inmates, died in their push for freedom. So frequent are the apparitions that a 'ghost cam' feeds images from the cellars to a screen in the bar.

Back on the south bank beside Lambeth's Tudor gatehouse to the Archbishop's Palace stands the Church of St Mary-at-Lambeth. Located close to the river in Lambeth Palace Road, the church has been converted to The Museum of Gardening History in recognition of the Tradescants, those intrepid travellers whose collection of curiosities formed the nucleus of Oxford's Ashmolean Museum. As father and son gardeners to Charles I and Charles II, they also brought back many garden plants now taken for granted, cultivating them in their Lambeth garden which became known as 'The Ark'. A charming knot garden has been established at St Mary's, containing only those plants available to seventeenth-century English gardeners, such as narcissus, lavender, muscari, violas and iris. There are also culinary and medicinal herbs and fragrant heritage roses.

The churchyard contains the elaborately carved tomb of the Tradescants. I have been unable to determine whether the drowned Hester Pooks Tradescant lies with them but her tormentor Elias Ashmole was definitely buried at St Mary's, though his grave is not on view (see page 54). According to tradition, dancing around the Tradescant tomb as Big Ben strikes midnight will summon up a ghost. I like to think it is the spirit of Hester, making sure Elias does not rest in peace. Mr Ashmole's demise in his mid seventies must have been caused by something drastic because he had previously survived smallpox, swine pox, plague, falling off a roof, falling into a fire, and being kicked in the head by a horse.

Australian visitors might be surprised to find that Admiral William Bligh is also buried here. Best remembered for the mutiny on the *Bounty* and for his harsh governorship of New South Wales, Bligh, like the Tradescants, had a profound knowledge of botany. He collected many specimens for Sir Joseph Banks to preserve and study at Kew Gardens and the inscription on his tomb reads: 'The celebrated navigator who first transplanted the Bread-fruit tree from Otaheite to the West Indies.' However, William Bligh's connection with botany has nothing to do with him being buried near the Tradescants. The admiral was living at Lambeth when his wife Elizabeth died in 1812, and a family plot was established at St Mary's. Bligh died five years later and was buried beside Elizabeth and the couple's day-old twin sons.

Bligh's tomb is made of locally made Coade stone. Around 1769, Mrs Eleanor Coade established a stone factory in Lambeth, where her greatest coup was to obtain the secret formula of an artificial stone, invented by Richard Holt in the early eighteenth century. The material was a mixture of clay, ground glass, flint and sand. It had the advantage of not shrinking when fired, and formed a type of porcelain which was completely weatherproof. When Eleanor died in 1840, the formula died with her and oddly enough scientists have never been able to reproduce it. The stone survives in various monuments around London, including the tomb of Mrs Coade's business partner William Sealey (also located at St Mary-at-Lambeth), but most notably in Coade's Lion.

Originally this giant lion served as the mascot of Lambeth's Lion Brewery. In 1966 it moved to its present position on the south side of Westminster Bridge, where Mrs Coade's factory once stood. Some years ago the lion became restless and apparently set off on its own version of the Lambeth Walk. Londoners were intrigued to notice a trail of red paw marks leading down the plinth and along the Albert Embankment. The prints finally disappeared over the wall of St Thomas's Hospital in Lambeth Palace Road, casting suspicion on high-spirited medical students.

Florence Nightingale established her Nursing School at old St Thomas's in 1860 and a small museum near the entrance to the new St Thomas's displays her personal effects, correspondence and published works. In 1861 an edition of Miss Nightingale's groundbreaking textbook, *Notes on Nursing,* appeared, with a section called 'Minding Baby'. No doubt it found its way to the Colonies and, to be honest, the following advice seems more appropriate for the Australian outback than for damp Victorian London:

> *But, of all things, don't burn baby's brains out by letting the sun bake its head when out, especially in its little cart, on a hot summer's day.*

When old St Thomas's Hospital closed down in 1862, an operating theatre in a garret was bricked up and not rediscovered until 1957. It had been built in 1821, with a viewing gallery so that students could observe proceedings. Visitors can now look down at the operating table, and at the sawdust-filled box underneath, which was used for the catching of blood. With no anaesthetics to blunt the pain, patients were blindfolded, gagged and bound to the table.

In July 1717 a newspaper published an account of the royal barge making its way along the Thames from Lambeth with fifty different instruments playing symphonies composed for the occasion by a Mr Hendel (George Frederick Handel). There are suggestions that Handel's *Water Music*, as it became known, was performed to drown out insulting comments from watermen who were notoriously disrespectful to royalty, particularly the unpopular George I. The article in the *Daily Courant* read:

> *On Wednesday evening* [the 17th] *at about 8, the King took Water at Whitehall in an open Barge ... and went up the River towards Chelsea. Many other Barges with Persons of Quality attended, and so great a Number of Boats, that the whole River in a manner was covered; a City Company's Barge was employ'd for the Musick, wherein were 50 Instruments of all sorts, who play'd all the way from Lambeth to Chelsea (While the Barges drove with the Tide without Rowing, as far as Chelsea) the finest symphonies, compos'd express for this Occasion by Mr Hendel; which his Majesty liked so well, that he caus'd it to be plaid over three times in going and returning.*

Uplifted by 'Mr Hendel's' new composition, King George and his party disembarked at Chelsea, where they enjoyed an elegant supper at a riverside villa.

Beyond the buildings of St Thomas's Hospital, steps lead up to Westminster Bridge and County Hall, once the headquarters of the Greater London Council but now a plush hotel. It is also home to the Saatchi Gallery which showcases the often confronting icons of Brit-art, including Tracey Emin's unmade bed and Damien Hirst's pickled shark. Westminster Bridge has an association with William Wordsworth, who stood upon an earlier version very early one September morning in 1802 and gazed at the city before him. He was inspired by the view of ships, towers, domes, theatres, temples … and houses:

> *The river glideth at his own sweet will:*
> *Dear God! The very houses seem asleep;*
> *And all that mighty heart is lying still.*

Across the river is Westminster itself, centre of English government for almost a thousand years. The tolling of Big Ben is as symbolic as the Houses of Parliament, and somehow reassuring. The clock's great hour bell was cast in 1856, but cracked a year later. It was recast at the Whitechapel Bell Foundry, only to fail again. This time it was decided not to recast but

© Shutterstock

The Houses of Parliament and Big Ben form a spectacular backdrop to fireworks over the Thames

to simply shift the cracked section away from the strike point of the clapper, and to reduce the clapper's weight. Big Ben fell silent again in 1976. As it tolled at 3.45 a.m. on 5 August, the chiming mechanism succumbed to metal fatigue and disintegrated. Bits of machinery flew all over the clock room, even piercing the ceiling. It took a year to repair the damage.

Big Ben looks down on a very busy scene. It is not surprising that the world's first traffic lights were installed at Westminster in 1868, long before the era of the motor car. A revolving, gas-filled lantern shone green or red to regulate the flow of horse buggies and pedestrians. As with Big Ben, there were teething troubles. The lights were hand-operated by a policeman and in the second week of operation they exploded, injuring the officer on duty.

The Duke of Wellington famously said the Houses of Parliament should be located on the river so that 'the populace cannot exact their demands by sitting down around you'. Perhaps the humanitarian William Morris was reacting to the Duke's words as he wrote his utopian tale *News from Nowhere*. Morris's fictional Londoners took advantage of the proximity of the Thames by turning the Houses of Parliament into a storage depot for animal dung, and a market for cabbages and turnips.

WESTMINSTER FOOL

175 g (6 oz) brioche loaf, thinly sliced
150 ml (¼ pint) sherry
300 ml (½ pint) single cream
300 ml (½ pint) milk
small blade of mace
5 large eggs
25 g (1 oz) caster sugar
1 tablespoon rosewater
freshly grated nutmeg

Lay the brioche in the bottom of a dish and pour over the sherry. Heat the milk and cream with the mace to just below boiling. Remove from heat. Cover and allow to infuse for 30 minutes. Make a custard with the eggs, sugar and the milk and cream mixture. Take out the mace. Add the rosewater to the custard and pour over the brioche. Grate some nutmeg over the top and cool. Serve chilled.

Sir Charles Barry designed the Gothic Houses of Parliament to replace the Royal Palace of Westminster, built around 1050. Parliament had sat in the Palace of Westminster since the thirteenth century; a tradition that very nearly ended on 5 November 1605. A scribbled note in the margin of the *Journals of the House* for that day records:

This last night the Upper House of Parliament was searched by Sir Thos. Knevett; and one Johnson [Johnson was an alias used by Guy Fawkes]*, a servant to Mr Thomas Percy, was there apprehended; who had placed thirty six barrels of gun powder in the vault under the House with a purpose to blow up the King, and the whole company, when they should there assemble.*

The Thames played its part in the plot as the barrels of gunpowder were ferried across from Lambeth and moved into the vault via the waterside Parliament Stairs. On 27 January 1606, eight of the conspirators, including Guy Fawkes, were taken by barge from the Tower to Westminster, where they were tried and sentenced to death by hanging. In a story ascribed to Sir Francis Bacon, who was present at the executions, one of the men, Sir Everard Digby, was taken down alive and had his heart cut out. It was held aloft with the cry, 'Here is the heart of a traitor!', to which the body is supposed to have replied, somewhat miraculously it has to be said, 'You lie!'

All English schoolchildren can recite the rhyme:

Please to remember the Fifth of November
Gunpowder Treason and plot
We know no reason why Gunpowder Treason
Should ever be forgot.

The plot is definitely not forgotten at Westminster. Before the annual State Opening of Parliament, a ritual search is still carried out by the Yeomen of the Guard.

At the height of the Civil War, the poet John Taylor commented on how empty Westminster Hall and the Law Courts had become:

You finde the Cookes leaning against the Dore-posts ruminating on those Halcion Termes, when whole herds of Clerkes, Solicitors and their Clyents, had wont to come with their sharpe-set noses, and stomaches from the hall, and devoure the Puddings and minc't Pyes by dozens, as swifty as a kennell of Hounds would lap up a dead horse.

In 1834, Old Palace at Westminster *was* destroyed, though not by political extremists. A fire broke out when officials tried to dispose of wooden tally sticks, used to record monies paid to the exchequer. In his role of social commentator, Charles Dickens pointed out that the cartloads of willow and hazel sticks could have been given to the poor as fuel. Instead, they were piled into the stove which heated the House of Lords and no one noticed that nearby panelling had ignited until it was too late. Only the Jewel Tower and Westminster Hall survived. Turner took the opportunity to make some quick watercolour sketches of the spectacular scene; his beloved Thames illuminated by fire instead of a rising or setting sun.

Westminster Abbey was built by Edward the Confessor on wasteland previously inhab-ited by lepers. Since 1065 all but two English monarchs have been crowned here, including Elizabeth II in 1952. Geoffrey Chaucer was buried at the abbey in 1400. He was followed by many famous literary figures, thereby creating Poet's Corner. Perhaps thinking of all those who might follow him, the dramatist Ben Jonson suggested a grave measuring 6x2 ft (2x0.5 m) was excessive and that a 2x2 ft plot would be fine for him. Accordingly, he was buried standing up. A gentleman called 'Spot' Ward also lies in Poet's Corner, though no one knows quite why. His only claim to fame appears to be that he successfully treated the injured thumb of King George II.

In the Museum of Westminster Abbey is a gold ring with a sardonyx cameo of Eliza-beth I. According to romantic legend, it was a gift from the Queen to her favourite, the Earl of Essex. Elizabeth promised that if ever Essex were to be charged with a crime, he would be pardoned upon return of the ring. In later years their relationship deteriorated to the point where Essex was tried for treason and sentenced to death. Elizabeth waited, but the ring did not appear and after changing her mind several times she signed the warrant for his execution. Essex was beheaded at the Tower of London on 25 February 1601, aged thirty-five. Apparently he had sent the ring but in a cruel twist of fate his messenger mistakenly passed it to Lady Nottingham, the Earl's great enemy, instead of to his cousin, Lady Scroope. Lady Nottingham deliberately kept the ring and only confessed to Eliza-beth on her death bed. The Queen allegedly replied: 'God may pardon you, I never can.'

The Thames Path leaves Westminster via the Victoria Embankment, where there is a river-side memorial to Sir Joseph Bazalgette, architect of the city's nineteenth-century sewage system. Before pollution began to affect London, members of the aristocracy loved to bathe in the river. In the eighteenth century the Earl of Pembroke received a letter humorously addressed to 'The Earl of Pembroke, in the Thames, over against Whitehall'. And in 1807 Lord Byron boasted:

Last week I swam in the Thames from Lambeth through the two bridges, Westminster and Blackfriars, a distance, including the different turns and tacks made on the way, of three miles! You see I am in excellent training …

Such pleasures ceased when water closets became fashionable. Previously, night carts had emptied earth closets and carried the contents out of the city via a notoriously messy and smelly route. However, in 1843 it was decided that all households should be connected to pipes which would carry sewage down the Thames and out to sea. It was a great idea in theory, but in practice the raw sewage simply floated up and down on the tide, right past the noses of Members of Parliament at Westminster.

By 1848 *Punch* magazine was railing about the pollution in a poem titled 'Dirty Father Thames', complaining:

And from thee is brewed our porter -
Thee, thou guilty puddle, sink!
Thou, vile cesspool, art the liquour,
Whence is made the beer we drink.

In 1858 a bill was passed allowing the outfall to be moved 10 miles (16 km) downstream to Barking. Joseph Bazalgette's grand plan, which cost the present-day equivalent of £6 billion, was to divert all the city drains into main sewers which ran along the riverbanks. The pipes were then covered and landscaped to create the Chelsea, Albert and Victoria Embankments. However, the outlet at Barking was still too close for comfort. Westminster may have breathed more easily, but only at the expense of underprivileged East-Enders. The cynical will draw their own conclusion as to why untreated sewage was still flowing into the river at Barking twenty years later; a situation that contributed to a tragedy of enormous proportions.

© Harpers Weekly, October 12 1878 (Wikipedia)

The carnage was horrific when the crowded steamer *Princess Alice* was hit by the collier *Bywell Castle* in 1878

At 8 p.m. on 3 September 1878, the crowded excursion steamer *Princess Alice* was hit by the iron-hulled collier *Bywell Castle*, on Barking Reach. The collision occurred only 300 yd (275 m) from shore but the steamer sank within four minutes and few people could swim. An inquiry found the water they drowned in was disgustingly polluted. It was not known how many people were on board, but the vessel was licensed to carry 936 passengers. Six-hundred-and-forty bodies were recovered, and many survivors died later from the effects of the contaminated water. Among the tragic stories was that of Benjamin and Emma Baker, from Somerset. They had been married eight days earlier and were on their honeymoon.

It is only now that moves are being made to upgrade the Victorian drainage system, which currently deals with 600 million gallons of sewage per day. At least a quarter of the old pipes are said to be leaking. Incidentally, the sewers are home to a horrifying sixty million rats, outnumbering the human population by more than seven to one.

Air pollution was also a problem in Victorian London. The fogs rising from the Thames today are ethereal mists compared with the dense smogs Charles Dickens described. In his novel *Bleak House*, Esther arrives from the country to find the city enveloped in an impenetrable shroud. She thinks there must be a fire but is told the brown haze is caused by a thick fog, known locally as a London Particular. Such fogs were also known as 'pea-soupers', which is why an old-fashioned recipe for pea soup is in turn called London Particular:

LONDON PARTICULAR

1 tablespoon butter
155 g (5 oz) thick cut, smoked back bacon, chopped
1 large onion, chopped
1 carrot, chopped
2 sticks celery, chopped
½ cup split peas (soaked overnight)
5 cups chicken stock
croutons
salt and pepper
several sprigs of fresh mint

In a large saucepan, fry the bacon lightly in the butter then add the onion, carrot and celery. Cook for a few more minutes. Add the drained split peas, stock and sprigs of mint. Season with salt and pepper. Bring to the boil, stirring occasionally. Cover and simmer for about an hour. Remove the mint and serve the soup scattered with croutons and grilled, chopped bacon.

Not everyone disliked the smog. In his autobiography published in 1841, Benjamin Haydon wrote:

So far from the smoke of London being offensive to me, it has always been to my imagination the sublime canopy that shrouds the City of the World.

Oscar Wilde also painted an evocative picture of London's fog in his poem, 'Symphony In Yellow':

Big barges full of yellow hay
Are moved against the shadowy wharf,
And, like a yellow silken scarf,
The thick fog hangs along the quay.

Horses provided the major means of transport around the city in Wilde's day and to keep them fed, hay barges plied the Thames daily. On a flood tide, a bale of straw was hung below the arches of bridges to warn bargemen of reduced headroom. The flat-bottomed hay barges had a very shallow draught and were thus able to navigate the upper reaches of the river. One in particular inspired the tale that after a heavy dew it could float across the meadows and tie up right beside a haystack.

Victoria Embankment continues on, past the offices of Whitehall and the Banqueting House, the last remnant of the old Whitehall Palace. The palace burned to the ground in 1698; a disaster supposedly caused by a maid drying clothes by an open fire. The Banqueting House was built by Inigo Jones in 1622 and has a wonderful ceiling painted by Paul Rubens. A scaffold was erected outside the building for the public execution of Charles I on 30 January 1649. The King was led to his death through a window of the Banqueting House, dressed in an extra undershirt to prevent him shivering in the winter chill and being labelled a coward. One person who did not attend was the Royalist John Evelyn, who wrote:

The Villanie of the Rebells proceeding now so far as to Tri, Condemn and murder our excellent King, the 30 of this month struck me with such horror that I kept the day of his Martyrdom a fast, and could not be present at that execrable wickednesse.

In 1660 Evelyn joyfully welcomed Charles II at the Restoration. A year later he watched the King make a grand procession down the Thames from Hampton Court to Whitehall, with his new bride, Catherine of Braganza.

Overlooking the Thames by nearby Charing Cross is the National Liberal Club, built in

1887 and featuring very ornate tiles. The Victorian politician Lord Birkenhead was not a member but was often seen entering the building. When confronted, he said he had always thought it was a public lavatory.

There is a touching love story associated with Charing Cross. In 1254, ten-year-old Eleanor of Castile married fifteen-year-old Edward, Prince of Wales (later Edward I). The couple were extremely happy together and when Eleanor died near Lincoln in 1270, a heart-broken Edward had her body brought back to London. Wherever the funeral procession halted overnight he ordered an elaborate memorial cross to be built. The final cross was built in London, at the spot romantics claim was called Charing after Edward's affectionate name for Eleanor: *'la cher reine'*.

Of the twelve original crosses, only three are left, including a superb example at Geddington, in Northamptonshire. In 1647 Cromwell's men knocked down Charing's cross and the site remained vacant until the Restoration. There is grim irony in that it then became the execution site for some of Cromwell's high-ranking officers. Samuel Pepys was among the onlookers when Major Harrison met his death. On 13 October 1660 he wrote: 'I went out to Charing Cross, to see Major-General Harrison hanged, drawn and quartered; which was done there, he looking as cheerful as any man could do in that condition.' The sentimental Victorians remembered Edward and Eleanor's love story and installed a replica cross, which still stands by Charing Cross railway station.

In the nearby Embankment Gardens is a memorial to Samuel Plimsoll, the British MP responsible for the adoption of the Plimsoll Line in 1876. The line is painted on the hull of a ship to indicate where the water-line should be if the vessel is safely loaded. Later the name plimsoll was given to a cheap canvas shoe which had a coloured line separating its rubber sole from a canvas upper. Plimsolls make ideal boating shoes, particularly as Samuel's safety principle can be applied. If water rises above the coloured line it is time to man the bilge pump, or abandon ship!

Downstream stands a far more ancient monument: Cleopatra's Needle, which dates from 1500 BC, when it was erected at Heliopolis in Egypt. It was given to Britain in 1819 but transporting the 68-ft (20-m) obelisk home proved quite a challenge. During a violent storm in the Bay of Biscay, it actually had to be cast adrift. Despite its antiquity, the Needle did not capture my imagination until I discovered there is a time capsule buried underneath it. Among other things, the capsule contains a portrait of Queen Victoria, a box of hairpins, a baby's bottle, a razor, a box of cigars, a hydraulic jack, and pictures of twelve of the country's most attractive women. It is fortunate Her Majesty was included separately because I fear she would not have featured among the twelve beauties. Perhaps they were selected from her eldest son's mistresses. Alfred Tennyson wrote a poem about the Needle which concluded:

I have seen the four great empires disappear,
I was when London was not. I am here.

However, I prefer a less distinguished rhyme, author unknown:

This monument one supposes,
Was looked upon by Moses.
It passed in time from the Greek to the Turks,
And was plonked down here by the Board of Works.

Damage to the plinths of the bronze sphinxes flanking the Needle was caused during the very first air attack on London, in September 1917.

Behind the Victoria Embankment Gardens is Adelphi Terrace where an eighteenth-century quack doctor called James Graham established his Temple of Health. It was adorned by scantily clad young 'goddesses', including a teenager called Emma Lyon who went on to become the mistress of Lord Nelson. For £50 per night, couples could sleep in Graham's giant 'celestial bed', which had a mattress stuffed with hair from the tails of prize stallions. Assisted by electrical currents passing across the headboard, it was claimed the bed could not only cure impotence but, in an early version of gene therapy, guarantee conception of the perfect child.

SOUTHBANK TO SOUTHWARK

Dwarfing Cleopatra's Needle across the river is the giant London Eye, the world's tallest Ferris wheel at 443 ft (135 m). On a clear day it is possible to see Windsor Castle. The components of the Eye were manufactured in various European countries and brought up the Thames by barge. Platforms were built in the river by Westminster Bridge and the wheel was assembled horizontally then lifted up from a hinged base. Finally, the capsules were fitted. The Eye has already become the subject of an urban myth. The story goes that when it began to move with its first paying passengers, the operators heard what sounded like a gust of wind and thought the wheel was creating a severe down-draft. However, it turned out to be the sound of blinds being drawn all over the city. Supposedly the Ministry of Defence closed theirs because they feared spies might ride the wheel armed with high-powered telescopes in an attempt to steal military secrets. High-rise apartment dwellers were more worried about their bedroom secrets.

Downstream, the brewery once reigned over by Mrs Coade's lion became the site of Royal Festival Hall, built for the Festival of Britain in 1951. The concert hall is just one in a series of stark concrete cultural centres, including the Hayward Gallery and, beyond Waterloo Bridge, the National Film Theatre. The Film Theatre stands on ground once occupied by Cupid's Garden, where the entertainment was often '18' rated. In 1691 a gardener at Arundel House in The Strand left his position with a parting gift of broken statuary. He spread a few arms and legs around his own backyard by Waterloo Bridge and created a Grecian-style pleasure garden, frequented by ladies of very easy virtue. There were also bowling greens, games of chance and drinking booths. In 1749, *Reeds Weekly Journal* reported a drunken argument in the skittle ground, during which a man had his eye struck out with a stick.

The final building in the South Bank arts complex is the multi-auditorium National Theatre. The Festival of Britain was held to cheer up war-weary Londoners but many people would now cheer if the buildings, often labelled 'concrete cankers', were removed. Never mind, there is a touch (albeit as light as an angel's breath) of Paris's Left Bank in the open-air bookstalls under Waterloo Bridge.

On 11 September 1978, this bridge was the scene of a James Bond-style murder. The Bulgarian dissident Georgi Markov was waiting for a bus on the bridge when he felt a sharp sting in his thigh. He died five days later and an autopsy revealed he had been poisoned by a substance called ricin, made from castor oil beans. A pellet hardly bigger than a pinhead was found in his body, apparently fired from an umbrella. The weapon was believed to have been supplied by the KGB, along with the deadly pellet of poison.

Ahead is Gabriel's Wharf, where old warehouses have been painted to look like domestic house fronts and the plaza is full of craft stalls and cafes. Another nearby refreshment spot is the Doggett's Coat and Badge pub, by Blackfriars Bridge. The coat and badge referred to in the pub's name are awarded to the winner of a single sculls race for apprentice watermen, which has been held on the river since 1715. The race was born out of Thomas Doggett's appreciation for the services of watermen, who transported Londoners in sometimes appalling weather conditions. It is held on the 4-mile, 5-furlong (6.5 km) stretch between London Bridge and Chelsea. Originally the competing boats were four-seater passenger wherries. The results are recorded as far back as 1780, when the winner was a young man called John Bradshaw who came from the district of, believe it or not, Pickled Herring.

The first Blackfriars Bridge opened in 1769. It was designed with elliptical arches by Scotsman Robert Mylne but only after some controversy, contributed to by none other than Samuel Johnson, who wrote several letters to the press in support of his friend John Gwyn's alternative design of semicircular arches. It was below this crossing that the river froze so completely in 1814 that an elephant was walked across! The bridge was rebuilt a century later and opened in 1869 by Queen Victoria, accompanied by her Scottish steward John Brown. Her Majesty probably wished she had stayed in her bolt-hole at Balmoral as she was extremely unpopular at the time and the pair were hissed at by the crowd. The design of the new bridge also attracted critics; blocks of masonry set on each corner were described rather wonderfully by a correspondent in the *Quarterly Review* as 'apropos of nothing, a well-known evidence of desperate imbecility'. The bridge is said to mark the point where salt water becomes fresh water and accordingly its supporting pillars are decorated with seabirds on the downriver side, freshwater birds on the upriver side.

A dramatic incident in Blackfriar's history occurred relatively recently. In 1982 the body of Italian banker Robert Calvi was found hanging from girders under the first arch on the north bank. His pockets were weighted with 11 lb (5 kg) of bricks and contained £15,000 in cash. Calvi was known as 'God's Banker' because he was the head of the Vatican Bank. At first it was presumed he had committed suicide, following investigations which had revealed a trail of murky financial deals. However, the case was reopened in 2002 and the following year it was decided that Calvi was already dead when he was suspended from the bridge, and that he was killed by the Mafia to cover up a money-laundering racket. Prosecutors in Rome recommended that four men be charged with his murder.

In 1962 a section of a Roman barge was found in the bed of the Thames close to Black-friars Bridge. Its cargo of Kentish ragstone was found at the same spot, leading experts to believe the barge sank while bringing stone from Maidstone to build the Wall of London. There was a stroke of luck for historians trying to date the barge, as a coin was found in the mast instep. It was dated AD 88 and placed so that the picture of the goddess Fortuna was pressed against the mast to ensure safe passage. Well, perhaps the crew escaped the sinking. It is also near here that the now-underground Fleet River flows into the Thames as a sewer, having risen on Hampstead Heath.

The name may be a little twee, but it would be a mistake not to make a detour to Ye Olde Cheshire Cheese pub in Fleet Street, haunt of literary figures such as Samuel Johnson, Charles Dickens, William Thackeray, Mark Twain and Oscar Wilde. In John Galsworthy's *Forsyte Saga,* Soames and Winifred Darcie lunch here with the lawyer Mr Bellby and are dismayed when the waiter arrives with their plates saying: 'I 'urried up the pudden sir, you'll find plenty o'lark in it to-day.'

Samuel Johnson's house is conveniently close by in Gough Square. A copy of his ground-breaking dictionary is on display and contains a satisfyingly succinct definition of a river: 'A land current of water bigger than a brook.' Battling with the commuter crush of British Rail and the Tube, we appreciated Johnson's pragmatic view of travel:

> *He that travels in theory has no inconvenience; he has shade and sunshine at his disposal and looks of gaiety. These ideas are indulged till the day of departure arrives, the chaise is called, and the progress of happiness begins. A few miles teach him the fallacies of imagination…*

A 360-yd (330-m) pedestrian bridge now links the north side of the Thames with the new Tate Modern at Bankside. It was London's first new river crossing in over 100 years, and 100,000 people walked across Millennium Bridge on its opening day, 10 June 2000, which might have caused what was described as 'a worrying and serious wobble'. The bridge closed within days and did not reopen for another two years. It is now suitably stable but I agree with comedian Billy Connolly's comment that a wobbly bridge would have been much more fun.

The Tate Modern gallery is housed in the old Bankside power station, another Gilbert Scott creation (see page 194). The striking architecture of the building threatens to over-shadow the art collection, particularly the massive entrance hall, which once housed the power station's turbine. The gallery has become one of the capital's most visited sites.

Ahead is Cardinal's Wharf, a cobbled close with two historic homes. One was the resi-dence of the provost of Southwark Cathedral and the other is thought to have been the home of Christopher Wren when he was building St Paul's Cathedral just across the river. It was under Paul's Pier Wharf that a fascinating Witches Bottle was found in 1953. The bottles were used in medieval times, not by witches but as a defence against them. They were filled with some of the victim's urine, the heart of an animal and a few iron nails. The bottles were then heated over a fire to boiling point, supposedly forcing any witch to reveal herself or die in agony.

For all the interest created by the opening of the Tate Modern, William Shakespeare remains the biggest drawcard at Bankside. In 1599 Thomas Platter wrote:

> On September 21st after lunch, about two o'clock, I and my party crossed the water, and there in the house with the thatched roof witnessed an excellent performance of the first Emperor Julius Caesar with a cast of some fifteen people; when the play was over, they danced very marvelously and gracefully together as is their want, two dressed as men and two as women.

Platter was referring to the Globe Theatre, which had opened in 1598. A production of Shakespeare's *Henry VIII* in 1613 went less smoothly. The entrance of the King was marked with the firing of a cannon but a spark flew into the thatched roof and burnt the theatre to the ground. An anonymous poet wrote a sonnet describing the disaster, with a warning couched in rather earthy terms:

> Bee warned, yow stage strutters all,
> Least yow again be catched,
> And such a burneing doe befall,
> As to them whose house was thatched;
> Forbeare your whoreing, breeding biles,
> And laye up that expense for tiles.

The reconstructed Globe officially opened in 1997. Fortunately the poet's warning was ignored and tile did not replace thatch. In fact, all the materials used were authentic and the dimensions of the theatre were recreated as accurately as possible. It reopened with a production of Shakespeare's *Two Gentlemen of Verona*. Of all the quotes about William Shakespeare, the following, from fellow dramatist George Bernard Shaw, is my favourite:

> With the possible exception of Homer, there is no eminent writer, not even Sir Walter Scott, whom I can despise so entirely as I despise Shakespeare when I measure my mind against his ... It would positively be a relief to me to dig him up and throw stones at him.

The Globe was not the only theatre on the South Bank in the sixteenth century. Play acting was associated with bawdy revelry and the theatres were located well away from the city, along with bull-baiting rings, taverns and brothels.

Perhaps it is appropriate that in Victorian times Barclay & Co, then the largest brewery in the world, extended from Southwark Bridge halfway to London Bridge. The brewery covered the site of the Globe Theatre. I should point out that Southwark also catered for teetotallers. In 1898 pedestrians could pause at a street lamp which had been adapted to dispense boiling water, cocoa or tea, on a penny-in-the-slot system.

In Borough High Street, Southwark, is London's last galleried coaching inn. The timber-framed George Inn dates from 1676, and was mentioned by Dickens in *Little Dorrit*. Its gently sagging open galleries overlook a cobbled courtyard, where Morris dancing and Shakespearean plays are sometimes performed in the summer. It is also an atmospheric place for a drink at Christmas, when they serve mulled wine. I was pleased to note that the restaurant menu features traditional English puddings such as Treacle Sponge and Spotted Dick. The latter is a calorie-filled, steamed suet roll studded with currants. In 2001 the Gloucestershire NHS caved in to political correctness and renamed it Spotted Richard on hospital menus. Fortunately sanity prevailed and the ludicrous decision was reversed a year later.

A frost fair was held by Southwark Bridge in 1564 after the Thames froze and, as a contemporary poet wrote:

The watermen, for want of rowing boats
Make use of booths to get their pence and groats.

The booths offered tankards of ale and brandy, Spanish wine called sack and dishes of freshly ground coffee. There was roast beef, goose, rabbit and capon and sweet dishes such as pancakes, hot codlins (apples) and plum cake. A delightfully fanciful account of a frost fair appears in Virginia Woolf's novel *Orlando*:

Lovers dallied upon divans spread with sables. Frozen roses fell in showers when the Queen and her ladies walked abroad. Coloured balloons hovered motionless in the air. Here and there burnt vast bonfires of cedar and oak wood, lavishly salted, so that the flames were of green, orange, and purple fire. But however fiercely they burnt, the heat was not enough to melt the ice which, though of singular transparency, was yet of the hardness of steel.

Disaster sometimes struck when the ice did eventually melt. Following a London frost fair in 1715, the poet John Gay wrote of an apple seller called Doll who was cut off in full voice, decapitated by a sheet of ice:

The cracking crystal yields, she sinks, she dies,
Her head, chopt off, from her lost shoulders flies:
Pippins she cried, but Death her voice confounds,
And Pip-Pip-Pip along the ice resounds.

During another big freeze in January 1814 crowds gathered at a frost fair held between London Bridge and Blackfriars. Enterprising stallholders sold 'Lapland Mutton' for a shilling a slice, or sixpence to simply watch it being cooked.

Frost fairs were held in London whenever the River Thames froze solid. Sadly, this no longer occurs

Southwark Bridge was the scene of a tragic accident in 1989, when the dredger *Bowbelle* hit the packed pleasure boat *Marchioness*. A twenty-first birthday party was being celebrated on board the *Marchioness* and fifty-one young people lost their lives. Continuing controversy over the cause of the accident resulted in an official inquiry in 2000. The findings of the investigation were heartbreaking for the friends and relatives of those who died. Among several contributing factors, it was found that neither vessel had an adequate look-out and that a rescue team took twenty minutes to arrive after being sent to the wrong place.

Downstream of Southwark Bridge is Winchester Palace, or what is left of it. Only the west wall of the medieval Bishops' Hall remains, its superb rose window an arresting sight against a background of office blocks. Nearby is Southwark Cathedral, also somewhat hemmed in by modern development. In 1607 the brother of William Shakespeare was buried here between the choir stalls, and nearby there is a memorial to William.

The Thames Path skirts around the cathedral to London Bridge and London Bridge City, a redevelopment centred around Hayes Wharf. The dock has been covered with a vaulted roof to form a shopping piazza. When Rob and I visited, chaffinches were singing in the potted trees and bathing in the water spouting from David Kemp's imaginative sculpture, 'The Navigators'. This wharf once stretched from London Bridge to Tower Bridge and was the storage point for vast quantities of New Zealand cheese and butter. It was one of the first wharves to install cold storage facilities.

Who knows how many versions of London Bridge have spanned the Thames? Initially they were constructed of wood but between 1176 and 1209 a stone bridge was built. It became a landmark, lined with houses, shops and a chapel. It was entered via spiked, fortified gates on which the decapitated heads of traitors were displayed, having been boiled, then dipped in tar to preserve them.

Such a fate befell Sir Thomas More, who was executed at Tower Hill in 1535. After a month, his grieving daughter Margaret Roper managed to bribe someone to throw the head down to her as she sat in a boat. According to legend she preserved it in spices and kept it safe until she herself died. The head was interred beside her at St Dunstan's Church in Canterbury.

Perhaps the old rhyme 'London Bridge Is Falling Down' inspired the following riddle:

As I was going o'er London Bridge,
I heard something crack;
And not a man in all of England
Can mend that!

The solution to the riddle was ice, but when the multi-arched bridge was demolished in 1832, the flow of the river increased and there were no more big freezes. The bridge was replaced

© Rob Conolly

Not only did the US buy the 'wrong' London Bridge, but several stones were left behind!

by a rather dull, granite crossing which was itself taken down in 1968 and sold to someone in the United States, who allegedly thought he was buying the far more impressive Tower Bridge! A English friend of mine remembers watching numbered sections of the bridge passing through her local railway station in open-sided carriages. A couple of stones from the first arch of Old London Bridge (the one sold to the US) can still be seen in the court-yard of St Magnus the Martyr Church, in Lower Thames Street. When we visited, a homeless person was lying below the stones in a sleeping bag, continuing a long and sad tradition of sleeping rough under the arches of London Bridge. The church, designed by Christopher Wren, was built at the foot of the old bridge between 1671 and 1676 after the previous building was destroyed in the Great Fire. It is the traditional church of the city's fishmongers.

Many treasures have been removed from the Thames, especially around the site of Old London Bridge. The discovery of a Roman bronze peacock was a piece of miraculous luck, but also a tribute to the observational powers of a collector called Charles Roach Smith. As dredgers brought up gravel from the riverbed, Roach Smith picked up a fragment of bronze which he was unable to identify. A year later he was watching buckets of sludge being trans-ferred to a barge when he picked out another piece of bronze. Something about its shape made him remember the earlier find. He fitted the two together to form the peacock, which is now held in the British Museum.

The river also yielded a pair of bronze forceps. The handles were decorated with busts of deities representing the days of the Roman week and the clamps were adorned with the heads of the Mother Goddess Cybele and the God Attis. According to legend, Cybele was in love with Attis but he was unfaithful and Cybele killed her rival in a fit of jealousy. Male readers may wish to cross their legs and take a sharp intake of breath at this point because a grief-stricken Attis was said to have castrated himself with forceps. Those found in the Thames have been associated with bizarre religious rites associated with the worship of the Mother Goddess. Apparently, young men aiming for the priesthood danced themselves into a frenzy then followed Attis's example.

In 2010 a copper alloy Roman disc was found in the river by Putney Bridge by an amateur archaeologist using a metal detector. It was later taken along to the Museum of London for recording and staff were amazed to see that it clearly depicted a couple performing a sexual act. It is thought the disc may have been a brothel token, with the numeral on the reverse representing either the fee paid by the client or the holder's place in a queue, in this case number fourteen. The rare disc has since been donated to the museum.

Treasure seekers are banned from digging around the area of Queenhithe Dock on the north bank of the Thames. It was from here panic-stricken victims of the Fire of London piled their belongings onto any available craft. Many of the overloaded boats sank at their moorings while jostling for space, and the riverbed still holds many items. Queenhithe Dock dates from AD 890 and is London's oldest. King John gave it to his mother Eleanor, whose brazen pleasure in collecting landing fees caused such fury that people lined London Bridge and stoned her barge as she was passing under the arches.

Roman tokens salvaged from the river. The image is explicit, but a spot of erosion spares some blushes!

Dowgate Pier was located between Southwark and London Bridge. The site features in an intriguing story concerning the Bank of England's only known 'break-in'. In 1836 a man wrote anonymously to the bank, telling officials he would meet them in the gold vaults at an appointed hour. The bankers were skeptical but duly assembled in the bullion room. Minutes later they saw a man push aside some floorboards and emerge from a drain, which he explained connected directly with the Thames at Dowgate. As a sewer worker, the man had a detailed knowledge of London's drains but since he had not taken advantage of the situation he was paid a reward of £800. However, the bank was unwilling to broadcast such a breach in security and dismissed reports about it as wild rumour. Proof that the incident had actually occurred was to come three years later. A letter written by the bank's architect to the Building Committee came to light. It was dated February 1839 and in part read:

> In May 1836, having had reason to apprehend danger from our sewers, it was discovered that an open and unobstructed sewer led directly from the gold vault down to Dowgate.

On the downriver side of London Bridge is the 202-ft (61.5-m) Monument, a Doric column designed by Christopher Wren to commemorate the Fire of London in 1666. If the monument were to be laid down, the flaming gilt urn on its summit would touch the spot in Pudding Lane where the fire broke out

We completed one of our day-long treks at the Monument and headed for home, although it was tempting to press on to the Tower of London and the Gothic grandeur of Tower Bridge.

Tower Bridge to Deptford

A flurry of autumn visitors and our own travels further afield interrupted our walk and it was almost Christmas by the time we began the final push to Greenwich. We were now a trio, as our friend Bill had joined us again.

Outside Tower Bridge station there were stalls selling roasted chestnuts, and old-fashioned toffee apples. I love the cultural diversity of London's modern street food but am tempted to mount a campaign to bring back other traditional favourites. Surely there would be a market for slabs of gilded gingerbread, or individual plum puddings, especially at Christmas. Miniature puddings were sold by street vendors until the mid nineteenth century, boiled in cotton bags and offered at a ha'penny each. And what of sugar plums, filled with exotic spices arriving from the Far East via the Thames?

SUGAR PLUMS

2 cups whole, peeled almonds
¼ cup honey
2 teaspoons grated orange zest
1 teaspoon ground cinnamon
½ teaspoon ground allspice
½ grated nutmeg
1 cup finely chopped dried apricots
1 cup finely chopped pitted dates

Toast almonds on a baking sheet at 175°C (350°F), for ten minutes or until golden brown. Cool and finely chop. Combine honey, orange zest, cinnamon, allspice and nutmeg in a bowl. Add almonds, apricots and dates. Mix well. Form heaped teaspoons of mixture into balls. Roll in sugar. Refrigerate in single layers between sheets of waxed paper in an airtight container. Will keep for about a month.

We took a short break from the walk to visit All Hallows Church. Though heavily restored, it is Saxon in origin. An arch in the south-west corner contains inscribed Roman tiles and there is also a legend that the heart of Richard I is buried here. Owing to All Hallows' close proximity to Tower Hill, headless bodies (including those of Archbishop Laud and Sir Thomas More) were held in the churchyard following executions. The church escaped damage during the Great Fire of London but was virtually destroyed by bombs in the Second World War II.

Samuel Pepys climbed All Hallows' tower after the Fire of London to witness 'the saddest sight of desolation'. His own house came through unscathed but Pepys had sensibly taken measures to protect his most prized possessions. On 4 September 1666 he buried his wine and his 'parmazen' cheese in the garden.

PEPYS' PARMESAN SAUCE

2 tablespoons butter
2 teaspoons flour
¾ cup whipping cream
½ cup grated parmeson cheese
dash of grated nutmeg
dash of pepper

Melt the butter in a skillet over medium heat. Add the flour and cook, stirring well. Add the cream, stirring vigorously until thick and smooth. Reduce heat and stir in the grated parmesan. Season with the nutmeg and pepper.

Pepys was a true *bon vivant,* and loved to impress with a good spread. In 1660 he entertained a handful of friends with fricassee of rabbit and chicken, a leg of boiled mutton, three carp, a side of lamb, a dish of roasted pigeon, four lobsters, three tarts, a lamprey pie, a dish of anchovies and various wines.

This feast marked the second anniversary of Samuel's operation for the removal of a kidney stone the size of a tennis ball. His survival may seem remarkable considering the lack of hygiene and crude surgery of the day, but the speed of the procedure helped. The stone was whisked out through a 3-in (7.5-cm) cut in under a minute. More importantly, Pepys was the first patient of the day and therefore the surgeon's hands and instruments were at their cleanest.

When the fire of London was first reported to the Lord Mayor, he dismissed it with the comment that 'a woman might piss it out', but of course he was wrong. Having begun in a baker's shop in Pudding Lane, the fire leapt across Fish Street then spread down to the

Thames. A pump by the arches of London Bridge burned before it could be put to use and the fire was further fuelled by the highly combustible contents of warehouses. As the diarist John Evelyn recorded: 'The coal and wood wharfs and magazines of oil, rosin etc. did infinite mischief.' Evelyn also described the destruction of St Paul's Cathedral. In what must have seemed like a scene from medieval warfare, he wrote of stones flying like grenades and molten lead from the cathedral's roof pouring down the streets, which became too hot to walk on.

Samuel Pepys also lived through the Great Plague and his account of the epidemic from 16 October 1665 has a powerful immediacy:

> *Thence I walked to the Tower. But Lord, how empty the streets are, and melancholy, so many poor sick people in the streets, full of sores, and so many sad stories overheard as I walk. Everyone talking of this dead, and that man sick, and so many in this place and so many in that. And they tell me that in Westminster there is never a physician, and but one apothecary left, all being dead.*

Pepys' family survived relatively unscathed and on New Year's Eve he could report that the city was filling again, and the shops reopening. He hoped the court would return to re-establish law and order, as the business district had become an unregulated rabble. In this he was a little optimistic. It was 1 February 1666 before King Charles and his family dared to leave Oxford.

From All Hallows Church, we followed in Pepys' footsteps to the tower, which is always full of schoolchildren scribbling furiously into dog-eared exercise books. Rob and I once chatted to a group of boys who shared some of their carefully gathered information. They told us about the stairs in the circular keep, which rise in a clockwise direction so that defenders were able to use their swords freely. In return I told them about George Trott, whose father was curator of the crown jewels between 1921 and 1951. George was raised in the tower and had the distinction of being whacked on the bottom by Queen Mary for giving cheek when she visited. She might have whacked a few more bottoms if she had known what liberties were being taken with the crown jewels. One day George and several other warders' sons went to watch the jewels being cleaned and as George's dad handed crowns to the royal jewellers, someone decided to try one on. In the end everyone had a go, young George and his mates included.

Worse liberties were taken with the crown jewels in the reign of Charles II, when the bold Captain Blood tried to make off with them. When captured he refused to speak to anyone but the King, which turned out to be a good move. Charles was disarmed by Blood's effrontery and not only gave him a pardon but a pension as well.

Children also revel in the gory details of executions and take great delight in placing their heads on an authentic chopping block. Anne Boleyn walked to her death at 8 a.m. on 19 May 1536. Mercifully, an expert executioner was sent over from Calais and she was dispatched with a single stroke of his sword, grateful that she had, in her own words, 'so little a neck'. Perhaps she was hoping for an eleventh-hour reprieve from the King because her final speech included the words: 'I pray God save the King and send him long to reign over you, for a gentler more merciful Prince there never was ...' But there was no reprieve for Anne and neither had anyone thought to order her a coffin. She was reputedly buried in an arrow box. I can imagine the Queen greeting her portly namesake Queen Anne (see page 167) two centuries later with the words: 'Welcome to the after-life, my dear, but what a mercy your coffin was tailor made!'

A few years later Henry's fifth wife Catherine Howard met the same fate as Anne Boleyn, and with equal dignity. The day before she was executed she called for a block to be brought to her apartment so that she would know exactly where to lay her head. Both Catherine and Anne were very brave, but the remarkable spirit of seventy-one-year-old Margaret, Countess of Salisbury, impresses me far more. About to be executed in 1541, the elderly Countess had to be chased around the scaffold by her axe-wielding executioner. Unfortunately there could only be one outcome and her death was a far messier affair than it might otherwise have been.

Perhaps the last word should go to the philosophical Sir Walter Raleigh, beheaded in the reign of James I. Raleigh positioned himself on the block with the comment: 'So the heart be right, it is no matter which way the head lies.' Raleigh was executed for conspiracy, though judging from the King's denunciation of smoking, he might also have been punishing Sir Walter for introducing tobacco to the country:

A custom loathsome to the eye, hateful to the nose, harmful to the brain, dangerous to the lungs, and in the black, stinking fume thereof, nearest resembling the horrible Stygian smoke of the pit that is bottomless.

The tower's yeoman wardens have long been called Beefeaters. Some say this was because beef formed a regular part of their daily rations. My friend Yvonne once telephoned a Beefeater on my behalf, to ask about the origin of the name and whether the beef ration story was true. He told her he had no idea. I have since heard an alternative theory: that Henry VIII established the warders as *boufitiers,* or guardians of the King's buffet. You would think any Beefeater worth his salt should have known that. Never mind, I prefer the story that King Henry tripped over a sentry in the dark one night and snapped: 'Forsooth, man, keep your b... feet out of the way!' He was probably at the end of his tether over his string of unsatisfactory wives, whose various fates can be remembered with the help of the following couplet:

One of the yeoman wardens at the Tower of London. The origins of their name, 'Beefeaters', is a matter of debate

Divorced, beheaded, died,
Divorced, beheaded, survived.

The moat surrounding the tower was drained in 1843 but on 7 January 1928 bleary-eyed Beefeaters woke to see it full of water again, the result of a tidal wave. During the Second World War's 'Dig for Victory' campaign, the moat was used to grow vegetables.

For the children's sake (yes, and my own!), I wish there was still a menagerie at the tower. Wild animals were kept as an amusement for royalty from the time of King John's reign (1199–1215). Among the early specimens were leopards, lions, a polar bear, eagles, owls and even an elephant. The lions appear to have prompted one of the first April Fools' Day hoaxes. In 1698 the aptly named *Dawks's News-letter* reported: 'Yesterday being the first of April, several persons were sent to the tower ditch to see the Lions washed.' The joke was repeated with small variations for centuries. In 1832 the lions were banished to Regents Park Zoo, allegedly after one foolhardy animal bit a soldier, but April Fools' hoaxes persisted until the mid nineteenth century. Tickets of admission were issued and visitors were asked to enter at the White Gate, which did not exist!

In 1965 the body of Sir Winston Churchill was carried from St Paul's Cathedral to Tower Wharf, for a final journey along the Thames. Yeomen of the guard formed a guard of honour as guns saluted and pipers on the hill played 'The Flowers Of The Forest'. At the riverside, Churchill was piped aboard a launch then carried upstream to the strains of 'Rule Britannia', from the band of the Royal Marines.

It was dark when we caught a bus back to Tower Bridge station at the end of our day's walk. Shining like a star among the soberly dressed commuters was a little West Indian girl in silver wellington boots and a purple mohair coat. She proudly showed us the Christmas decorations she had made at school, including a sleigh daubed with glue and glitter which

© Look and Learn/Peter Jackson Collection

A tiger thrills young visitors to the Tower of London Menagerie

LLOYDS COFFEE HOUSE.

This Thameside coffee house evolved into Lloyd's of London

she 'flew' through the air to the lusty accompaniment of 'Jingle Bells'. We were thoroughly enjoying her performance but just as she was getting into full swing, her mother told her to sit down and be quiet. Afterwards, Bill and I agreed we should have stood on our seats and finished the carol ourselves.

Rob and I returned to Tower Hill a few days later and I tried to pinpoint the site of Edward Lloyd's coffee house. It was established circa 1688 by the river in Great Tower Street and became a favourite spot for merchants and ship owners to meet and conduct business. Wealthy individuals shared the risk of insuring ships and their cargoes, with Edward Lloyd providing reliable maritime information. The establishment slowly evolved into the giant marine insurance company Lloyd's of London, now located within a landmark building in nearby Lime Street.

The old coffee house also served tea and exotic fruit sherbets, 'made in Turkie, of lemons, roses, and violets perfumed'. Here is a modern take on sherbet, served as a celebration punch.

CHAMPAGNE SHERBET PUNCH

1 bottle champagne
3 cups pineapple juice
¼ cup lemon juice
4 cups frozen pineapple sherbet

Mix the lemon and pineapple juice in a punch bowl. Before serving add the sherbet scoop by scoop then pour in the champagne. Stir gently. (Makes about 20 servings.)

With the coffee house long gone, the best alternative for those in search of refreshment and society is to wander along to the Hung, Drawn and Quartered pub (26–27 Old Tower Street). There is still a link with the old days because this ale and pie establishment is popular with insurance 'suits' from Lloyd's. The macabre name appears in a quote on the pub's sign: 'I went to see Major General Harrison being hung, drawn and quartered. He was looking as cheerful as any man could in that condition – Samuel Pepys, 12 October 1660.' Major Harrison was one of the Parliamentarians who signed Charles I's death warrant. Following the Restoration, he was tried for regicide and executed at Charing Cross (see page 206). Inside, a hangman's noose dangles above the bar. Continuing the historical theme the walls are hung with portraits of bygone English kings and queens, including a seriously bloated and dyspeptic Henry VIII.

Along with boutique ales, the pub serves London Pride beer and cider, though sadly no sherbet. Its house pie, lamb with coriander and lemon, receives warm recommendations from patrons.

Meanwhile the Thames Path continues along the south bank under an arch of Tower Bridge to Butler's Wharf, and hence to the stark white buildings of the Design Museum. But let me pause here for a word (or two) about this iconic bridge. After an eight-year period of construction, it opened on 30 June 1894, though not of course to universal approval. The artist Sir Frank Brangwyn commented: 'A more absurd structure than the Tower Bridge has never been thrown across a strategic river.' And architect H. H. Statham declared it represented 'the vice of tawdriness and pretentiousness'. It has also been the subject of an elaborate practical joke. On 1 April 2010 the *Daily Mail* ran a story stating that the bridge had been sold to a Utah billionaire for $200 million (£133 million); clearly America's revenge for having been 'sold a pup' regarding London Bridge in 1968. It was to be dismantled over the summer months and, while it was understood that the public would be upset, the paper reported that the offer had been considered far too generous to refuse. The intention was that the bridge would form part of a British-inspired theme park, where it would be rebuilt as part of a rollercoaster, 'with tracks twinng around its famous turrets and sweeping beneath its rising roadway'.

The ability for the lower span to be raised for shipping almost created a disaster in December 1952 when the southern bascule of the bridge began to open just as a double-decker red bus was crossing from that direction. Displaying nerves of steel, the quick-thinking driver accelerated and 'flew' over a 3-ft (1-m), gap. His bus then dropped 6 ft (2 m) to the northern side, which had not begun to move. Miraculously, there were no serious injuries.

On 3 June 2012 the bridge was the focal point in Queen Elizabeth's Diamond Jubilee river pageant: a spectacular flotilla comprising over 1,000 vessels. The bascules rose in salute as the flower-decked royal barge passed below. At 6 p.m. they were lowered in a moving finale in which fireworks exploded and the London Philharmonic Orchestra performed the National Anthem.

Few people are aware that there was once a tunnel below Tower Bridge. In Charles Dickens Jnr's quirky *Dictionary of the Thames,* it is described as an iron tube, 7 ft (2.5 m) feet in diameter, which was driven through the riverbed between Tower Hill on the left bank and Vine Street on the right. The tunnel opened in 1870 and originally contained a twelve-seater 'tram omnibus' attached to an endless cable which drew passengers through. However, the project was a financial failure and after only three months the operating company folded and the tunnel became a pedestrian crossing.

Dickens Snr would surely have admired his son's turn of phrase in the following explanation of its limitations as a walkway:

> ... *after subtracting from its diameter the amount necessary to afford a sufficient width of platform, there is not much headroom left, and it is not advisable for any but the briefest of Her Majesty's lieges to attempt the passage in high-heeled boots, or with a hat to which he attaches any value.*

The footway received some adverse publicity in 1888. A man was spotted inside wielding a knife, and this at the height of fears over the Jack the Ripper murders. It finally became redundant when the bridge opened, although today it serves a useful purpose by carrying water mains and telecommunication cables.

Social history is my abiding passion, but it can make a refreshing change to look at the very new instead of the old. On my first visit to the riverside Design Museum, a group of Dutch designers were exhibiting a range of innovative household items. I was intrigued by a small-scale domestic urinal, with a placard explaining in plain terms how it had been possible to produce something so compact:

At home one does not find a urinal as repulsive and will be inclined to stand more closely. One will not wait as long, have less pressure on the bladder and so be able to pee in a more controlled manner.

Not to be outdone, Delft designer Marian Loth exhibited a women's urinal called 'The Lady P'. Featuring a bowl shaped to fit the female form, her objective was to reduce queues at women's toilets by allowing them to urinate in public without embarrassment … hmm, I don't think so, Marian! Mind you, some unpleasant brushes with stinging nettles could be avoided if the units were installed along remote sections of the Thames Path. Of course, there is an enduring urban myth that pregnant women in the UK are allowed to relieve themselves anywhere without penalty, including into a policeman's helmet.

The exhibits reminded me that in medieval times anyone caught short in the street could pay a small sum to a roving latrine attendant for the use of a bucket and the privilege of being screened from the public by a voluminous cloak. This may well have been where the saying 'to spend a penny' originated. The bucket brigade lost a good deal of its trade when Lord Mayor Dick Whittington built his 128-seater 'House of Easement' over the Thames, in the fifteenth century.

A footbridge leads over St Saviour's Lock to Mill Street, Bermondsey and Jacob's Island. Setting the scene for the death of the murderer Bill Sikes in *Oliver Twist*, Charles Dickens wrote:

Near to that part of the Thames on which the church at Rotherhithe abuts, where the buildings on the banks are dirtiest and the vessels on the river blackest with the dust of colliers and the smoke of close-built low-roofed houses, there exists the filthiest, the strangest, the most extraordinary of the many localities that are hidden in London ….

He identifies the place as Jacob's Island, which became isolated at high tide:

… surrounded by a muddy ditch six or eight feet deep and fifteen or twenty wide when the tide is in, once called Mill Pond, but known in these days as Folly Ditch.

Trying to escape his attackers by lowering himself from a roof into Folly Ditch, Sikes overbalances and falls 35 ft (10 m). The rope under his arms slips to his neck and hangs him.

We paused to photograph the unique statue of Dr Alfred Salter (1873–1945). In the early 1900s Salter, a committed social reformer, established a pioneering health service for the poor of Bermondsey, who were succumbing to diseases such as cholera and typhoid. Sculptor Diane Gorvin placed the old man on a bench, waving to a bronze vision of his daughter Joyce, who died from scarlet fever aged only nine. In November 2011 the lifesize figure of

Dr Salter was stolen and has probably been melted down for scrap metal, a truly unconscionable act. Little Joyce and her pet cat had to be 'taken into care' by the council.

Ahead is Cherry Garden Pier, a reminder that before industrialization there were meadows and orchards by the river. If Samuel Pepys ever decided not to take a boat to his office at the Deptford shipyards, he could have strolled along grassy paths, eating cherries as he climbed over country stiles.

The church at Rotherhithe mentioned by Dickens is St Mary's. Its churchyard is the resting place of Christopher Jones, the master of the *Mayflower*. Opposite is a pub called The Mayflower, built on the site of The Shippe Inn, from where the Pilgrim Fathers left in 1620.

Nearby, the site of a former charity school is marked by the figures of two eighteenth-century schoolchildren. The writer Sylvia Townsend Warner recalled taking a friend to see the figures in 1928. Afterwards they wandered into Prince Street, with its row of eighteenth-century captains' houses and spoke to an old lady who lived in one quite happily, despite it being infested with rats. She had grown up in Rotherhithe and spoke of the anger aroused by Marc and Isambard Brunel's pioneering tunnel, which allowed outsiders to walk under the Thames and take jobs from local men.

Many lives were lost during construction of the tunnel, both by drowning and from the effects of breathing impure air. When work resumed after the first major flooding in 1827, a banquet was held underground, as a show of confidence and resolve. The unique scene was captured by artist George Jones. A year later, during another flood, Isambard Brunel was badly injured while trying to save his workers. The foot tunnel finally opened in 1843, and was soon lined with street-stalls. Fairs were even held in the underpass, which now carries the tube train.

Downstream at Cumberland Wharf is a bronze statue called 'Sunbeam Weekly and the Pilgrim's Pocket' by the artist Peter McLean. A newsboy from the 1930s reads the history of the American nation in the magazine; from the arrival of the *Mayflower* through to the twentieth century. A bearded pilgrim gazes in awe over the boy's shoulder at images of cowboys and American automobiles. Today, intending emigrants can drop a coin in the elderly pilgrim's pocket and wish for a smoother path in life.

The very last cows on our Thames Path journey were residents of Surrey Docks' city farm, where children can mingle with domestic animals such as goats, pigs, sheep, cows and ducks. I wondered whether the ducks were descended from those that once nested on the river beside the working docks. Somehow the birds were able to calculate which timber-stacked barges would remain undisturbed long enough for them to hatch and raise a brood.

Huge quantities of timber went up in smoke here after Docklands was bombarded during the Second World War. Across the river at the West India Docks, onlookers reported seeing burning sugar oozing from the buildings like a lava flow. Extinguishing fires was particularly difficult if the Thames was at low tide because many fire-fighting barges were inoperable. One of the worst days for the docks was 7 September 1940, dubbed Black Saturday, when the pall of smoke from German bombs could be seen all over London. A total of 430 people died on Black Saturday and 10,000 were left homeless. By New Year's Day 1941, the death toll in London exceeded 13,000. Nature provided a touching memorial for those who died. In soil exposed to the light after homes were destroyed, wildflowers appeared, such as scarlet pimpernel, wild columbine and sorrel.

Sewage pipes were also destroyed during the Blitz, adding to river pollution caused by a leap in London's population during the 1930s. A survey twenty years later revealed the Thames was completely devoid of fish from Kew to Gravesend. Conversely, rats thrived in riverside mud. In the late 1950s a pair of kestrels nesting in the roof of the Savoy Hotel raised their young on Thames rats. Fortunately water purity has improved enormously and the river now supports 119 fish species. In 2004 the tally briefly hit 120 when a piranha was found at Dagenham, dropped onto a boat by a seagull.

Salmon had disappeared from the Thames at least a century before the Second World War. It has been suggested that gas lighting was a contributing factor as deadly cyanide residue from the gas found its way into the river. Ironically, medieval apprentices complained of being fed too much salmon! Oysters were plentiful as well, and certainly not considered a luxury, as they are today. In the eighteenth century Samuel Johnson regularly fed them to his favourite cat, Hodge. Pickled oysters were a great favourite, as was stew made from the shellfish and their liquor plus milk, butter, parsley and pepper.

The following is an old-fashioned recipe for oyster pie. The cook's own judgment must be used regarding quantities of the ingredients, based on the size of the pie dish used.

© Kiva Atkinson

Oysters were once so plentiful in the Thames that Samuel Johnson fed them to his cat!

OYSTER AND EGG PIE

prepared shortcrust pastry to line and top the pie
potatoes
oysters
hard-boiled eggs
butter
salt and pepper
milk

Line a pie dish with pastry. Par boil the potatoes, slice and place a layer in the bottom of the dish. Add a layer of oysters and a layer of sliced, hard-boiled egg. Season each layer with salt and pepper and a few small knobs of butter. Repeat layers until the dish is full. Cover with milk and top with a pastry lid. Bake in a moderate oven until golden brown.

A boundary stone signals the end of Rotherhithe parish and the entrance to Deptford, where Queen Elizabeth I knighted Sir Francis Drake on board his ship *The Golden Hind* after Drake's circumnavigation of the world between 1577 and 1580. It was Elizabeth's father Henry VIII who established the Royal Naval Dockyard here, which originally covered 30 acres (12 hectares). *The Golden Hind* had been built at Deptford (she was originally called *The Pelican*) and following Drake's investiture the ship became a tourist attraction at the dockyard, with day-trippers even able to enjoy meals on board. Eventually the ship fell into ruin but several chairs were made from its timbers and in 1662 the keeper of naval stores at Deptford, John Davies, presented one to Oxford's Bodleian Library. A poem written for the occasion by Abraham Cowley acknowledges the appropriateness of timber from the *Golden Hind* being fashioned into a chair:

> *Drake & his ship, could not have wished from Fate*
> *A more blest Station, or more blest Estate.*
> *For Lo! A Seate of endless Rest is giv'n*
> *To her in Oxford, and to him in Heav'n.*

The chair remains at Oxford in the university's oldest teaching room, the fifteenth-century Divinity Hall.

The ships of another famous explorer, Captain James Cook, were outfitted and provisioned at Deptford before he set out for the South Seas in 1768. Along with the usual hardtack biscuits, dried peas and salted pork, the holds of the ships were loaded with large quantities of sauerkraut, which it was hoped would prevent scurvy in the tropics. The sauer-kraut was probably imported from Germany but the hardtack (or ship's biscuits) would have been produced at Deptford's Royal Victualling Yard. Cast-iron ovens embedded in brick arches were used to bake the biscuits until 1906, and the victualling yard itself did not close until the 1960s. Cook's flagship *Endeavour* also held crates of laying hens, but fresh eggs and roast chicken disappeared from the captain's table after the crates were swept overboard during a storm in the Bay of Biscay.

Based on information gathered during Cook's travels, the east coast of Australia was chosen as an appropriate site for a penal colony. In 1788 the eleven ships of the First Fleet sailed into Sydney Harbour carrying some 770 convicts and several hundred soldiers and sailors. Sydney's Maritime Museum displays a handful of pebbles taken from the bed of the Thames and used as shingle ballast in HMS *Sirius*, flagship of the fleet. Perhaps I should keep quiet about the stones in case the British government asks Australia to return them, just as the Greeks are pressing for the return of the Elgin Marbles.

Samuel Pepys was a frequent visitor to Deptford in his role as Secretary to the Admiralty. He is remembered in the high-rise Pepys Estate, site of the former Royal Victualling Yard, with its warehouses full of dry goods such as mustard, pepper and powdered chocolate. There were also a slaughterhouse, milling facilities, a meat-salting complex and a vast eighteenth-century rum depot, which still stands.

We were reminded of the darker side of the Thames as we walked by the estate because a body had been found floating in front of the property a couple of days earlier, at St George's Stairs. According to police the victim had been hit on the head then manually strangled. There was a Jack the Ripper flavour about the case because a later news report suggested the limbs had been 'disarticulated' perhaps by a butcher or a mortician.

Pepys' diary records his dalliance with the wife of the Deptford shipping yard carpenter, William Bagwell. Bagwell was shamefully compliant in the affair, no doubt hoping for promotion. Conveniently for Pepys, the couple lived locally, and on 20 December 1664 he wrote:

> *... walked, without being observed, with Bagwell home to his house and there was very kindly used, and the poor people did get a dinner for me in their fashion – of which I also eat very well. After dinner I found occasion of sending him abroad; and then alone avec elle ...*

In his secret code of jumbled foreign tongues, Pepys then describes his adulterous act with Mrs Bagwell. The dinner provided by the carpenter's wife may well have concluded with a baked lemon custard known as Deptford Pudding. Lemon zest gives the pudding a delicious tang, and it is very light in texture, which would have suited Pepys' after-dinner exertions.

DEPTFORD PUDDING

breadcrumbs made from 6 slices white bread, crusts removed
2 eggs, separated
60 g (2 oz) sugar
½ pint milk
grated rind of a lemon
3 teaspoons lemon juice

Preheat oven to 180°C (350°F). Butter an ovenproof dish. In a bowl, beat the egg yolks, sugar and milk and stir in the breadcrumbs, lemon rind and juice. Beat the egg whites until they stand in soft peaks then fold into the mixture. Turn into the ovenproof dish. Stand the pudding in a baking tin filled with enough hot water to come halfway up the dish. Bake for 30–40 minutes until well risen and golden. Serve immediately.

Deptford was also the home of Pepys' friend and fellow diarist John Evelyn for over forty years, from 1652 to 1694. Evelyn lived by the river at Sayes Court, which stood until 1729 on a spot now known as Sayes Court Park. He was a passionate gardener and a respected author on the subject (I was amused to read his warning not to over-water indoor plants during winter, advice garden writers are still trying to drum into their readers three centuries down the track). John Evelyn's own garden was a showplace, with a grove of French walnuts, holly and lilac hedges, and all manner of English native trees. He also grew figs, grapes, stone-fruit, asparagus and strawberries. His glass beehive attracted a visit from King Charles II and fascinated Samuel Pepys.

It is a pity no one warned Evelyn against renting out his property. In 1678 he leased Sayes Court to the young Peter Mikhailov, who was to become Peter the Great, Tsar of Russia. Mikhailov's purpose in taking a house in Deptford was that he wanted to study ship building at the nearby royal docks (part of Evelyn's land had actually been purchased for use as the victualling yard). The idea must have sounded reasonable enough to a prospective landlord but Evelyn's bailiff soon reported: 'There is a housefull of people, and right nasty.' It was no exaggeration as the carousing Peter and his friends ruined Mrs Evelyn's best sheets, broke windows and furniture and, worst of all, wrecked Sayes Court's garden. As it turned out, John Evelyn was lucky. None other than Christopher Wren was called in to assess the damage and full compensation was paid by the government. It should also be said that the future Tsar managed to learn a great deal at the shipyards and went on to establish Russia's navy.

Deptford later became the location for the foreign cattle market. More cows passed through the market than were ever milked for syllabubs at Petersham. For many years all cattle from abroad were landed and slaughtered here, and it was not a pretty sight. A guide to the Thames published in 1891 described the area as an unsavoury shambles which 'no person of nice tastes should think of visiting'.

At Deptford's Church of St Nicholas, passersby are reminded of their own mortality by a charnel house in the churchyard and grinning skulls on the entrance pillars. Thoughts of heavenly retribution probably caused Sam Pepys to avert his gaze, especially after an interlude with Mrs Bagwell.

DOCKLANDS

Following the north bank route from the tower, the Thames Path leads into St Katharine Docks, which has its origins in the tenth century when the Saxon King Edgar granted 13 acres (5 hectares) to thirteen knights for the purposes of trading in foreign goods. Between 1825 and 1828 the riverside moorings at St Katharine were replaced by an extensive system of enclosed docks and many new warehouses were built. Slum housing was cleared during the redevelopment and 11,000 local residents were displaced. Rubbing salt into their wounds, rubble from demolished homes was used to build mansions in Belgravia. Luxury cargo handled at St Katharine reflected the taste of the Victorians, particularly decorative animal by-products such as ivory, feathers and tortoise shell. One of the old warehouses has been transformed into the galleried Dickens Inn, which reputedly sells more beer than any other London pub.

Enclosed docks were built to provide more space for ships than the open river allowed, but also to offer better protection against theft. Pilfering from ships and warehouses was rife and at one time dockworkers had their pockets sewn up to prevent them stealing valuable spices. After the police station at neighbouring Wapping was built, Victorian street urchins had so many brushes with the law they cheekily corrupted a familiar line from the Lord's Prayer into 'Lead us not into Thames Station'. Much of the temptation to steal was due to abject poverty. Men lined up each day to compete for poorly paid casual work and in August 1889 the appalling conditions led to a dispute, and the first Port of London shutdown since 1797. One of the leading figures supporting the strikers was John Burns, from the New Union movement. He was commemorated in an updated version of the satirical rhyme originally written about Faringdon's Henry Pye:

Sing a song of sixpence [6d being the hourly rate the men were demanding]
Dockers on the strike.
Guinea pigs are hungry,
As the greedy pike.
Till the docks are opened,
Burns for you will speak.
Courage lads, and you will win,
Well within the week.

But after a fortnight without resolution, the strikers and their families were running out of food. It was a contribution of £30,000 from Australian dockers that helped them hold out until their demands were met: sixpence an hour and improved working conditions. The dispute was significant in that it led to the formation of the Dockers' Union and the beginning of the Trade Union Movement. John Burns went on to become an MP and keen historian of London. He is responsible for the most well-known words ever uttered about the River Thames: 'The St Lawrence is water, the Mississippi is muddy water, but the Thames is liquid history.'

When dockworkers walked off the job again during the 1926 General Strike, the government responded by using warships to transport blackleg labour down the Thames at night. The strike collapsed within days, prompting the novelist Arnold Bennett to write: 'The General Strike now seems pitiful – a pathetic attempt of underdogs who hadn't a chance when the over-dogs really set themselves to win.'

Len Bates worked for the Port of London Authority for many years, both before and after the Second World War. His book *Thames Cavalcade* is a tribute to the working river, which finally died when container ships arrived, requiring deeper water. Bates tells a story about the wool stores, which received some 200,000 bales a year from Australia, New Zealand and South Africa. Fleeces were displayed prior to the annual auction sales, providing the perfect field trip for schoolchildren. According to Mr Bates, one prim schoolmistress learned more about the story of wool than she bargained for. Having shown the class examples of scoured and greasy wool, the foreman held up a fleece which he said was a mixture of sheep and goat hair. 'Oh, how did that come about?' the teacher asked, to which the leering foreman replied, 'Haven't you ever had a night on the tiles?'

In Wapping High Street is the Town of Ramsgate pub, so named because fishermen from the port of Ramsgate in Kent used to unload their boats nearby. The infamous Captain Blood was arrested on the road outside the pub in 1671 (see page 220) and a century later convicts bound for Australia were held in its cellars. Close by is Wapping Old Stairs, with more historical links. Dick Turpin is said to have fired his last shot from the stairs and it was here that 'Hanging' Judge Jeffreys was apprehended. Jeffreys was trying to flee to France after his 'Bloody Assizes' of 1685 where participants in Monmouth's rebellion were tried and sentenced to death. Rob and I made our way down the slippery steps and stood by the water's edge. The tide was going out and despite all the redevelopment in Docklands, the ghosts of the past still lingered in the muddy smell of the riverbed, and in the sound of the Thames coursing through polished pebbles:

The river tide lapping,
Like the ghost of some sailorman's wooden leg tapping,
And the creak of the mast, and the brown sail a-flapping
Of a topsail barge dropping
By Wapping Old Stairs.

Further along the High Street at Wapping New Stairs, the ghosts are said to be those of pirates and cutthroats hanged at Execution Dock for committing crimes on the high seas. The gallows were set up on the shore in front of a crowd of expectant onlookers. Afterwards the bodies were smeared with pitch and placed in an iron gibbet cage. The cage was chained to a stake at the low water mark until three tides had washed over the corpse. A report from 1557 read:

The vii day of Aprell was hanged at the low-water marke at Wapying beyond St Kath-
eryn's vii men for robbing at see.

Among those who 'danced the hempen jig' was a murdering pirate, Captain William Kidd, in 1701. The last public executions at Wapping took place as recently as 1830. Sailors who blanched at the spectacle could bring the colour back to their cheeks with a cup of hot grog, invented by Admiral Sir Edward Vernon. The Admiral's aim was to save money by diluting his crew's rum ration, although the lime juice in the following recipe might have helped prevent scurvy. The name grog came from the cloak Vernon wore; a rough silk and wool blend fabric known as grogram.

HOT GROG

50 ml (2 fl oz) dark rum
50 ml (2 fl oz) lime juice
1 teaspoon brown sugar
2 cloves
1 cinnamon stick

Gently heat all ingredients in a saucepan. Strain into a teacup. Serves one sailor.

Wherever there are sailors, especially those full of hot grog, there are women ready to take their money in return for a good time. It is said that J. M. W. Turner visited the mean streets of Wapping to sketch prostitutes and their clients. None of the pictures have survived but it is presumed they were among folios of 'obscene pictures' destroyed at the request of the National Gallery trustees.

Beyond the famous Prospect of Whitby pub the path detours around the Shadwell Basin and the canoeing centre at Shadwell Pierhead. It was at Shadwell that Captain James Cook met his future wife, a local girl called Elizabeth Batts. At the time, Cook was employed on Tyne–Thames coal carriers, which unloaded at Wapping. The couple married in 1762, when James was thirty-four and Elizabeth just twenty. Their first home was at 126 Upper Shadwell and their first child, James, was christened in Shadwell's St Paul's Church.

It was coal fires that contributed to the smog wreathing the quays in Oscar Wilde's poem, but coal had many other uses. In 1856 an eighteen-year-old called William Perkin was experimenting with coal tar in a makeshift laboratory at Shadwell. He was trying to make artificial quinine and in the process produced a dark sludge which he discovered could dye silk a unique, light purple. Perkin called the new colour mauve (French for the colour of the mallow flower). The coal-based dye was referred to as aniline, and inspired a comic verse in *Punch*:

> *Oil and ointment and wax and wine,*
> *And the lovely colours called aniline;*
> *You can make anything from a salve to a star,*
> *If you only know how, from black coal-tar.*

The discovery led to a mania for mauve among ladies of fashion in Paris and London.

Limehouse Basin was a dock built to serve the Regent's Canal, which enters the Thames here. A ship builder called Duncan Dunbar established a wharf at Limehouse in the mid nineteenth century and his name will strike a chord with Australians, especially Sydneysiders. Dunbar's ships took emigrants on the then three-month trip to New South Wales, returning home laden with goods from the Far East. On 20 August 1857, his namesake ship *The Dunbar* was heading into Sydney Harbour during a violent storm when it was wrecked on the cliffs below South Head: 121 people drowned, the sole survivor being a sailor called James Johnson, who clung to the rocks for thirty-six hours before being rescued. Johnson was later employed at a New South Wales' lighthouse and in a strange coincidence he helped rescue the sole survivor of another wreck, nine years later.

Beyond Limehouse is the giant warehouse at West India Docks which opened in 1803 as the world's longest brick building. Now one of Britain's oldest-surviving warehouses, it houses the Museum of Docklands, where 2,000 years of Thames history comes to life. Among the Roman artifacts is a wooden barrel lid from AD 50–70, still coated in the pitch used to seal the contents. The Romans imported a wide range of goods into Britain including glassware from Italy, marble from Turkey, fish oil from Spain, wine from Italy and dried fruits from Palestine. The Viking raiders are represented by a battle axe found near London Bridge. From Tudor times there is an iron pennant from a wherry, decorated with the Tudor rose.

My favourite section of the museum covers the eighteenth century, when the sailing ships of the East India Company returned to England with their holds full of exotic produce. On display are the private papers of Thomas Bartlett, a captain's steward who served on a number of the company's ships. Bartlett was allowed to indulge in a little private trade and it is fascinating to read his handwritten shopping lists, which included sweetmeats, spices, silk, chinaware, and various articles of oriental furniture.

In 2003, modern 'mudlarkers' fished a handful of coins from the shores of the Thames. They were examined by the British Museum and found to be seventeenth-century Javanese coins, brought to London as a souvenir in the very early days of the East India Company. They were among the first coins minted in Java.

It is a shock to walk from the evocative Museum of Docklands to the outside world, especially with the towers of the Canary Wharf development looming up ahead. Canary Wharf opened in 1992 and is the most powerful symbol of docklands regeneration. In February 1996 it was a target of terrorism. The IRA claimed responsibility for a half-ton truck bomb which killed two people and seriously injured many others.

I felt slightly nervous as we ventured on into Millwall, though not from fear of a terrorist attack. Thirty years earlier a friend and I had been engulfed by a surging mass of Millwall football fans on their way to do battle with a rival club. We managed to escape unscathed when the mounted police arrived, but the mob's bloodcurdling battle cry entered my psyche.

Thankfully all was quiet on the riverfront as we made our way past Burrells Wharf, and on to the yard where the giant steamship *Great Eastern* was built. Designed by Isambard Kingdom Brunel in 1858, the ship was 225 yd (207 m) long, six times larger than any vessel afloat. She was touted as 'the Crystal Palace of the sea', capable of carrying 4,000 passengers. During the dangerous work of riveting, young children were employed to crawl into confined areas behind the ship's iron shell. After much argument, it was decided to launch the *Great Eastern* sideways, and even then it took several attempts to manoeuvre her into the Thames. On the first attempt she moved a mere 4 ft (1.5 m).

Bad omens surrounded the ship from the start. There were serious financial disputes during construction and on Brunel's final visit to the yard on 5 September 1859 he suffered a serious stroke. Ten days later, as the steamship made her way down the English Channel, one of her huge boilers burst, killing six men. Brunel died shortly after hearing the news. Public confidence was shaken by the explosion, and there were also stories that the *Great Eastern* was haunted. From the time she was launched, strange tapping noises were heard coming from the bowels of the ship but despite repeated investigations no cause was ever found. Many believed the mystery was solved in 1888, when she was finally broken up. Workmen found two skeletons in the bilge, a riveter's hammer lying beside them. One of the skeletons was that of a child.

The Ferry House pub marks the point where a ferry once crossed the river to Greenwich. Thames Path walkers travel *below* the river via the Greenwich foot tunnel, which opened in 1902 allowing South London dockers to find employment on the Isle of Dogs. It emerges on the south bank close to where the *Cutty Sark* is moored.

GREENWICH TO THE THAMES BARRIER

The sleek tea-clipper *Cutty Sark* was the last of her kind, built in 1869 for the lucrative tea trade. Tea was still a luxury item in the nineteenth century and there were huge financial rewards in being the first to get the new season's crop to the London markets from China. The Victorians even used tea as a flavouring in a popular summer dessert:

EARL GREY CREAM

15 g (½ oz) loose Earl Grey tea (China tea flavoured with oil of bergamot)
300 ml (½ pint) milk
2 eggs, separated
2 tablespoons sugar
1 tablespoon gelatine
3 tablespoons warm water
150 ml (¼ pint) double cream

Place the tea and the milk in a pan and gently bring to the boil. Remove from the heat and allow to infuse for 5–10 minutes. Strain through a fine sieve. Beat the egg yolks into the sugar and stir in the milk. Dissolve the gelatine in the warm water and stir into the mixture. Whisk the egg white to soft peaks and gently fold in. Pour into a glass serving dish and, when set, decorate with rosettes of whipped cream. Serve with fresh fruit.

Later the *Cutty Sark* carried an equally valuable cargo of Australian wool. She once made the trip from Sydney to the Lizard Peninsula in sixty-seven days, powered only by the wind. The name *Cutty Sark* means 'short chemise' and comes from the Robbie Burns' poem 'Tom O'Shanter'. In the poem, the chemise is worn by a swift and beautiful witch called Nannie, who chases the drunken Tom home, grabbing the tail of his horse as he escapes across a river. The ship's figurehead represents Nannie in her chemise:

Her cutty sark O' Paisley Harn [linen],
That while a lassie she had worn,
In Longitude tho' sorely scanty,
It was her best and she was vauntie [proud]

At one stage the clipper was owned by Portuguese interests, who translated the name *Cutty Sark* to *Pequina Camisola,* or Little Shirt. Apparently sailors used to amuse themselves by making a horse-tail from frayed rope, to put in Nannie's outstretched hand.

Close by is a tiny craft with the beautiful and fitting name, *Gypsy Moth IV.* In 1966, sixty-four-year-old Francis Chichester set off in this yacht to complete a single-handed voyage around the world. He returned in triumph nine months and one day later, to the acclaim of the nation – and a knighthood. My family and I watched Chichester's public investiture on television in Australia, but it was only later that I appreciated the full historical significance of the occasion. Sir Francis was knighted by Elizabeth II, in the same location and with the same sword used by Elizabeth I to knight Sir Francis Drake. Asked what had prompted his spirit of adventure, Chichester replied 'Because it intensifies life', an understatement if ever there was one!

On Christmas Eve 1805 the body of another British naval hero, Horatio Nelson, was brought up the Thames to the Seamen's Hospital at Greenwich, where it lay in state in the Painted Hall. During the voyage home from Trafalgar, his body had been preserved in alcohol; brandy as far as Gibraltar, then spirit of wine. Nelson's heroic death aroused such emotion that the public queued back to the City of London for the chance to file past the coffin. On 8 January, drums and trumpets played funeral dirges as a mile-long procession of black-draped barges conveyed his remains from Greenwich to Whitehall, then on to St Paul's Cathedral for burial.

Nelson relics were so greatly prized that, inevitably, they were stolen. While the body lay in the Painted Hall, someone hid behind a statue then sneaked out to lift the dead hero's gold watch and seal, and to prise the jewels from the scabbards of his dress swords. In 1950, a spectacular diamond ornament given to Nelson by the Sultan of Turkey disappeared from the National Maritime Museum. Fortunately the most poignant and personal mementoes remain, including Nelson's bloodied and bullet-pierced battle jacket. Also on display are the matching gold rings in the form of clasped hands which Nelson secretly exchanged with Emma Hamilton at a communion service in London.

Long before Nelson's sailing ship *Victory* went into battle against the French, the stretch of river from Greenwich to Westminster had been used to test an early version of a submarine. It was invented by Cornelis Drebbel in 1620. The vessel was powered by twelve oarsmen in a greased leather rowing capsule, with the oars protruding from leather valves. Drebbel had managed to come up with a method of purifying the air inside the submarine, enabling the crew to breathe. According to a contemporary riddle the submarine was designed for the same purpose as later versions: to sink enemy ships.

> It is an Automa, runnes under water,
> With a snug nose, and has a nimble taile
> Made like an auger, with which taile she wrigles
> Betwixt the coasts of a ship and sinkes it straight.

From around 1700, fun fairs were held in Greenwich Park. By the middle of the century the crowds were enormous and so badly behaved that respectable people stayed away. The rest had a wonderful time: drinking to excess, gawping at freak shows and spending their pennies on cheap fairings. A favourite toy was a little wooden wheel which could be rolled down an unsuspecting person's buttocks to produce a highly embarrassing sound. However, the cheapest and most infamous entertainment was for men and women to hold hands and charge down the park's Castle Hill, ending up at the bottom in an indelicate tangle of limbs. Naturally the pompous Victorians were not amused and put a stop to the fairs in 1857.

Greenwich Park is crowned by the Royal Observatory, designed by Christopher Wren in 1675 and famous as the site of the prime meridian of longitude and the basis for Greenwich Mean Time. Beyond the park is the Trafalgar Tavern, renowned for whitebait suppers attended by literary figures such as Dickens, Thackeray and Wilkie Collins and also popular with cabinet ministers of the nineteenth century. One of them, Lord Palmerston, proposed a toast with the words: 'Let us all imitate this very wise little fish – drink a lot and say nothing.' Whitebait are still served at the Trafalgar. They are caught in the Thames estuary on the flood tide, using a fine net, and were once used as bait to catch whiting – hence the name.

Charles Dickens Jnr mentioned the Trafalgar Tavern in a humorous commentary on Greenwich's more expansive fish dinners:

> The typical fish dinner of London is the extraordinary entertainment offered at Greenwich – perhaps the most curious repast ever invented by the ingenuity of the most imaginative hotel-keeper. Main courses of fish prepared in every conceivable way, followed by ducks and peas, beans and bacon cutlets, and other viands, so arranged as to stimulate a pleasing if somewhat expensive thirst, are washed down at these Gargantuan feeds by the choicest brands known to civilization ... only two houses can be recommended for this kind of sport – the 'Trafalgar' and the 'Ship'.

Shellfish continue to be harvested in the estuary as well, and a small cockle fleet operates

Our walking companion Bill Wilson tries to reattach a Thames Path sign at Greenwich

from the village of Leigh-on-Sea, on the Essex shore. I have been told that whelks and winkles in particular should be eaten on a pebble beach, preferably while wearing plimsolls and shivering in a string vest!

Greenwich Palace was the birthplace of Henry VIII and also of his daughters Mary and Elizabeth. Elizabeth's mother Anne Boleyn left from the palace by barge in 1533 for her coronation. It was a spectacular procession as a contemporary account reveals:

> *And so all the lords with the mayor and all the guilds of London brought her by water from Greenwich to the Tower of London, and there the king's grace received her as she landed, and then over a thousand guns were fired at the Tower, and others were fired at Limehouse, and on other ships lying in the Thames.*

In 1536 Anne made the same journey along the Thames to the tower, this time to await execution. Ironically, the barge used had once belonged to the woman she supplanted in Henry VIII's affections, Catherine of Aragon. The palace was abandoned in the seventeenth century.

Accompanied by Bill, Rob and I set out very early one morning to complete the final stretch of the Thames Path. We realized our journey was nearing its end when we came to a sign reading: GREENWICH PENINSULAR ½M THAMES BARRIER 1¾M. A bolt had come loose and the sign was swinging in the breeze. Bill stood on a bench to fix it but despite his efforts, or perhaps because of them, it fell into my arms. I pointed it in the direction of the Flood Barrier while Rob grabbed the camera and took a couple of hasty shots. We were worried that we might be mistaken for middle-aged vandals, although it was actually opportunistic theft that had crossed my mind. To Bill's relief the sign would not fit under my coat so we left it on the bench and headed for the Millennium Dome. It had appeared on the horizon looking like a futuristic pencil holder from the Design Museum's gift shop.

At the time the Dome was built, the British were enjoying a dig at the French, boasting that the Eiffel Tower could be laid end to end inside the Dome with metres to spare. However, pride was tempered by concern over what the Dome might contain and whether it would live up to expectations. Goaded by suggestions that silence indicated a complete absence of ideas, organizers finally disclosed that visitors would walk through a giant human body. Presumably they were inspired by artist Damien Hirst's Turner Prize exhibit where the public passed through the middle of a cow. Sadly, the Dome was a bit of a flop and by mid 2000 there was talk of selling the contents to Australia.

The greatest excitement at the Dome occurred on 8 November 2000, when an audacious attempt was made to steal a flawless 203-carat diamond known as the Millennium Star, being displayed in the Money Zone. Would-be thieves drove a mechanized digger through a wall

Millennium Village, where bold architecture is softened by waterways rich in wildlife

of the building. They were armed with smoke grenades, stink bombs and nail guns detonated by gunpowder. A high-powered motor boat had been stationed in the Thames for a quick get-away. However, having been tipped off well in advance, police had stationed themselves in the building disguised as cleaners. They moved in just as the gang tried to smash their way into the display case of gems, reported to have a combined worth of about £350 million. 'I was only 12 inches from pay day,' one man boasted to officers. However, he was actually 12 inches from a collection of fakes as the priceless diamond and its eleven smaller companions had been substituted with cheap crystals.

During the summer of 1658, the Thames itself provided Greenwich with a tourist attraction. John Evelyn wrote:

> *A large whale was taken betwixt my land butting on the Thames and Greenwich ...*
> *black skin'd like coach leather, very small eyes, greate taile 58 foot long 16ft high.*

In recent years the once heavily industrialized peninsula has undergone urban renewal on a massive scale, in conjunction with an ambitious plan to bring birdlife back to the area. Iron barriers were removed from the riverbanks to establish reed beds; a habitat for birds such as reed buntings and sedge warblers.

Returning in 2010 we noticed an incredible change in the area. Although it could not be called a complete success, the Dome has evolved into an entertainment centre with music venues, bars, restaurants and a roller-skating rink. Nearby, the Greenwich Peninsula Ecology Park has been established, butting up against the giant apartment complex of Millennium Village. The park's 4 acres (1.5 hectares) of marshes and waterways are fed by a freshwater bore. They attract an impressive range of wildlife which can be inspected at close quarters from boardwalks and bird hides. Entrance to this idyllic area is free. The juxtaposition of a tranquil, reed-fringed lake against the bold playfulness of modern residential architecture completely captured my imagination.

With construction of the Dome still underway, on our initial walk the Thames Path had been temporarily re-routed. Although there were detour signs along the mesh boundary fences, they were small and easily overlooked, particularly after it began to rain. Immersed in a discussion about the best way to roast a goose, we blundered through increasingly sticky mud to a dead end.

By the time we were back on track, a mist had rolled in and the river completely disappeared. Bill began to look tired and emotional and I was desperately trying to keep the hem of my coat clean. Thank God I hadn't lumbered myself with that Thames Path sign. I tried to think positive thoughts about reed buntings and sedge warblers but deep down I feared the millennium project might prevent us reaching our goal after all.

We were greatly relieved when the temporary path finally turned back to the Thames … and the iconic Flood Barrier. Floods were being documented in London as early as 1099 when it was recorded 'Thames much flooded on Festival of St Martin'. In 1236, Stow's Chronicles of England mentioned the bizarre effects of another serious flood: '… in the great Palace of Westminster, men did row with wherries in the midst of the Hall.' Samuel Pepys also wrote of abnormally high tides inundating the city.

In January 1953 a violent storm coincided with a huge surge tide, creating havoc right down the east coast of the country. Central London was saved only because floodwaters escaped to low-lying areas in the estuary such as Canvey Island, where there were fifty-three deaths. A memorial stone at the Barrier pays tribute to more than 2,100 people who drowned in countries around the North Sea. In the aftermath of the disaster, levy banks were raised at Canvey Island, which actually increased the risk to the city. Seventy-nine square miles (127 km) were considered to be under threat if a tide of 1953 proportions reoccurred. Twelve months later, a committee established to investigate the problem came up with the idea of a moveable flood barrier. However, thirty years passed before their ambitious plan came to fruition.

The gleaming covers protecting the Barrier's hydraulic machinery have a skin of steel

© Rob Conolly

Hooded 'Knights of the Barrier' protect London from dangerous tidal surges

plates with a slightly rippled finish that reflects the light. Underneath is a triple skin of European redwood. Their double curved design is said to have been influenced by the sails of the Sydney Opera House and some say they look like upturned boats. However, to me the covers have a reassuring resemblance to the armoured hoods of knights, standing shoulder to shoulder across the river.

The project's massive construction cost of £480 million has been more than justified. In its first twelve years of operation the underwater gates were raised twenty-nine times to protect London from high water levels and tidal surges. Although the four main gates weigh a massive 3,700 tons each, they can be in place within thirty minutes, effectively holding back the tide. The Barrier was officially opened by Queen Elizabeth II, who must have been tempted to turn to her husband and say: 'My word, Philip, this is one in the eye for old Canute!'

Underneath the control centre is a long etching in a concrete wall by the artist Simon Read. Called 'Profile Of The River Thames', it charts the Thames Path all the way from the source. I secretly hoped the chairman of the Thames Authority might be on hand to present us with a badge of achievement but I suppose he only turns up if he knows you are coming.

Never mind, we shook hands with Bill and celebrated in the visitors' centre over what we affectionately dubbed a Reading Special: a pot of tea and chips. Returning recently, I was disappointed to find that chips had been deemed unhealthy and removed from the menu. I ordered baked beans on toast as a substitute and the Cockney chef, sensing my disappointment, kindly offered to substitute white bread for the regulation wholemeal.

One-hundred-and-eighty miles (288 km) down and no more to go. Perhaps it was just as well, because it was bloody cold. As Ezra Pound wrote in a parody of the old song written by the monks at Reading Abbey:

Winter is icummen in,
Lhude sing Goddamn,
Raineth drop and staineth slop,
And how the wind doth ramm!

It was time to go home and light the fire.

EPILOGUE

Technically, our journey was not quite complete. As Thomas Platter pointed out in 1599, London is 60,000 paces from the ocean. Having stood at the dry source of the Thames in Gloucestershire, it seemed only right that we should travel the extra distance (albeit by car) to watch the river empty into the North Sea.

Just beyond the Flood Barrier is the Greenwich suburb of Woolwich, where Henry VIII established his naval dockyards in 1512. In August 1845 the *London Times* reported that the Woolwich Steam Packet Company's vessels *Nymph* and *Fairy* had brought down 195 convicts from Millbank Prison, including my Shadbolt relatives (see page 196). What heart-breakingly ironic names for a cargo of human misery. The men were put aboard the *Mayda,* then lying at Woolwich ready to transport them to Norfolk Island. Ominously, this ship's name was just one letter short of what later became the international distress signal of MAYDAY. Despite a calm passage, the ship lost its topmast and foremast-head and from the very beginning there was an extraordinary amount of illness on board. It was a situation Surgeon Kilroy was at a loss to explain, although he later mentioned the 'nauseous and astringent' taste of the drinking water, stored in oak barrels. A far greater hazard was that, according to normal practice, the barrels had been filled from the polluted Thames.

Like many others, my great-great-grandfather George Shadbolt fell ill with dysentery. His life was saved by the surgeon who, perhaps spotting something decent in the young man, kept him on the sick list for an unusually long period; from mid September until the end of October. A special note in Kilroy's report of the voyage states this was 'to allow him the benefit of a hospital diet and a daily allowance of wine'.

The decision to continue our journey allowed me to make a pilgrimage to Greenhithe, where Isabella Beeton died (see page 141). In the autumn of 1861 Isabella and her husband moved to a small farmhouse at Greenhithe called Mount Pleasant, located close to the Thames. Isabella's sister Charlotte intensely disliked the property, describing it as 'that nasty, damp house down by the river'. There was a hint of prophesy in her words as Isabella died at Mount Pleasant of puerperal fever in July 1865, following the birth of her fourth child.

Contrary to the widely held image of Mrs Beeton as a middle-aged matron, she was just twenty-eight. It was at Greenhithe that Isabella wrote her *Dictionary of Every-Day Cookery*, published in the year of her death. One of the final recipes was for whiting, which can be caught in the Thames estuary:

WHITING AUX FINES HERBES

Ingredients – 1 bunch of sweet herbs chopped very fine; butter. Mode – Clean and skin the fish, fasten the tails in the mouths, and lay them in a baking-dish. Mince the herbs very fine, strew them over the fish, and place small pieces of butter over; cover with another dish and let them simmer in a Dutch oven for ¼ hour or 20 minutes. Turn the fish once or twice, and serve with the sauce poured over. Time - ¼ hour or twenty minute. Average Cost – 4d. each. Seasonable all year, but best from October to March. Sufficient – 1 small whiting for each person.

Sheerness on Kent's Isle of Sheppey is considered the last Thames settlement but Rob and I chose to view the estuary from the tip of the neighbouring peninsula, the Isle of Grain. This prompted us to visit desolate Cooling Marshes, where Charles Dickens set the scene for Pip's dramatic encounter with the convict in the opening scene of *Great Expectations*. As Pip explained: 'Ours was the marsh country, down by the river, within, as the river wound, twenty miles of the sea.' The village churchyard held the bodies of Pip's five infant brothers, in graves so narrow he called them 'stone lozenges' and suggested the boys must all have been born dead, lying on their backs with their hands in their pockets. Dickens based his fiction on a poignant group of not five but thirteen graves, which can still be seen in Cooling church-yard. The stone tombs are scarcely more than 1 ft (30 cm) in length, with ten belonging to a single family: the eighteenth-century Comports.

In his *Dictionary of the Thames,* Dickens' son Charles wrote of the benefits of hot punch as protection against 'aguish' country such as that found in the Thames marshes. He even provided his own recipe:

MR DICKENS THE YOUNGER'S ANTI-AGUE PUNCH
Take a common earthenware painter's pipkin [pot], glazed inside, of almost a large tumbler capacity. Put in three lumps of sugar, about a third of the peel of a lemon, a glass of old rum, and a glass of brandy. Set fire to the mixture, and let it burn well for about two minutes, carefully stirring the while. Then add the juice of half a lemon strained through muslin, blow out the fire and fill up with boiling water. Pour into a tumbler and drink as soon as you can. You will find it eminently comforting. Prevention is better than cure.

Charles Dickens' 'stone lozenges' in Cooling churchyard, arguably the most moving sight in our long journey

From Cooling we made our way eastward until the road ran out in the remote village of Grain. During the First World War, soldiers returning from abroad were stationed here. Some were infected with malaria and the presence of the anopheles mosquito in the river marshes led to the disease spreading to the local community. It was the last-known malaria epidemic in the UK, with half of Grain's children becoming infected. The epidemic may well have resulted in more 'stone lozenges', and in fact several soldiers are buried in the local church-yard.

We parked the car and walked down to Grain's shingle beach. I picked up a souvenir pebble as we watched container ships entering and leaving the estuary. The ships cross an imaginary line stretching from nearby Sheerness across to Southend-on-Sea in Essex. This line marks the end of the Port of London Authority's jurisdiction and is the true end of the Thames.

SELECT BIBLIOGRAPHY

Ackroyd, Peter, *Thames: Secret River* (Chatto & Windus, 2007)

Briggs, Martin, *Down the Thames* (Herbert Jenkins Ltd, 1949)

Beeton, Isabella, *Mrs Beeton's Book of Household Management* (Cassell, 2000)

Blamey, Marjorie & Fitter, Richard, *Wild Flowers* (Collins Gem, 1980)

Buchanan, Ian (Ed.), *Buckinghamshire* (Philip's County Guides, 1994)

Burton, Maurice, *Guide to the Mammals of Britain & Europe* (Treasure Press, 1976)

Carroll, Lewis, *Alice's Adventure in Wonderland* and *Through the Looking Glass, and What Alice Found There* (Macmillan, 1911)

Dickens, Charles (Jnr), *Dickens' Dictionary of London, 1884: (sixth year); an unconventional handbook* (Macmillan, 1884)

Dickens, Charles (Jnr), *Dickens' Dictionary of the Thames, 1883: From its Source to the Nore, 1883* (Macmillan, 1883)

Emmons, Ron, *Walks Along the Thames Path* (New Holland, 2001)

Field Guide to the Birds of Britain (Reader's Digest, 1981)

Fraser, Antonia, *Faith & Treason: The Gunpowder Plot* (Doubleday, 1996)

Fraser, Antonia, *The Lives of the Kings & Queens of England* (Weidenfeld & Nicolson, 1975)

Grahame, Kenneth, *The Wind in the Willows* (Methuen, 1951)

Grigson, Geoffrey, *The Shell Country Book* (Phoenix House, 1962)

Hatts, Leigh, *The Thames Path* (Cicerone Press, 1998)

The Hidden Places of the Thames Valley (Travel Publishing, 1999)

Jerome, Jerome K., *Three Men in a Boat: To Say Nothing of the Dog* (J. M. Dent, 1957)

Lehmann, Rosamond, *The Swan in the Evening: Fragments of an Inner Life* (Collins, 1968)

The National Trust Handbook (National Trust, 2011)

Peel, J. H. B., *Portrait of the Thames* (Robert Hale, 1967)
Pepys, Samuel, *The Diary of Samuel Pepys* (G. Bell, 1918–19)

Sharp, David, *The Thames Path* (Aurum Press, 2001)

www.beatlesinterviews.org (see 1964-07-00), Beatles/A Hard Day's Night, Promo Interview

INDEX